MYRTLEFIELD
HOUSE

CLAIMING TO ANSWER

THE QUEST FOR REALITY AND SIGNIFICANCE

BOOK 5

CLAIMING TO ANSWER

HOW ONE PERSON BECAME THE RESPONSE TO OUR DEEPEST QUESTIONS

DAVID GOODING
JOHN LENNOX

Myrtlefield House
Belfast, Northern Ireland

Cover design: Frank Gutbrod.
Interior design and composition: Sharon VanLoozenoord.

Published by The Myrtlefield Trust
PO Box 2216
Belfast, N Ireland, BT1 9YR
w: www.myrtlefieldhouse.com
e: info@myrtlefieldhouse.com

ISBN: 978-1-912721-20-7 (hbk.)
ISBN: 978-1-912721-21-4 (pbk.)
ISBN: 978-1-912721-22-1 (PDF)
ISBN: 978-1-912721-23-8 (Kindle)
ISBN: 978-1-912721-24-5 (EPUB without DRM)
ISBN: 978-1-912721-30-6 (box set)

23 22 21 20 19   10 9 8 7 6 5 4 3 2 1

DEDICATED TO OUR YOUNGER FELLOW STUDENTS,

REMEMBERING THAT WE WERE ONCE STUDENTS — AND STILL ARE

CONTENTS

BOOK 5: CLAIMING TO ANSWER

HOW ONE PERSON BECAME THE RESPONSE TO OUR DEEPEST QUESTIONS

ILLUSTRATIONS

SERIES PREFACE

The average student has a problem—many problems in fact, but one in particular. No longer a child, he or she is entering adult life and facing the torrent of change that adult independence brings. It can be exhilarating but sometimes also frightening to have to stand on one's own feet, to decide for oneself how to live, what career to follow, what goals to aim at and what values and principles to adopt.

How are such decisions to be made? Clearly much thought is needed and increasing knowledge and experience will help. But leave these basic decisions too long and there is a danger of simply drifting through life and missing out on the character-forming process of thinking through one's own worldview. For that is what is needed: a coherent framework that will give to life a true perspective and satisfying values and goals. To form such a worldview for oneself, particularly at a time when society's traditional ideas and values are being radically questioned, can be a very daunting task for anyone, not least university students. After all, worldviews are normally composed of many elements drawn from, among other sources, science, philosophy, literature, history and religion; and a student cannot be expected to be an expert in any one of them, let alone in all of them (indeed, is anyone of us?).

Nevertheless we do not have to wait for the accumulated wisdom of life's later years to see what life's major issues are; and once we grasp what they are, it is that much easier to make informed and wise decisions of every kind. It is as a contribution to that end that the authors offer this series of books to their younger fellow students. We intend that each book will stand on its own while also contributing to the fuller picture provided by the whole series.

So we begin by laying out the issues at stake in an extended introduction that overviews the fundamental questions to be asked, key voices to be listened to, and why the meaning and nature of ultimate reality matter to each one of us. For it is inevitable that each one of us will, at some time and at some level, have to wrestle with the fundamental questions of our existence. Are we meant to be here, or is it really by accident that we are? In what sense, if any, do we matter, or are we simply rather insignificant specks inhabiting an insubstantial corner of our galaxy? Is there a purpose in it all? And if indeed it does matter, where would we find reliable answers to these questions?

In Book 1, *Being Truly Human*, we consider questions surrounding the value of humans. Besides thinking about human freedom and the dangerous way it is often devalued, we consider the nature and basis of morality and how other moralities compare with one another. For any discussion of the freedom humans have to choose raises the question of the power we wield over other humans and also over nature, sometimes with disastrous consequences. What should guide our use of power? What, if anything, should limit our choices, and to what extent can our choices keep us from fulfilling our full potential and destiny?

The realities of these issues bring before us another problem. It is not the case that, having developed a worldview, life will unfold before us automatically and with no new choices. Quite the opposite. All of us from childhood onward are increasingly faced with the practical necessity of making ethical decisions about right and wrong, fairness and injustice, truth and falsity. Such decisions not only affect our individual relationships with people in our immediate circle: eventually they play their part in developing the social and moral tone of each nation and, indeed, of the world. We need, therefore, all the help we can get in learning how to make truly ethical decisions.

But ethical theory inevitably makes us ask what is the ultimate authority behind ethics. Who or what has the authority to tell us: you ought to do this, or you ought not to do that? If we cannot answer that question satisfactorily, the ethical theory we are following lacks a sufficiently solid and effective base. Ultimately, the answer to this question unavoidably leads us to the wider philosophical question: how are we related to the universe of which we form a part? What is the nature of ultimate reality? Is there a creator who made us and built into us our moral awareness, and requires us to live according to his laws? Or, are human beings the product of mindless, amoral forces that care nothing about ethics, so that as a human race we are left to make up our own ethical rules as best we can, and try to get as much general agreement to them as we can manage, either by persuasion or even, regretfully, by force?

For this reason, we have devoted Book 2, *Finding Ultimate Reality*, to a discussion of Ultimate Reality; and for comparison we have selected views and beliefs drawn from various parts of the world and from different centuries: the Indian philosophy of Shankara; the natural and moral philosophies of the ancient Greeks, with one example of Greek mysticism; modern atheism and naturalism; and finally, Christian theism.

The perusal of such widely differing views, however, naturally provokes further questions: how can we know which of them, if any, is true? And what is truth anyway? Is there such a thing as absolute truth? And how should we recognise it, even if we encountered it? That, of course, raises the fundamental question that affects not only scientific and philosophical theories, but our day-to-day experience as well: how do we know anything?

The part of philosophy that deals with these questions is known as epistemology, and to it we devote Book 3, *Questioning Our Knowledge*. Here we pay special attention to a theory that has found wide popularity in recent times, namely, postmodernism. We pay close attention to it, because if it were true (and we think it isn't) it would seriously affect not only ethics, but science and the interpretation of literature.

When it comes to deciding what are the basic ethical principles that all should universally follow we should observe that we are not the first generation on earth to have thought about this question. Book 4, *Doing What's Right*, therefore, presents a selection of notable but diverse ethical theories, so that we may profit from their insights that are of permanent value; and, at the same time, discern what, if any, are their weaknesses, or even fallacies.

But any serious consideration of humankind's ethical behaviour will eventually raise another practical problem. As Aristotle observed long ago, ethics can tell us what we ought to do; but by itself it gives us no adequate power to do it. It is the indisputable fact that, even when we know that something is ethically right and that it is our duty to do it, we fail to do it; and contrariwise, when we know something is wrong and should not be done, we nonetheless go and do it. Why is that? Unless we can find an answer to this problem, ethical theory—of whatever kind—will prove ultimately ineffective, because it is impractical.

Therefore, it seemed to us that it would be seriously deficient to deal with ethics simply as a philosophy that tells us what ethical standards we ought to attain to in life. Our human plight is that, even when we know that something is wrong, we go and do it anyway. How can we overcome this universal weakness?

Jesus Christ, whose emphasis on ethical teaching is unmistakable, and in some respects unparalleled, nevertheless insisted that ethical teaching is ineffective unless it is preceded by a spiritual rebirth (see Gospel of John 3). But this brings us into the area of religion, and many people find that difficult. What right has religion to talk about ethics, they say, when religion has been the cause of so many wars, and still leads to much violence? But the same is true of political philosophies—and it does not stop us thinking about politics.

Then there are many religions, and they all claim to offer their adherents help to fulfil their ethical duties. How can we know if they are true, and that they offer real hope? It seems to us that, in order to know whether the help a religion offers is real or not, one would have to practise that religion and discover it by experience. We, the authors of this book, are Christians, and we would regard it as impertinent of us to try to describe what other religions mean to their adherents. Therefore, in Book 5, *Claiming to Answer*, we confine ourselves to stating why we think the claims of the Christian gospel are valid, and the help it offers real.

However, talk of God raises an obvious and very poignant problem: how can there be a God who cares for justice, when, apparently, he makes no attempt to put a stop to the injustices that ravage our world? And how can it be thought that there is an all-loving, all-powerful, and all-wise creator when so many people suffer such bad things, inflicted on them not just by man's cruelty but by natural disasters and disease? These are certainly difficult questions. It is the purpose of Book 6, *Suffering Life's Pain*, to discuss these difficulties and to consider possible solutions.

It only remains to point out that every section and subsection of the book is provided with questions, both to help understanding of the subject matter and to encourage the widest possible discussion and debate.

DAVID GOODING
JOHN LENNOX

ANALYTICAL OUTLINE

CLAIMING TO
ANSWER

SERIES INTRODUCTION

Our worldview . . . includes our views,
however ill or well thought out, right or
wrong, about the hard yet fascinating
questions of existence and life: What am
I to make of the universe? Where did it
come from? Who am I? Where did I come
from? How do I know things? Do I have any
significance? Do I have any duty?

THE SHAPING OF A WORLDVIEW
FOR A LIFE FULL OF CHOICES

In this introductory section we are going to consider the need for each one of us to construct his or her own worldview. We shall discuss what a worldview is and why it is necessary to form one; and we shall enquire as to what voices we must listen to as we construct our worldview. As we set out to examine how we understand the world, we are also trying to discover whether we can know the ultimate truth about reality. So each of the subjects in this series will bring us back to the twin questions of what is real and why it matters whether we know what is real. We will, therefore, need to ask as we conclude this introductory section what we mean by 'reality' and then to ask: what is the nature of ultimate reality?[1]

WHY WE NEED A WORLDVIEW

There is a tendency in our modern world for education to become a matter of increasing specialisation. The vast increase of knowledge during the past century means that unless we specialise in this or that topic it is very difficult to keep up with, and grasp the significance of, the ever-increasing flood of new discoveries. In one sense this is to be welcomed because it is the result of something that in itself is one of the marvels of our modern world, namely, the fantastic progress of science and technology.

But while that is so, it is good to remind ourselves that true education has a much wider objective than this. If, for instance, we are to understand the progress of our modern world, we must see it against

---

[1] Please note this Introduction is the same for each book in the series, except for the final section— Our Aim.

the background of the traditions we have inherited from the past and that will mean that we need to have a good grasp of history.

Sometimes we forget that ancient philosophers faced and thought deeply about the basic philosophical principles that underlie all science and came up with answers from which we can still profit. If we forget this, we might spend a lot of time and effort thinking through the same problems and not coming up with as good answers as they did.

Moreover, the role of education is surely to try and understand how all the various fields of knowledge and experience in life fit together. To understand a grand painting one needs to see the picture as a whole and understand the interrelationship of all its details and not simply concentrate on one of its features.

Moreover, while we rightly insist on the objectivity of science we must not forget that it is we who are doing the science. And therefore, sooner or later, we must come to ask how we ourselves fit into the universe that we are studying. We must not allow ourselves to become so engrossed in our material world and its related technologies that we neglect our fellow human beings; for they, as we shall later see, are more important than the rest of the universe put together.[2] The study of ourselves and our fellow human beings will, of course, take more than a knowledge of science. It will involve the worlds of philosophy, sociology, literature, art, music, history and much more besides.

Educationally, therefore, it is an important thing to remember— and a thrilling thing to discover—the interrelation and the unity of all knowledge. Take, for example, what it means to know what a rose is: *What is the truth about a rose?*

To answer the question adequately, we shall have to consult a whole array of people. First the scientists. We begin with the *botanists*, who are constantly compiling and revising lists of all the known plants and flowers in the world and then classifying them in terms of families and groups. They help us to appreciate our rose by telling us what family it belongs to and what are its distinctive features.

Next, the *plant breeders* and *gardeners* will inform us of the history of our particular rose, how it was bred from other kinds, and the conditions under which its sort can best be cultivated.

---

[2] Especially in Book 1 of this series, *Being Truly Human.*

FIGURE I.1. A Rose.

In William Shakespeare's play *Romeo and Juliet,* the beloved dismisses the fact that her lover is from the rival house of Montague, invoking the beauty of one of the best known and most favourite flowers in the world: 'What's in a name? that which we call a rose / By any other name would smell as sweet'.

Reproduced with permission of ©iStock/OGphoto.

Then, the *chemists, biochemists, biologists* and *geneticists* will tell us about the chemical and biochemical constituents of our rose and the bewildering complexities of its cells, those micro-miniaturised factories which embody mechanisms more complicated than any built by human beings, and yet so tiny that we need highly specialised equipment to see them. They will tell us about the vast coded database of genetic information which the cell factories use in order to produce the building blocks of the rose. They will describe, among a host of other things, the processes by which the rose lives: how it photosynthesises sunlight into sugar-borne energy and the mechanisms by which it is pollinated and propagated.

After that, the *physicists* and *cosmologists* will tell us that the chemicals of which our rose is composed are made up of atoms which themselves are built from various particles like electrons, protons and neutrons. They will give us their account of where the basic material in the universe comes from and how it was formed. If we ask how such knowledge helps us to understand roses, the cosmologists may well point out that our earth is the only planet in our solar system that is able to grow roses! In that respect, as in a multitude of other respects, our planet is very special—and that is surely something to be wondered at.

But when the botanists, plant breeders, gardeners, chemists, biochemists, physicists and cosmologists have told us all they can, and it is a great deal which would fill many volumes, even then many of us will feel that they will scarcely have begun to tell us the truth about roses. Indeed, they have not explained what perhaps most of us would think is the most important thing about roses: the beauty of their form, colour and fragrance.

Now here is a very significant thing: scientists can explain the astonishing complexity of the mechanisms which lie behind our senses of vision and smell that enable us to see roses and detect their scent. But we don't need to ask the scientists whether we ought to consider roses beautiful or not: we can see and smell that for ourselves! We perceive this by *intuition*. We just look at the rose and we can at once see that it is beautiful. We do not need anyone to tell us that it is beautiful. If anyone were so foolish as to suggest that because science cannot measure beauty, therefore beauty does not exist, we should simply say: 'Don't be silly.'

But the perception of beauty does not rest on our own intuition alone. We could also consult the *artists*. With their highly developed sense of colour, light and form, they will help us to perceive a depth and intensity of beauty in a rose that otherwise we might miss. They can educate our eyes.

Likewise, there are the *poets*. They, with their finely honed ability as word artists, will use imagery, metaphor, allusion, rhythm and rhyme to help us formulate and articulate the feelings we experience when we look at roses, feelings that otherwise might remain vague and difficult to express.

Finally, if we wanted to pursue this matter of the beauty of a rose deeper still, we could talk to the *philosophers*, especially experts in aesthetics. For each of us, perceiving that a rose is beautiful is a highly subjective experience, something that we see and feel at a deep level inside ourselves. Nevertheless, when we show a rose to other people, we expect them too to agree that it is beautiful. They usually have no difficulty in doing so.

From this it would seem that, though the appreciation of beauty is a highly subjective experience, yet we observe:

1.   there are some objective criteria for deciding what is beautiful and what is not;
2.   there is in each person an inbuilt aesthetic sense, a capacity for perceiving beauty; and
3.   where some people cannot, or will not, see beauty, in, say, a

rose, or will even prefer ugliness, it must be that their internal capacity for seeing beauty is defective or damaged in some way, as, for instance, by colour blindness or defective shape recognition, or through some psychological disorder (like, for instance, people who revel in cruelty, rather than in kindness).

Now by this time we may think that we have exhausted the truth about roses; but of course we haven't. We have thought about the scientific explanation of roses. We have then considered the value we place on them, their beauty and what they mean to us. But precisely because they have meaning and value, they raise another group of questions about the moral, ethical and eventually spiritual significance of what we do with them. Consider, for instance, the following situations:

First, a woman has used what little spare money she had to buy some roses. She likes roses intensely and wants to keep them as long as she can. But a poor neighbour of hers is sick, and she gets a strong feeling that she ought to give at least some of these roses to her sick neighbour. So now she has two conflicting instincts within her:

1. an instinct of self-interest: a strong desire to keep the roses for herself, and
2. an instinctive sense of duty: she ought to love her neighbour as herself, and therefore give her roses to her neighbour.

Questions arise. Where do these instincts come from? And how shall she decide between them? Some might argue that her selfish desire to keep the roses is simply the expression of the blind, but powerful, basic driving force of evolution: self-propagation. But the altruistic sense of duty to help her neighbour at the expense of loss to herself—where does that come from? Why ought she to obey it? She has a further problem: she must decide one way or the other. She cannot wait for scientists or philosophers, or indeed anyone else, to help her. She has to commit herself to some course of action. How and on what grounds should she decide between the two competing urges?

Second, a man likes roses, but he has no money to buy them. He sees that he could steal roses from someone else's garden in such a way that he could be certain that he would never be found out. Would it be wrong to steal them? If neither the owner of the roses, nor the police, nor the courts would ever find out that he stole them, why shouldn't he steal them? Who has the right to say that it is wrong to steal?

Third, a man repeatedly gives bunches of roses to a woman whose husband is abroad on business. The suspicion is that he is giving her roses in order to tempt her to be disloyal to her husband. That would be adultery. Is adultery wrong? Always wrong? Who has the right to say so?

Now to answer questions like these in the first, second, and third situations thoroughly and adequately we must ask and answer the most fundamental questions that we can ask about roses (and indeed about anything else).

Where do roses come from? We human beings did not create them (and are still far from being able to create anything like them). Is there a God who designed and created them? Is he their ultimate owner, who has the right to lay down the rules as to how we should use them?

Or did roses simply evolve out of eternally existing inorganic matter, without any plan or purpose behind them, and without any ultimate owner to lay down the rules as to how they ought to be used? And if so, is the individual himself free to do what he likes, so long as no one finds out?

So far, then, we have been answering the simple question 'What is the truth about a rose?' and we have found that to answer it adequately we have had to draw on, not one source of knowledge, like science or literature, but on many. Even the consideration of roses has led to deep and fundamental questions about the world beyond the roses.

It is our answers to these questions which combine to shape the framework into which we fit all of our knowledge of other things. That framework, which consists of those ideas, conscious or unconscious, which all of us have about the basic nature of the world and of ourselves and of society, is called our worldview. It includes our views, however ill or well thought out, right or wrong, about the hard yet fascinating questions of existence and life: What am I to make of the universe? Where did it come from? Who am I? Where did I come from? How do I know things? Do I have any significance? Do I have any duty? Our worldview is the big picture into which we fit everything else. It is the lens through which we look to try to make sense of the world.

Our worldview is the big picture into which we fit everything else. It is the lens through which we look to try to make sense of the world.

ASKING THE FUNDAMENTAL QUESTIONS

'He who will succeed', said Aristotle, 'must ask the right questions'; and so, when it comes to forming a worldview, must we.

It is at least comforting to know that we are not the first people to have asked such questions. Many others have done so in the past (and continue to do so in the present). That means they have done some of the work for us! In order to profit from their thinking and experience, it will be helpful for us to collect some of those fundamental questions which have been and are on practically everybody's list. We shall then ask why these particular questions have been thought to be important. After that we shall briefly survey some of the varied answers that have been given, before we tackle the task of forming our own answers. So let's get down to compiling a list of 'worldview questions'. First of all there are questions about the universe in general and about our home planet Earth in particular.

The Greeks were the first people in Europe to ask scientific questions about what the earth and the universe are made of, and how they work. It would appear that they asked their questions for no other reason than sheer intellectual curiosity. Their research was, as we would nowadays describe it, disinterested. They were not at first concerned with any technology that might result from it. Theirs was pure, not applied, science. We pause to point out that it is still a very healthy thing for any educational system to maintain a place for pure science in its curriculum and to foster an attitude of intellectual curiosity for its own sake.

But we cannot afford to limit ourselves to pure science (and even less to technology, marvellous though it is). Centuries ago Socrates perceived that. He was initially curious about the universe, but gradually came to feel that studying how human beings ought to behave was far more important than finding out what the moon was made

FIGURE I.2. *The School of Athens* by Raphael.

Italian Renaissance artist Raphael likely painted the fresco *Scuola di Atene* (The School of Athens), representing Philosophy, between 1509 and 1511 for the Vatican. Many interpreters believe the hand gestures of the central figures, Plato and Aristotle, and the books each is holding respectively, *Timaeus* and *Nicomachean Ethics*, indicate two approaches to metaphysics. A number of other great ancient Greek philosophers are featured by Raphael in this painting, including Socrates (eighth figure to the left of Plato).

Reproduced from Wikimedia Commons.

of. He therefore abandoned physics and immersed himself in moral philosophy.

On the other hand, the leaders of the major philosophical schools in ancient Greece came to see that you could not form an adequate doctrine of human moral behaviour without understanding how human beings are related both to their cosmic environment and to the powers and principles that control the universe. In this they were surely right, which brings us to what was and still is the first fundamental question.[3]

First fundamental worldview question

What lies behind the observable universe? Physics has taught us that things are not quite what they seem to be. A wooden table, which looks solid, turns out to be composed of atoms bound together by powerful forces which operate in the otherwise empty space between them. Each atom turns out also to be mostly empty space and can be modelled from one point of view as a nucleus surrounded by orbiting electrons. The nucleus only occupies about one billionth of the space of the atom. Split the nucleus and we find protons and neutrons. They turn out to be composed of even stranger quarks and gluons. Are these the basic building blocks of matter, or are there other even more mysterious elementary building blocks to be found? That is one of the exciting quests of modern physics. And even as the search goes on, another question keeps nagging: what lies behind basic matter anyway?

The answers that are given to this question fall roughly into two groups: those that suggest that there is nothing 'behind' the basic matter of the universe, and those that maintain that there certainly is something.

Group A.   There is nothing but matter. It is the prime reality, being self-existent and eternal. It is not dependent on anything or on anyone. It is blind and purposeless; nevertheless it has within it the power to develop and organise itself—still blindly and purposelessly—into all the variety of matter and

---

[3]   See Book 4: *Doing What's Right.*

life that we see in the universe today. This is the philosophy of materialism.

Group B. Behind matter, which had a beginning, stands some uncreated self-existent, creative Intelligence; or, as Jews and Muslims would say, God; and Christians, the God and Father of the Lord Jesus Christ. This God upholds the universe, interacts with it, but is not part of it. He is spirit, not matter. The universe exists as an expression of his mind and for the purpose of fulfilling his will. This is the philosophy of theism.

Second fundamental worldview question

This leads us to our second fundamental worldview question, which is in three parts: *how did our world come into existence, how has it developed, and how has it come to be populated with such an amazing variety of life?*

Again, answers to these questions tend to fall into two groups:

Group A. Inanimate matter itself, without any antecedent design or purpose, formed into that conglomerate which became the earth and then in some way (not yet observed or understood) as a result of its own inherent properties and powers by spontaneous generation spawned life. The initial lowly life forms then gradually evolved into the present vast variety of life through the natural processes of mutation and natural selection, mechanisms likewise without any design or purpose. There is, therefore, no ultimate rational purpose behind either the existence of the universe, or of earth and its inhabitants.

Group B. The universe, the solar system and planet Earth have been designed and precision engineered to make it possible for life to exist on earth. The astonishing complexity of living systems, and the awesome sophistication of their mechanisms, point in the same direction.

It is not difficult to see what different implications the two radically different views have for human significance and behaviour.

Third fundamental worldview question

The third fundamental worldview question comes, again, as a set of related questions with the answers commonly given to central ideas falling into two groups: *What are human beings? Where do their rationality and moral sense come from? What are their hopes for the future, and what, if anything, happens to them after death?*

Group A.   *Human nature.* Human beings are nothing but matter. They have no spirit and their powers of rational thought have arisen out of mindless matter by non-rational processes.

Morality. Man's sense of morality and duty arise solely out of social interactions between him and his fellow humans.

Human rights. Human beings have no inherent, natural rights, but only those that are granted by society or the government of the day.

Purpose in life. Man makes his own purpose.

The future. The utopia dreamed of and longed for will be brought about, either by the irresistible outworking of the forces inherent in matter and/or history; or, alternatively, as human beings learn to direct and control the biological processes of evolution itself.

Death and beyond. Death for each individual means total extinction. Nothing survives.

Group B.   *Human nature.* Human beings are created by God, indeed in the image of God (according, at least, to Judaism, Christianity and Islam). Human beings' powers of rationality are derived from the divine 'Logos' through whom they were created.

Morality. Their moral sense arises from certain 'laws of God' implanted in them by their Creator.

14

Human rights. They have certain inalienable rights which all other human beings and governments must respect, simply because they are creatures of God, created in God's image.

Purpose in life. Their main purpose in life is to enjoy fellowship with God and to serve God, and likewise to serve their fellow creatures for their Creator's sake.

The future. The utopia they long for is not a dream, but a sure hope based on the Creator's plan for the redemption of humankind and of the world.

Death and beyond. Death does not mean extinction. Human beings, after death, will be held accountable to God. Their ultimate state will eventually be, either to be with God in total fellowship in heaven; or to be excluded from his presence.

These, very broadly speaking, are the questions that people have asked through the whole of recorded history, and a brief survey of some of the answers that have been, and still are, given to them.

The fundamental difference between the two groups of answers

Now it is obvious that the two groups of answers given above are diametrically opposed; but we ought to pause here to make sure that we have understood what exactly the nature and cause of the opposition is. If we were not thinking carefully, we might jump to the conclusion that the answers in the A-groups are those given by science, while the answers in the B-groups are those given by religion. But that would be a fundamental misunderstanding of the situation. It is true that the majority of scientists today would agree with the answers given in the A-groups; but there is a growing number of scientists who would agree with the answers given in the B-groups. It is not therefore a conflict between science and religion. It is a difference in the basic philosophies which determine the interpretation of the evidence which science provides. Atheists will interpret that evidence in one way; theists (or pantheists) will interpret it in another.

This is understandable. No scientist comes to the task of doing research with a mind completely free of presuppositions. The atheist does research on the presupposition that there is no God. That is his basic philosophy, his worldview. He claims that he can explain everything without God. He will sometimes say that he cannot imagine what kind of scientific evidence there could possibly be for the existence of God; and not surprisingly he tends not to find any.

The theist, on the other hand, starts by believing in God and finds in his scientific discoveries abundant—overwhelming, he would say—evidence of God's hand in the sophisticated design and mechanisms of the universe.

> We pick up ideas, beliefs and attitudes from our family and society, often without realising that we have done so, and without recognising how these largely unconscious influences and presuppositions control our reactions to the questions with which life faces us.

It all comes down, then, to the importance of recognising what worldview we start with. Some of us, who have never yet thought deeply about these things, may feel that we have no worldview, and that we come to life's questions in general, and science in particular, with a completely open mind. But that is unlikely to be so. We pick up ideas, beliefs and attitudes from our family and society, often without realising that we have done so, and without recognising how these largely unconscious influences and presuppositions control our reactions to the questions with which life faces us. Hence the importance of consciously thinking through our worldview and of adjusting it where necessary to take account of the evidence available.

In that process, then, we certainly must listen to science and allow it to critique where necessary and to amend our presuppositions. But to form an adequate worldview we shall need to listen to many other voices as well.

VOICES TO BE LISTENED TO

So far, then, we have been surveying some worldview questions and various answers that have been, and still are, given to them. Now we must face these questions ourselves, and begin to come to our own decisions about them.

Our worldview must be our own, in the sense that we have personally thought it through and adopted it of our own free will. No one has the right to impose his or her worldview on us by force. The days are rightly gone when the church could force Galileo to deny what science had plainly taught him. Gone, too, for the most part, are the days when the State could force an atheistic worldview on people on pain of prison and even death. Human rights demand that people should be free to hold and to propagate by reasoned argument whatever worldview they believe in—so long, of course, that their view does not injure other people. We, the authors of this book, hold a theistic worldview. But we shall not attempt to force our view down anybody's throat. We come from a tradition whose basic principle is 'Let everyone be persuaded in his own mind.'

So we must all make up our own minds and form our own worldview. In the process of doing so there are a number of voices that we must listen to.

The voice of intuition

The first voice we must listen to is intuition. There are things in life that we see and know, not as the result of lengthy philosophical reasoning, nor as a result of rigorous scientific experimentation, but by direct, instinctive intuition. We 'see' that a rose is beautiful. We instinctively 'know' that child abuse is wrong. A scientist can sometimes 'see' what the solution to a problem is going to be even before he has worked out the scientific technique that will eventually provide formal proof of it.

A few scientists and philosophers still try to persuade us that the laws of cause and effect operating in the human brain are completely deterministic so that our decisions are predetermined: real choice is not possible. But, say what they will, we ourselves intuitively know that we do have the ability to make a free choice, whether, say, to read a book, or to go for a walk, whether to tell the truth or to tell a lie. We know we are free to take either course of action, and everyone else knows it too, and acts accordingly. This freedom is such a part of our innate concept of human dignity and value that we (for the most part) insist on being treated as responsible human beings and on treating others as such. For that reason, if we commit a crime, the magistrate will first enquire

17

(*a*) if, when we committed the crime, we knew we were doing wrong; and (*b*) whether or not we were acting under duress. The answer to these questions will determine the verdict.

We must, therefore, give due attention to intuition, and not allow ourselves to be persuaded by pseudo-intellectual arguments to deny (or affirm) what we intuitively know to be true (or false).

On the other hand, intuition has its limits. It can be mistaken. When ancient scientists first suggested that the world was a sphere, even some otherwise great thinkers rejected the idea. They intuitively felt that it was absurd to think that there were human beings on the opposite side of the earth to us, walking 'upside-down', their feet pointed towards our feet (hence the term 'antipodean') and their heads hanging perilously down into empty space! But intuition had misled them. The scientists who believed in a spherical earth were right, intuition was wrong.

The lesson is that we need both intuition and science, acting as checks and balances, the one on the other.

The voice of science

Science speaks to our modern world with a very powerful and authoritative voice. It can proudly point to a string of scintillating theoretical breakthroughs which have spawned an almost endless array of technological spin-offs: from the invention of the light bulb to virtual-reality environments; from the wheel to the moon-landing vehicle; from the discovery of aspirin and antibiotics to the cracking of the genetic code; from the vacuum cleaner to the smartphone; from the abacus to the parallel computer; from the bicycle to the self-driving car. The benefits that come from these achievements of science are self-evident, and they both excite our admiration and give to science an immense credibility.

Yet for many people the voice of science has a certain ambivalence about it. For the achievements of science are not invariably used for the good of humanity. Indeed, in the past century science has produced the most hideously efficient weapons of destruction that the world has ever seen. The laser that is used to restore vision to the eye can be used to guide missiles with deadly efficiency. This development has led in recent times to a strong anti-scientific reaction. This is understandable; but we need to guard against the obvious fallacy of blaming science for the misuse made of its discoveries. The blame for the devastation caused by the atomic bomb, for instance, does not chiefly lie with the scientists who discovered the possibility of atomic fission and fusion, but with the politicians who for reasons of global conquest insisted on the discoveries being used for the making of weapons of mass destruction.

Science, in itself, is morally neutral. Indeed, as scientists who are Christians would say, it is a form of the worship of God through the reverent study of his handiwork and is by all means to be encouraged. It is for that reason that James Clerk Maxwell, the nineteenth-century Scottish physicist who discovered the famous equations governing electromagnetic waves which are now called after him, put the following quotation from the Hebrew Psalms above the door of the Cavendish Laboratory in Cambridge where it still stands: 'The works of the LORD are great, sought out of all them that have pleasure therein' (Ps 111:2).

We must distinguish, of course, between science as a method of investigation and individual scientists who actually do the investigation. We must also distinguish between the facts which they establish beyond (reasonable) doubt and the tentative hypotheses and theories which they construct on the basis of their initial observations and experiments, and which they use to guide their subsequent research.

These distinctions are important because scientists sometimes mistake their tentative theories for proven fact, and in their teaching of students and in their public lectures promulgate as established fact what has never actually been proved. It can also happen that scientists advance a tentative theory which catches the attention of the media who then put it across to the public with so much hype that the impression is given that the theory has been established beyond question.

> Scientists sometimes mistake their tentative theories for proven fact, and in their teaching of students and in their public lectures promulgate as established fact what has never actually been proved.

Then again, we need to remember the proper limits of science. As we discovered when talking about the beauty of roses, there are things which science, strictly so called, cannot and should not be expected to explain.

Sometimes some scientists forget this, and damage the reputation of science by making wildly exaggerated claims for it. The famous mathematician and philosopher Bertrand Russell, for instance, once wrote: 'Whatever knowledge is attainable, must be attained by scientific methods; and what science cannot discover, mankind cannot know.'[4] Nobel laureate Sir Peter Medawar had a saner and more realistic view of science. He wrote:

> There is no quicker way for a scientist to bring discredit upon himself and on his profession than roundly to declare—particularly when no declaration of any kind is called for—that science knows or soon will know the answers to all questions worth asking, and that the questions that do not admit a scientific answer are in some way nonquestions or 'pseudoquestions' that only simpletons ask and only the gullible profess to be able to answer.[5]

Medawar says elsewhere: 'The existence of a limit to science is, however, made clear by its inability to answer childlike elementary questions having to do with first and last things—questions such as "How did everything begin?"; "What are we all here for?"; "What is the point of living?"' He adds that it is to imaginative literature and religion that we must turn for answers to such questions.[6]

However, when we have said all that should be said about the limits of science, the voice of science is still one of the most important voices to which we must listen in forming our worldview. We cannot, of course, all be experts in science. But when the experts report their findings to students in other disciplines or to the general public, as they increasingly do, we all must listen to them; listen as critically as we listen to experts in other fields. But we must listen.[7]

The voice of philosophy

The next voice we must listen to is the voice of philosophy. To some people the very thought of philosophy is daunting; but actually anyone

---

[4] Russell, *Religion and Science*, 243.
[5] Medawar, *Advice to a Young Scientist*, 31.
[6] Medawar, *Limits of Science*, 59–60.
[7] Those who wish to study the topic further are directed to the Appendix in this book: 'The Scientific Endeavour', and to the books by John Lennox noted there.

who seriously attempts to investigate the truth of any statement is already thinking philosophically. Eminent philosopher Anthony Kenny writes:

> Philosophy is exciting because it is the broadest of all disciplines, exploring the basic concepts which run through all our talking and thinking on any topic whatever. Moreover, it can be undertaken without any special preliminary training or instruction; anyone can do philosophy who is willing to think hard and follow a line of reasoning.[8]

Whether we realise it or not, the way we think and reason owes a great deal to philosophy—we have already listened to its voice!

Philosophy has a number of very positive benefits to confer on us. First and foremost is the shining example of men and women who have refused to go through life unthinkingly adopting whatever happened to be the majority view at the time. Socrates said that the unexamined life is not worth living. These men and women were determined to use all their intellectual powers to try to understand what the universe was made of, how it worked, what man's place in it was, what the essence of human nature was, why we human beings so frequently do wrong and so damage ourselves and society; what could help us to avoid doing wrong; and what our chief goal in life should be, our *summum bonum* (Latin for 'chief good'). Their zeal to discover the truth and then to live by it should encourage—perhaps even shame—us to follow their example.

Secondly, it was in their search for the truth that philosophers from Socrates, Plato, and Aristotle onwards discovered the need for, and the rules of, rigorous logical thinking. The benefit of this to humanity is incalculable, in that it enables us to learn to think straight, to expose the presuppositions that lie sometimes unnoticed behind even our scientific experiments and theories, to unpick the assumptions that lurk in the formulation and expressions of our opinions, to point to fallacies in our argumentation, to detect instances of circular reasoning, and so on.

However, philosophy, just like science, has its proper limits. It cannot tell us what axioms or fundamental assumptions we should

---

8   Kenny, *Brief History of Western Philosophy*, xi.

adopt; but it can and will help us to see if the belief system which we build on those axioms is logically consistent.

There is yet a third benefit to be gained from philosophy. The history of philosophy shows that, of all the many different philosophical systems, or worldviews, that have been built up by rigorous philosophers on the basis of human reasoning alone, none has proved convincing to all other philosophers, let alone to the general public. None has achieved permanence, a fact which can seem very frustrating. But perhaps the frustration is not altogether bad in that it might lead us to ask whether there could just be another source of information without which human reason alone is by definition inadequate. And if our very frustration with philosophy for having seemed at first to promise so much satisfaction, and then in the end to have delivered so little, disposes us to look around for that other source of information, even our frustration could turn out to be a supreme benefit.

The voice of history

Yet another voice to which we must listen is the voice of history. We are fortunate indeed to be living so far on in the course of human history as we do. Already in the first century AD a simple form of jet propulsion was described by Hero of Alexandria. But technology at that time knew no means of harnessing that discovery to any worthwhile practical purpose. Eighteen hundred years were to pass before scientists discovered a way of making jet engines powerful enough to be fitted to aircraft.

When in the 1950s and 1960s scientists, working on the basis of a discovery of Albert Einstein's, argued that it would be possible to make laser beams, and then actually made them, many people mockingly said that lasers were a solution to a non-existent problem, because no one could think of a practical use to which they could be put. History has proved the critics wrong and justified the pure scientists (if pure science needs any justification!).

In other cases history has taught the opposite lesson. At one point the phlogiston theory of combustion came to be almost universally accepted. History eventually proved it wrong.

Fanatical religious sects (in spite, be it said, of the explicit prohibition of the Bible) have from time to time predicted that the end of the world would take place at such-and-such a time in such-and-such a place. History has invariably proved them wrong.

In the last century, the philosophical system known as logical positivism arose like a meteor and seemed set to dominate the philosophical landscape, superseding all other systems. But history discovered its fatal flaw, namely that it was based on a verification principle which allowed only two kinds of meaningful statement: *analytic* (a statement which is true by definition, that is a tautology like 'a vixen is a female fox'), or *synthetic* (a statement which is capable of verification by experiment, like 'water is composed of hydrogen and oxygen'). Thus all metaphysical statements were dismissed as meaningless! But, as philosopher Karl Popper famously pointed out, the Verification Principle itself is neither analytic nor synthetic and so is meaningless! Logical positivism is therefore self-refuting. Professor Nicholas Fotion, in his article on the topic in *The Oxford Companion to Philosophy*, says: 'By the late 1960s it became obvious that the movement had pretty much run its course.'[9]

Earlier still, Marx, basing himself on Hegel, applied his dialectical materialism first to matter and then to history. He claimed to have discovered a law in the workings of social and political history that would irresistibly lead to the establishment of a utopia on earth; and millions gave their lives to help forward this process. The verdict has been that history seems not to know any such irresistible law.

History has also delivered a devastating verdict on the Nazi theory of the supremacy of the Aryan races, which, it was promised, would lead to a new world order.

History, then, is a very valuable, if sometimes very disconcerting, adjudicator of our ideas and systems of thought. We should certainly pay serious heed to its lessons and be grateful for them.

But there is another reason why we should listen to history. It introduces us to the men and women who have proved to be world leaders of thought and whose influence is still a live force among us today. Among them, of course, is Jesus Christ. He was rejected, as we know, by his contemporaries and executed. But, then, so was Socrates. Socrates' influence has lived on; but Christ's influence has been and still is infinitely greater than that of Socrates, or of any other world leader.

---

[9] Fotion, 'Logical Positivism'.

It would be very strange if we listened, as we do, to Socrates, Plato, Aristotle, Hume, Kant, Marx and Einstein, and neglected or refused to listen to Christ. The numerous (and some very early) manuscripts of the New Testament make available to us an authentic record of his teaching. Only extreme prejudice would dismiss him without first listening to what he says.

> History introduces us to the men and women who have proved to be world leaders of thought and whose influence is still a live force among us today. . . . It would be very strange if we listened, as we do, to Socrates, Plato, Aristotle, Hume, Kant, Marx and Einstein, and neglected or refused to listen to Christ.

The voice of divine self-revelation

The final voice that claims the right to be heard is a voice which runs persistently through history and refuses to be silenced in claiming that there is another source of information beyond that which intuition, scientific research and philosophical reasoning can provide. That voice is the voice of divine self-revelation. The claim is that the Creator, whose existence and power can be intuitively perceived through his created works, has not otherwise remained silent and aloof. In the course of the centuries he has spoken into our world through his prophets and supremely through Jesus Christ.

Of course, atheists will say that for them this claim seems to be the stuff of fairy tales; and atheistic scientists will object that there is no scientific evidence for the existence of a creator (indeed, they may well claim that assuming the existence of a creator destroys the foundation of true scientific methodology—for more of that see this book's Appendix); and that, therefore, the idea that we could have direct information from the creator himself is conceptually absurd. This reaction is, of course, perfectly consistent with the basic assumption of atheism.

However, apparent conceptual absurdity is not proof positive that something is not possible, or even true. Remember what we noticed earlier, that many leading thinkers, when they first encountered the suggestion that the earth was not flat but spherical, rejected it out of hand because of the conceptual absurdities to which they imagined it led.

In the second century AD a certain Lucian of Samosata decided to debunk what he thought to be fanciful speculations of the early scientists and the grotesque traveller's tales of so-called explorers. He wrote a book which, with his tongue in his cheek, he called *Vera historia* (A True Story). In it he told how he had travelled through space to the moon. He discovered that the moon-dwellers had a special kind of mirror by means of which they could see what people were doing on earth. They also possessed something like a well shaft by means of which they could even hear what people on earth were saying. His prose was sober enough, as if he were writing factual history. But he expected his readers to see that the very conceptual absurdity of what he claimed to have seen meant that these things were impossible and would forever remain so.

Unknown to him, however, the forces and materials already existed in nature, which, when mankind learned to harness them, would send some astronauts into orbit round the moon, land others on the moon, and make possible radio and television communication between the moon and the earth!

We should remember, too, that atomic radiation and radio frequency emissions from distant galaxies were not invented by scientists in recent decades. They were there all the time, though invisible and undetected and not believed in nor even thought of for centuries; but they were not discovered until comparatively recent times, when brilliant scientists conceived the possibility that, against all popular expectation, such phenomena might exist. They looked for them, and found them.

Is it then, after all, so conceptually absurd to think that our human intellect and rationality come not from mindless matter through the agency of impersonal unthinking forces, but from a higher personal intellect and reason?

An old, but still valid, analogy will help us at this point. If we ask about a particular motor car: 'Where did this motor car begin?' one answer would be, 'It began on the production lines of such-and-such a factory and was put together by humans and robots.'

Another, deeper-level, answer would be: 'It had its beginning in the mineral from which its constituent parts were made.'

But in the prime sense of beginning, the motor car, of which this particular motor car is a specimen, had its beginning, not in the factory, nor in its basic materials, but in something altogether different:

in the intelligent mind of a person, that is, of its inventor. We know this, of course, by history and by experience; but we also know it intuitively: it is self-evidently true.

Millions of people likewise have felt, and still do feel, that what Christ and his prophets say about the 'beginning' of our human rationality is similarly self-evidently true: 'In the beginning was the Logos, and the Logos was with God, and the Logos was God. . . . All things were made by him . . .' (John 1:1–2, our trans.). That is, at any rate, a far more likely story than that our human intelligence and rationality sprang originally out of mindless matter, by accidental permutations, selected by unthinking nature.

Now the term 'Logos' means both rationality and the expression of that rationality through intelligible communication. If that rational intelligence is God and personal, and we humans are endowed by him with personhood and intelligence, then it is far from being absurd to think that the divine Logos, whose very nature and function it is to be the expression and communicator of that intelligence, should communicate with us. On the contrary, to deny a priori the possibility of divine revelation and to shut one's ears in advance to what Jesus Christ has to say, before listening to his teaching to see if it is, or is not, self-evidently true, is not the true scientific attitude, which is to keep an open mind and explore any reasonable avenue to truth.[10]

Moreover, the fear that to assume the existence of a creator God would undermine true scientific methodology is contradicted by the sheer facts of history. Sir Francis Bacon (1561–1626), widely regarded as the father of the modern scientific method, believed that God had revealed himself in two great Books, the Book of Nature and the Book of God's Word, the Bible. In his famous *Advancement of Learning* (1605), Bacon wrote: 'Let no man . . . think or maintain, that a man can search too far, or be too well studied in the book of God's word, or in the book of God's works; divinity or philosophy; but rather let men endeavour an endless progress or proficience in both.'[11] It is this quotation which Charles Darwin chose to put at the front of *On the Origin of Species* (1859).

---

[10] For the fuller treatment of these questions and related topics, see Book 5 in this series, *Claiming to Answer*.

[11] Bacon, *Advancement of Learning*, 8.

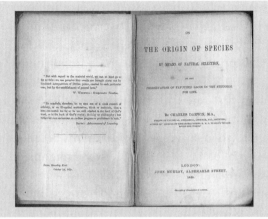

FIGURE I.3.
On the Origin of Species (1859)
by Charles Darwin.

One of the book epigraphs
Charles Darwin selected for
his magnum opus is from
Francis Bacon's *Advancement
of Learning* (1605).

Reproduced from Dennis O'Neil.

Historians of science point out that it was this theistic 'Two-Book' view which was largely responsible for the meteoric rise of science beginning in the sixteenth century. C. S. Lewis refers to a statement by one of the most eminent historians of all time, Sir Alfred North Whitehead, and says: 'Professor Whitehead points out that centuries of belief in a God who combined "the personal energy of Jehovah" with "the rationality of a Greek philosopher" first produced that firm expectation of systematic order which rendered possible the birth of modern science. Men became scientific because they expected Law in Nature and they expected Law in Nature because they believed in a Legislator.'[12] In other words, theism was the cradle of science. Indeed, far from thinking that the idea of a creator was conceptually absurd, most of the great leaders of science in that period did believe in a creator.

Johannes Kepler	1571–1630	Celestial mechanics
Blaise Pascal	1623–62	Hydrostatics
Robert Boyle	1627–91	Chemistry, Gas dynamics
Isaac Newton	1642–1727	Mathematics, Optics, Dynamics
Michael Faraday	1791–1867	Magnetism
Charles Babbage	1791–1871	Computer science
Gregor Mendel	1822–84	Genetics
Louis Pasteur	1822–95	Bacteriology
Lord Kelvin	1824–1907	Thermodynamics
James Clerk Maxwell	1831–79	Electrodynamics, Thermodynamics

---

[12] Lewis, *Miracles*, 110.

All of these famous men would have agreed with Einstein: 'Science without religion is lame, religion without science is blind.'[13] History shows us very clearly, then, that far from belief in God being a hindrance to science, it has provided one of the main impulses for its development.

Still today there are many first-rate scientists who are believers in God. For example, Professor William D. Phillips, Nobel laureate for Physics 1997, is an active Christian, as is the world-famous botanist and former Director of the Royal Botanic Gardens, Kew in London, Sir Ghillean Prance, and so is the geneticist Francis S. Collins, who was the Director of the National Institutes of Health in the United States who gained recognition for his leadership of the international Human Genome Project which culminated in 2003 with the completion of a finished sequence of human DNA.[14]

But with many people another objection arises: if one is not sure that God even exists, would it not be unscientific to go looking for evidence for God's existence? Surely not. Take the late Professor Carl Sagan and the Search for Extra Terrestrial Intelligence (the SETI project), which he promoted. Sagan was a famous astronomer, but when he began this search he had no hard-and-fast proven facts to go on. He proceeded simply on the basis of a hypothesis. If intelligent life has evolved on earth, then it would be possible, perhaps even likely, that it would have developed on other suitable planets elsewhere in the universe. He had no guarantee that it was so, or that he would find it, even if it existed. But even so both he and NASA (the National Aeronautics and Space Administration) thought it worth spending great effort, time and considerable sums of money to employ radio telescopes to listen to remote galaxies for evidence of intelligent life elsewhere in the universe.

Why, then, should it be thought any less scientific to look for an intelligent creator, especially when there is evidence that the universe bears the imprint of his mind? The only valid excuse for not seeking for God would be the possession of convincing evidence that God does not, and could not, exist. No one has such proof.

---

[13] Einstein, 'Science and Religion'.
[14] The list could go on, as any Internet search for 'Christians in science' will show.

But for many people divine revelation seems, nonetheless, an utter impossibility, for they have the impression that science has outgrown the cradle in which it was born and somehow proved that there is no God after all. For that reason, we examine in greater detail in the Appendix to this book what science is, what it means to be truly scientific in outlook, what science has and has not proved, and some of the fallacious ways in which science is commonly misunderstood. Here we must consider even larger questions about reality.

> The only valid excuse for not seeking for God would be the possession of convincing evidence that God does not, and could not, exist. No one has such proof.

THE MEANING OF REALITY

One of the central questions we are setting out to examine is: can we know the ultimate truth about reality? Before we consider different aspects of reality, we need to determine what we mean by 'reality'. For that purpose let's start with the way we use the term in ordinary, everyday language. After that we can move on to consider its use at higher levels.

In everyday language the noun 'reality', the adjective 'real', and the adverb 'really' have several different connotations according to the contexts in which they are used. Let's think about some examples.

First, in some situations the opposite of 'real' is 'imaginary' or 'illusory'. So, for instance, a thirsty traveller in the Sahara may see in the distance what looks to him like an oasis with water and palm trees, when in fact there is no oasis there at all. What he thinks he sees is a mirage, an optical illusion. The oasis is not real, we say; it does not actually exist.[15] Similarly a patient, having been injected with powerful drugs in the course of a serious operation, may upon waking up from the anaesthetic suffer hallucinations, and imagine she sees all kinds of weird creatures stalking round her room. But if we say, as we do, that these things which

---

[15] Mirages occur 'when sharp differences in temperature and therefore in density develop between thin layers of air at and immediately above the ground. This causes light to be bent, or refracted, as it travels through one layer to the next. . . . During the day, when a warm layer occurs next to the ground, objects near the horizon often appear to be reflected in flat surfaces, such as beaches, deserts, roads and water. This produces the shimmering, floating images which are commonly observed on very hot days.' *Oxford Reference Encyclopaedia*, 913.

she imagines she sees, are not real, we mean that they do not in actual fact exist. We could argue, of course, that something is going on in the patient's brain, and she is experiencing impressions similar to those she would have received if the weird creatures had been real. Her impressions, then, are real in the sense that they exist in her brain; but they do not correspond with the external reality that the patient supposes is creating these sense impressions. The mechanisms of her brain are presenting her with a false picture: the weird creatures do not exist. She is not seeing *them*. They are not real. On the basis of examples like this (the traveller and the patient) some philosophers have argued that none of us can ever be sure that the sense impressions which we think we receive from the external world are true representations of the external world, and not illusions. We consider their arguments in detail in Book 3 in this series, *Questioning Our Knowledge*, dealing with epistemology and related matters.

To sum up so far, then: neither the traveller nor the patient was perceiving external reality as it really was. But the reasons for their failure were different: with the traveller it was an external illusion (possibly reinforced by his thirst) that made him misread reality and imagine there was a real oasis there, when there wasn't. With the patient there was nothing unusual in the appearance of her room to cause her disordered perception. The difficulty was altogether internal to her. The drugs had distorted the perception mechanisms of her brain.

From these two examples we can learn some practical lessons:

1. It is important for us all to question from time to time whether what we unthinkingly take to be reality is in fact reality.
2. In cases like these it is external reality that has to be the standard by which we judge whether our sense perceptions are true or not.
3. Setting people free from their internal subjective misperceptions will depend on getting them, by some means or other, to face and perceive the external, objective reality.

Second, in other situations the opposite of 'real', in everyday language, is 'counterfeit', 'spurious', 'fraudulent'. So if we describe a piece of metal as being 'real gold', we mean that it is genuine gold, and not something such as brass that looks like gold, but isn't. The practical importance of being able to discern the difference between what is real in this sense and what is spurious or counterfeit, can easily be illustrated.

Take coinage, for instance. In past centuries, when coins were made (or supposed to be made) of real gold, or real silver, fraudsters would often adulterate the coinage by mixing inferior metal with gold or silver. Buyers or sellers, if they had no means of testing whether the coins they were offered were genuine, and of full value, or not, could easily be cheated.

Similarly, in our modern world counterfeiters print false bank notes and surreptitiously get them into circulation. Eventually, when the fraud is discovered, banks and traders refuse the spurious bank notes, with the result that innocent people are left with worthless pieces of paper.

Or, again, a dishonest jeweller might show a rich woman a necklace made, according to him, of valuable gems; and the rich, but unsuspecting, woman might pay a large price for it, only to discover later on that the gems were not real: they were imitations, made of a kind of glass called paste, or strass.

Conversely, an elderly woman might take her necklace, made of real gems, to a jeweller and offer to sell it to him in order to get some money to maintain herself in her old age. But the unscrupulous jeweller might make out that the gems were not as valuable as she thought: they were imitations, made of paste; and by this deceit he would persuade the reluctant woman to sell him the necklace for a much lesser price than it was worth.

Once more it will be instructive to study the underlying principles at work in these examples, because later on, when we come to study reality at a higher level, they could provide us with helpful analogies and thought models.[16]

Notice, then, that these last three examples involve significantly different principles from those that were operating in the two which we studied earlier. The oasis and the weird creatures were not real, because they did not actually exist in the external world. But the spurious coins, the fraudulent bank notes, and the genuine and the imitation gems, all

---

[16] See especially in Book 2: *Finding Ultimate Reality*.

existed in the external world. In that sense, therefore, they were all real, part of the external reality, actual pieces of matter.

What, then, was the trouble with them? It was that the fraudsters had claimed for the coins and the bank notes a value and a buying power that they did not actually possess; and in the case of the two necklaces the unscrupulous jewellers had on both occasions misrepresented the nature of the matter of which the gems were composed.

The question arises: how can people avoid being taken in by such spurious claims and misrepresentations of matter? It is not difficult to see how questions like this will become important when we come to consider the matter of the universe and its properties.

In modern, as in ancient, times, to test whether an object is made of pure gold or not, use is made of a black, fine-grained, siliceous stone, called a touchstone. When pure gold is rubbed on this touchstone, it leaves behind on the stone streaks of a certain character; whereas objects made of adulterated gold, or of some baser metal, will leave behind streaks of a different character.

In the ancient world merchants would always carry a touchstone

FIGURE I.4. A Touchstone.

First mentioned by Theophrastus (c.372–c.287 BC) in his treatise *On Stone*, touchstones are tablets of finely grained black stones used to assay or estimate the proportion of gold or silver in a sample of metal. Traces of gold can be seen on the stone.

Reproduced from Mauro Cateb/Flickr.

with them; but even so it would require considerable knowledge and expertise to interpret the test correctly. When it comes to bank notes and gems, the imitations may be so cleverly made that only an expert could tell the difference between the real thing and the false. In that case non-experts, like ourselves, would have to depend on the judgments of experts.

But what are we to do when the experts disagree? How do we decide which experts to trust? Is there any kind of touchstone that ordinary people can use on the experts themselves, or at least on their interpretations?

There is one more situation worth investigating at this point before we begin our main study.

Third, when we are confronted with what purports to be an account of something that happened in the past and of the causes that led to its happening, we rightly ask questions: 'Did this event really take place? Did it take place in the way that this account says it did? Was the alleged cause the real cause?' The difficulty with things that happened in the past is that we cannot get them to repeat themselves in the present, and watch them happening all over again in our laboratories. We have therefore to search out and study what evidence is available and then decide which interpretation of the evidence best explains what actually happened.

This, of course, is no unusual situation to be in. Detectives, seeking to solve a murder mystery and to discover the real criminal, are constantly in this situation; and this is what historians and archaeologists and palaeontologists do all the time. But mistakes can be made in handling and interpreting the evidence. For instance, in 1980 a man and his wife were camping in the Australian outback, when a dingo (an Australian wild dog) suddenly attacked and killed their little child. When, however, the police investigated the matter, they did not believe the parents' story; they alleged that the woman herself had actually killed the child. The courts found her guilty and she was duly sentenced. But new evidence was discovered that corroborated the parents' story, and proved that it really was a dingo that killed the infant. The couple was not fully and finally exonerated until 2012.

Does this kind of case mean, then, that we cannot ever be certain that any historical event really happened? Or that we can never be sure as to its real causes? Of course not! It is beyond all doubt that, for instance, Napoleon invaded Russia, and that Genghis Khan besieged Beijing (then called Zhongdu). The question is, as we considered earlier: what kind of evidence must we have in order to be sure that a historical event really happened?

But enough of these preliminary exercises. It is time now to take our first step towards answering the question: can we know the ultimate truth about reality?

WHAT IS THE NATURE OF ULTIMATE REALITY?

We have thought about the meaning of reality in various practical situations in daily life. Now we must begin to consider reality at the higher levels of our own individual existence, and that of our fellow human beings, and eventually that of the whole universe.

Ourselves as individuals

Let's start with ourselves as individuals. We know we exist. We do not have to engage in lengthy philosophical discussion before we can be certain that we exist. We know it intuitively. Indeed, we cannot logically deny it. If I were to claim 'I do not exist', I would, by stating my claim, refute it. A non-existent person cannot make any claim. If I didn't exist, I couldn't even say 'I do not exist', since I have to exist in order to make the claim. I cannot, therefore, logically affirm my own non-existence.[17]

There are other things too which we know about ourselves by intuition.

First, we are self-conscious, that is, we are aware of ourselves as separate individuals. I know I am not my brother, or my sister, or my next-door neighbour. I was born of my parents; but I am not just an extension of my father and mother. I am a separate individual, a human being in my own right. My will is not a continuation of their will, such that, if they will something, I automatically will the same thing. My will is my own.

My will may be conditioned by many past experiences, most of which have now passed into my subconscious memory. My will may well be pressurised by many internal desires or fears, and by external circumstances. But whatever philosophers of the determinist school may say, we know in our heart of hearts that we have the power of choice. Our wills, in that sense, are free. If they weren't, no one could ever be held to be guilty for doing wrong, or praised for doing right.

Second, we are also intuitively aware of ourselves as persons, intrinsically different from, and superior to, non-personal things. It is not a

---

[17] We call this law of logic the law of non-affirmability.

question of size, but of mind and personality. A mountain may be large, but it is mindless and impersonal. It is composed of non-rational matter. We are aware of the mountain; it is not aware of us. It is not aware of itself. It neither loves nor hates, neither anticipates nor reflects, has no hopes nor fears. Non-rational though it is, if it became a volcano, it might well destroy us, though we are rational beings. Yet we should not conclude from the fact that simply because such impersonal, non-rational matter is larger and more powerful that it is therefore a higher form of existence than personal, rational human beings. But it poignantly raises the question: what, then, is the status of our human existence in this material world and universe?

Our status in the world

We know that we did not always exist. We can remember being little children. We have watched ourselves growing up to full manhood and womanhood. We have also observed that sooner or later people die, and the unthinking earth, unknowingly, becomes their grave. What then is the significance of the individual human person, and of his or her comparatively short life on earth?

Some think that it is Mankind, the human race as a whole, that is the significant phenomenon: the individual counts for very little. On this view, the human race is like a great fruit tree. Each year it produces a large crop of apples. All of them are more or less alike. None is of any particular significance as an individual. Everyone is destined for

FIGURE I.5. An Apple.

Apple trees take four to five years to produce their first fruit, and it takes the energy from 50 leaves to produce one apple. Archaeologists have found evidence that humans have been enjoying apples since before recorded history.

Reproduced with permission of ©iStock/ChrisBoswell.

a very short life before, like the rest of the crop, it is consumed and forgotten; and so makes room for next year's crop. The tree itself lives on, producing crops year after year, in a seemingly endless cycle of birth, growth and disappearance. On this view then, the tree is the permanent, significant phenomenon; any one individual apple is of comparatively little value.

Our origin

But this view of the individual in relation to the race, does not get us to the root of our question; for the human race too did not always exist, but had a beginning, and so did the universe itself. This, therefore, only pushes the question one stage further back: to what ultimately do the human race as a whole, and the universe itself, owe their existence? What is the Great Reality behind the non-rational matter of the universe and behind us rational, personal, individual members of the human race?

Before we begin to survey the answers that have been given to this question over the centuries, we should notice that though science can point towards an answer, it cannot finally give us a complete answer. That is not because there is something wrong with science; the difficulty lies in the nature of things. The most widely accepted scientific theory nowadays (but not the only one) is that the universe came into being at the so-called Big Bang. But the theory tells us that here we encounter a singularity, that is, a point at which the laws of physics all break down. If that is true, it follows that science by itself cannot give a scientific account of what lay before, and led to, the Big Bang, and thus to the universe, and eventually to ourselves as individual human beings.

Our purpose

The fact that science cannot answer these questions does not mean, of course, that they are pseudo-questions and not worth asking. Adam Schaff, the Polish Marxist philosopher, long ago observed:

> What is the meaning of life? What is man's place in the universe? It seems difficult to express oneself scientifically on such hazy topics.

And yet if one should assert ten times over that these are typical pseudo-problems, *problems would remain.*[18]

Yes, surely problems would remain; and they are life's most important questions. Suppose by the help of science we could come to know everything about every atom, every molecule, every cell, every electrical current, every mechanism in our body and brain. How much further forward should we be? We should now know what we are made of, and how we work. But we should still not know what we are made for.

Suppose for analogy's sake we woke up one morning to find a new, empty jeep parked outside our house, with our name written on it, by some anonymous donor, specifying that it was for our use. Scientists could describe every atom and molecule it was made of. Engineers could explain how it worked, and that it was designed for transporting people. It was obviously intended, therefore, to go places. But where? Neither science as such, nor engineering as such, could tell us where we were meant to drive the jeep to. Should we not then need to discover who the anonymous donor was, and whether the jeep was ours to do what we liked with, answerable to nobody, or whether the jeep had been given to us on permanent loan by its maker and owner with the expectation that we should consult the donor's intentions, follow the rules in the driver's handbook, and in the end be answerable to the donor for how we had used it?

That surely is the situation we find ourselves in as human beings. We are equipped with a magnificent piece of physical and biological engineering, that is, our body and brain; and we are in the driver's seat, behind the steering wheel. But we did not make ourselves, nor the 'machine' we are in charge of. Must we not ask what our relationship is to whatever we owe our existence to? After all, what if it turned out to be that we owe our existence not to an impersonal what but to a personal who?

To some the latter possibility is instinctively unattractive if not frightening; they would prefer

> Must we not ask what our relationship is to whatever we owe our existence to? After all, what if it turned out to be that we owe our existence not to an impersonal what but to a personal who?

---

[18] Schaff, *Philosophy of Man*, 34 (emphasis added).

to think that they owe their existence to impersonal material, forces and processes. But then that view induces in some who hold it its own peculiar *angst*. Scientist Jacob Bronowski (1908–74) confessed to a deep instinctive longing, not simply to exist, but to be a recognisably distinct individual, and not just one among millions of otherwise undifferentiated human beings:

> When I say that I want to be myself, I mean as the existentialist does that I want to be free to be myself. This implies that I want to be rid of constraints (inner as well as outward constraints) in order to act in unexpected ways. Yet I do not mean that I want to act either at random or unpredictably. It is not in these senses that I want to be free, but in the sense that I want to be allowed to be different from others. I want to follow my own way—but I want it to be a way recognisably my own, and not zig-zag. And I want people to recognise it: I want them to say, 'How characteristic!'[19]

Yet at the same time he confessed that certain interpretations of science roused in him a fear that undermined his confidence:

> This is where the fulcrum of our fears lies: that man as a species and we as thinking men, will be shown to be no more than a machinery of atoms. We pay lip service to the vital life of the amoeba and the cheese mite; but what we are defending is the human claim to have a complex of will and thoughts and emotions—to have a mind. . . .
>
> The crisis of confidence . . . springs from each man's wish to be a mind and a person, in face of the nagging fear that he is a mechanism. The central question I ask is this: Can man be both a machine and a self?[20]

Our Search

And so we come back to our original question; but now we clearly notice that it is a double question: not merely to what or to whom

---

[19] Bronowski, *Identity of Man*, 14–5.
[20] Bronowski, *Identity of Man*, 7–9.

does humanity as a whole owe its existence, but what is the status of the individual human being in relation to the race as a whole and to the uncountable myriads of individual phenomena that go to make up the universe? Or, we might ask it another way: what is our significance within the reality in which we find ourselves? This is the ultimate question hanging over every one of our lives, whether we seek answers or we don't. The answers we have for it will affect our thinking in every significant area of life.

These, then, are not merely academic questions irrelevant to practical living. They lie at the heart of life itself; and naturally in the course of the centuries notable answers to them have been given, many of which are held still today around the world.

If we are to try to understand something of the seriously held views of our fellow human beings, we must try to understand their views and the reasons for which they hold them. But just here we must sound a warning that will be necessary to repeat again in the course of these books: those who start out seriously enquiring for truth will find that at however lowly a level they start, they will not be logically able to resist asking what the Ultimate Truth about everything is!

In the spirit of truthfulness and honesty, then, let us say directly that we, the authors of this book, are Christians. We do not pretend to be indifferent guides; we commend to you wholeheartedly the answers we have discovered and will tell you why we think the claims of the Christian gospel are valid, and the help it offers real. This does not, however, preclude the possibility of our approaching other views in a spirit of honesty and fairness. We hope that those who do not share our views will approach them in the same spirit. We can ask nothing more as we set out together on this quest—in search of reality and significance.

OUR AIM

Our small contribution to this quest is set out in the 6 volumes of this series. In this, the fifth book in the series, we consider evidence for the claims of the Christian gospel. We first compare some of the answers that the world's major religions provide and ask whether, as is commonly thought, all religions are leading to the same goal. We then consider the question of the historicity of the New Testament, including external sources that refer to its key events, as well as the accuracy of its own documents. We then turn to Jesus Christ and the question of whether he was a real figure in history or only a product of religious myth supported by literary fiction. We then consider the idea that Christ came back from the dead and whether anyone should believe in that, or in any other, miracle in our day. And, finally, we consider the specific evidence for the resurrection of Christ, that miracle upon which the truth of Christianity rests and in which both the hope and the judgement of the world are promised.

CHAPTER 1

DO ALL RELIGIONS LEAD TO THE SAME GOAL?

Without its distinctive doctrines and beliefs a religion would cease to exist as a religion. Moreover, people must be free honestly to publicise what they sincerely believe to be true, provided always they do it by peaceful means; and both truth and logic demand that they should be free to assert that what contradicts the truth is not true.

INTRODUCTION

More or less religion?

When anyone appears to claim that religion is the remedy for the human race's faults and failings, and the cure for the moral confusion, cynicism and nihilism from which the world suffers, the claim, to many people, must seem, to say the least, problematical, if not altogether incredible. Look at the history of religions, they say. Religion has been the cause of endless wars, misery and bloodshed. And is it not the clash of world religions that at this present moment is fomenting international strife and terrorism? The fact is that Christendom in the Crusades raised its armies and slaughtered Muslims, Turks and Jews in disputes over sacred lands and sites. Catholicism in the *auto-da-fés* of Spain tortured and burned both Jews and Protestants; and Protestants in their turn in other countries fought Catholic armies and executed Catholic 'heretics'. Hindus and Muslims still fight each other over the possession of holy sites. And does not the dispute over possession of the Temple Mount in Jerusalem still threaten world peace? To all of which we could add that in the twentieth century secular ideologies of both the East and West were pursued and enforced with all the absolutism of virtual religious and messianic zeal—with the result that large economies were ruined and multimillions died. Surely, say many, we need less religion, not more.

Others are not so sure. They have experienced the barren inability of atheism, naturalism and secularism to provide either a firm basis, or an adequate motivation, for private and public morality. Instinctively they feel that religion, with its spiritual dimension, could provide that basis, and stimulate sufficiently strong faith, hope and courage, to achieve private and public unselfishness, altruism, and morality necessary for the cohesion of both family and society. At least religion could do this, they feel, if (but it's a very big if) all religions could be persuaded to stop fighting each other, and work together for the common good.

So far so good; and in the light of Christ's prohibition on the use of force either to defend or to promote his kingdom and truth (see John 18:36–37), all Christians will blush with shame at the thought of people in the name of Christ waging war on other religions and trying to impose the Christian gospel by force of any kind.[1]

A common argument for mutual tolerance

But now there enters another argument, and it goes like this:

1. It has been the stressing of differences between the various religions that has been, and still is, responsible for stirring up animosity and hatred between people of different faiths.
2. Such stressing of the differences between religions is foolish, since all religions are essentially aiming at the same goal. They may be following different paths; but they are paths up the same mountain, and they are all aiming at, and will eventually arrive at, the same summit.
3. The duty of all religions and religious people, therefore, is to agree to, and to preach, the fact that they all lead to the same God, that all aim at the same goal, and that their differences are minimally important. Thus all can, and should, work together for the common good.

This triple argument is undoubtedly attractive; but its cogency depends on the truth or otherwise of the three assumptions it makes:

1. that the chief goal at which all religions aim is to get people to behave well towards one another;
2. that all religions would agree that this is their chief goal; and
3. that all religions would accept that their distinctive doctrines and beliefs are minimally important.

Assumption 1 gains plausibility because teaching people to observe a moral code is precisely what all mature religions set out

---

[1] For a fuller discussion of Christ's prohibition, see Ch. 8—'Truth on Trial' in Book 3: *Questioning Our Knowledge.*

to do; and all these moral codes have a good deal in common, e.g. kindness to little children and to the elderly, almsgiving to the poor, care for orphans and for the sick, respect for one's fellow human beings, honesty in commerce, truth-telling, unselfishness, good citizenship, etc.

Even so, one would have to remember that not all religions have been, or are, particularly concerned with morality. The ancient classical religions of Greece and Rome worshipped gods and goddesses who were represented in their myths as behaving far more immorally than the people who worshipped them. Serious ethical teaching in the ancient classical world was the province, not of religion, but of philosophy.

Similarly, ancestor or spirit worship, which is still widely practised even among scientifically and technologically advanced nations, is not solely (or even, perhaps, chiefly) concerned with showing loving respect to the memory of one's departed relatives, but also in great part with cajoling their spirits by the appropriate rites to stay in the spirit world and not to cause trouble by returning and haunting the homes of their living descendants. Or again, in some places, sacrifices and offerings are made to the gods (as we have ourselves witnessed) in order to persuade them to grant success in the football lottery, or to bribe them to favour oneself and be against one's business competitors.

But let's leave this aside, and return to the observation that mature religions are seriously concerned with teaching and encouraging people to behave well towards one another. But what follows from that?

Assumption 2 supposes that all these mature religions would agree that their main purpose is to encourage people to treat each other well and to do their duty to society. But the assumption is not true. The religions themselves would not agree with it; and they have a right not to. Religion is not simply moral philosophy. Though true religion is concerned, as the Christian New Testament puts it, 'to visit orphans and widows in their affliction' (Jas 1:27), there's more to religion than that. Religion's prime concern is with God, or the gods, and with the human race's right relations with him, or them. An atheist can be seriously and sincerely concerned to live and work for the good of his fellow-citizens; and most atheists, we presume, are. But an atheist's attitude to God is seriously astray. Let's use an analogy to illustrate the point.

In centuries gone by, the seas of the world were sailed by many pirate ships. In some of those ships the pirates doubtless behaved very well towards one another and had rigorous and well-kept rules to ensure that the booty they captured was fairly shared out. In that sense they may well have been satisfied with the standard of morality they had achieved. But that would have overlooked the fundamental fact that they were pirates in rebellion against the lawful government on land! If that government had caught them, their excellent moral behaviour towards one another would not have saved them from hanging.

If there is a supreme being, a Creator to whom we owe our very life and breath, our first duty is to him, to 'love him with all our heart, soul and strength' as Judaism's Bible puts it (see Deut 6:5), and then secondly, to 'love your neighbour as yourself' (Lev 19:18). The second commandment is closely entailed by the first, so much so that the New Testament argues: 'If anyone says, "I love God", and hates his brother, he is a liar; for he who does not love his brother whom he has seen cannot love God whom he has not seen' (1 John 4:20). But that does not mean that so long as I have treated my brother well, it does not matter if I have ignored God, rejected his authority, refused him my love, obedience and loyalty, and denied his very existence. And if I have treated God so, when he finally calls me to account, it will be no excuse to plead that nevertheless I have behaved well to my fellow human beings.

If there is a supreme being, a Creator to whom we owe our very life and breath, our first duty is to him, to 'love him with all our heart, soul and strength' . . .

Assumption 3—that all religions would be prepared to accept that their distinctive doctrines and beliefs are minimally important—is offensive to their adherents' intelligence and integrity. In addition, it borders on the absurd. Without its distinctive doctrines and beliefs a religion would cease to exist as a religion. Moreover, people must be free honestly to publicise what they sincerely believe to be true, provided always they do it by peaceful means; and both truth and logic demand that they should be free to assert that what contradicts the truth is not true. No religion is going to accept that its doctrines are merely a form of pragmatism in which it does not matter in the end whether they are true or not.

By that same token, no religion has the right to take offence, if others question the truth of its beliefs. Religions that use the power of the State to forbid anyone publicly to question the truth of their doctrines, merely advertises thereby the weakness of those doctrines. Such questioning by no means calls into doubt the sincerity of those who believe those doctrines; but in no other department of life would any responsible person be content to take sincerity as a guarantee of either truth or safety. All forms of medical practice, for instance, have by definition the same goal, namely the healing of the sick. But not all medicines are equally potent or equally safe. Some are poison. We should not be wise to swallow the contents of a bottle indiscriminately simply because the label bore the word 'medicine'. We all believe in the objectivity of truth where medicine is concerned. In the same way we cannot afford to assume that a religion is true just because it labels itself 'a religion'.

The facts

Our task now, then, is to answer honestly the question that stands at the head of this chapter: 'Do all religions lead to the same goal?' For that purpose we shall consider five major religions: Hinduism, Buddhism, Judaism, Christianity and Islam. We shall consider what they believe and teach concerning matters that are necessarily fundamental to any and all religions.[2]

WHAT THE MAJOR RELIGIONS MEAN BY 'GOD'

Hindu religion

We have considered the views of Hindu philosophy on this topic in an earlier book in this series.[3] Here we consider Hindu religion.

It is claimed by some that original Hindu religion was monotheistic. Certainly popular Hinduism still believes in a supreme Being

---

[2] We are, of course, aware that there are many other religions in the world; but a survey of them all would be impossible in this chapter, and would, in any case, simply demonstrate the same point: that world religions disagree over fundamental issues. Students, however, should check for themselves the accuracy of our account by reference to detailed studies and encyclopaedias.

[3] See Ch. 1—'Indian Pantheistic Monism', Book 2: *Finding Ultimate Reality*.

called Brahman, who (or which) is largely unknowable. But alongside of that, Hindus believe in literally thousands of gods and goddesses, the elephant god, Ganesha, included; and these they tend to worship rather than Brahman. There are abundant temples to all the other gods and goddesses; temples to Brahman, however, are rare, or non-existent. Of course, any one person cannot worship all these deities; people concentrate on one or more to whom they are specially devoted.

Popular Hindu religion, like philosophical Hinduism, also holds the doctrine of pantheism, that everyone and everything is identical with God.[4] The doctrine runs into enormous difficulties, as we see in the following statement by Sri Ramakrishna:

> God alone is, and it is He who has become this universe ... 'As the snake I bite, as the healer I cure.' God is the ignorant man and God is the enlightened man. God as the ignorant man remains deluded. Again He as the guru gives enlightenment to God in the ignorant.[5]

Ravi Zacharias well brings out the implications of this doctrine for other religions:

> The question arises, then, that when Buddha rejected the Vedas [the sacred Scriptures of Hinduism] was he God in ignorance or God in enlightenment? When Mohammed posited monotheism and the way of submission to Allah, was he God in ignorance or God in enlightenment? So runs the sequence of questions when all that exists is God.[6]

The doctrine also inevitably carries the implication that evil, as well as good, is God. Judaism, Christianity and Islam recoil in horror from this.

Buddhism

Original Buddhism split from Hinduism. Strictly speaking it is not a religion: it does not concern itself, or necessarily believe in, any god

---

[4] See the discussions of pantheism in Chs. 1 and 2 in Book 2: *Finding Ultimate Reality*.
[5] Isherwood, *Vedanta for Modern Man*, 222.
[6] *Jesus Among Other Gods*, 162.

at all. It is a philosophy which offers its adherents a body of doctrine (*The Three Pitakas*) and a set of psychological disciplines calculated to deliver them from the tyranny of desire and to lead them into a way of life increasingly free from turmoil, stress and fear, and also into peaceful relations with their fellow men and women.

Mahayana (or, Popular) *Buddhism.* This form of Buddhism, of which there are many varieties, is much influenced by Hinduism, and in consequence believes in multitudinous deities.

Judaism, Christianity and Islam

Positively believing in God, they must, and do, consider original Buddhism's disregard (or denial) of God's existence as a form of the human race's fundamental sin. Being also monotheistic, Judaism, Christianity and Islam will never agree with Hinduism's and Mahayana Buddhism's worship of thousands of gods. They hold that it is a grave sin thus to compromise the oneness of the One True God.

WHAT THE MAJOR RELIGIONS TEACH ABOUT THE MATERIAL WORLD

Mainline Judaism, Christianity and Islam

All three believe that the material creation as it left the hand of the Creator was good, and that our material bodies are likewise essentially good, designed and created by the deliberate intention of the One True God himself. Though spoiled by sin and subject to corruption and death, they will one day be resurrected and glorified.

Hinduism and Mahayana Buddhism

These two religions teach the very opposite. They teach that the material world and our material bodies were not the direct creation of the supreme deity, though they emanated from It (or, Him). They were the creation of some lesser deity, or some lesser form of the supreme deity; and matter is undesirable, if not positively evil. Accordingly the human race's wisdom is to escape as far as possible from the taint of their material bodies and to strive on an upward path of spirituality until they are finally free from matter altogether, attain moksha, enter nirvana, and becomes one with the pure World-Soul.

All three monotheistic faiths regard this devaluation of the human body as a virtual insult to the Creator. Christianity holds also that it is utterly irreconcilable with the incarnation of the Son of God in a human body, his bodily resurrection and ascension into heaven, the eventual resurrection and glorification of the bodies of his people, and the redemption and restoration of the whole creation.

Already, then, it is obvious that we are dealing here, not with minor differences but with two fundamentally irreconcilable worldviews.

WHAT ANSWER DO THE MAJOR RELIGIONS HAVE TO THE PROBLEM OF GUILT?

The problem stated

It is true, as we have already noticed, that when it comes to the basic principles of morality, all mature religions teach more or less the same. Compare, for instance, the Five Precepts of Buddhism with the Ten Commandments of Judaism. In a word, all religions teach us that we ought to be good. Our human predicament, however, is that we have not been good. We have sinned against God, broken his laws, and incurred their penalties. We have sinned against our fellow men and women, and have done them damage. We have sinned against ourselves; and if we are indeed God's creatures, then to sin against our fellow creatures and against ourselves is also a grievous sin against the Creator.

The result is—whether our consciences are still working and register our guilt, or whether they have ceased to function, and so fail to register it—we are, in objective fact, guilty. If we are to have soundly based peace with our Creator, we need release from our guilt. Thus any religion worthy of the name must have some answer to this problem of guilt.

But how? It is clearly no use telling men and women that their past sin and guilt do not matter and can conveniently be forgotten. For in the end that would mean that the people against whom they have sinned do not matter, the damage they have done doesn't matter, and that conscience is a mere mental weakness that can be suppressed with impunity. God will never take that view.

Nor can there be any thought of our somehow compensating God for our sins. If we could do our duty perfectly, love and serve God with all our heart, mind, soul and strength, we should still have nothing left over to compensate God with.

Every man and woman urgently needs, therefore, a solution to this problem that can uphold their own moral standards and their sense of justice, as well as—and above all—God's standards, and yet at the same time bring them forgiveness and justly release them from the chains of past guilt. What do the major religions say?

The doctrine of karma, reincarnation and the transmigration of souls

The way of dealing with guilt propounded by eastern pantheistic religions such as Hinduism and Buddhism is the doctrine of karma. This teaching maintains that every evil deed or sin a person does brings an inevitable amount of deserved suffering upon him or her. It is the principle of 'what you sow, you reap'. Moreover, the suffering cannot end until the full amount of it, determined by the law of karma, has been endured, or paid off, in some way.

In this context the idea of forgiveness is irrelevant. Indeed it makes no sense; and in consequence, in some forms of Buddhism there is no such thing as forgiveness. The law of karma is thought of as an impersonal principle, like, say, the law of gravity. Sin, therefore, is not like sin against the law of a personal Creator God, who of his mercy can forgive the guilt of sin. The impersonal law of karma dictates that the only way a man can be freed from the consequence of his sin is himself to suffer the necessary amount of suffering deserved by his sin. He can expect no outside help. 'No one can purify another.'[7]

The law of karma goes on to say that when a man dies and his soul leaves his body, if by that time he has not suffered enough to satisfy the law of karma, his soul must come back to earth and be reincarnated in another human body. (The doctrine of the transmigration of the soul teaches that if the man in his lifetime has behaved very badly, his soul

---

[7] Zaehner, *The Concise Encyclopaedia of Living Faiths*, 265.

may be reincarnated in the body of some beast.) This cycle must then be repeated, if need be many times over, until the man has suffered enough to work off all his karma, and so can be released from having to be reincarnated ever again thereafter.

But see what this means. If a child is born disabled, the doctrine of reincarnation will say that this is because this child (or his soul) sinned in a previous incarnation and by the time it came to die, it had not suffered enough to work off its karma. Therefore it had to be reincarnated so that it could continue to suffer. No one, however, can tell the child what sins they were which he did in his previous incarnations for which he now suffers, nor how many previous incarnations he has been through already and still has not suffered enough to work off his karma. What hope has he, therefore, that in this present incarnation he will not sin further and so make endless further incarnations necessary? Moreover, it would not actually be helpful to try to alleviate the child's sufferings, for that would cut down the amount of suffering that the child must go through in order to fulfil its karma.

In many eyes this is a very cruel doctrine. It carries, moreover, the corollary that a man who from childhood has enjoyed splendid health and prosperity, can, according to this doctrine, claim to have deserved this prosperity because he lived a better previous life than the child, even if his present prosperity has been secured by crooked financial dealings. Furthermore, this doctrine has undoubtedly helped to buttress and to justify the caste system.

Judaism, Christianity and Islam deny that to be born into this world is a penalty for having sinned in a previous incarnation.

Judaism, Christianity and Islam, therefore, resolutely reject this doctrine. They would deny that to be born into this world is a penalty for having sinned in a previous incarnation. To imply any such thing is surely an insult to life itself and a slander on the Creator. When Christ encountered a man blind from birth, and was asked, 'Rabbi, who sinned, this man or his parents, that he was born blind?' Jesus answered [emphatically], 'It was not that this man sinned, or his parents...' (John 9:1–3).

If a woman through promiscuity contracts AIDS, her newborn child may be infected, and as a result will suffer greatly in its short life. In that sense, children do suffer as the result of the sins of their forebears. But

Judaism, Christianity and Islam will none of them say that this is the child's fault because of sins it did in a previous incarnation.

THE QUESTION OF SALVATION IN THE THREE MONOTHEISTIC FAITHS

Our brief survey so far has demonstrated some of the fundamental differences between Judaism, Christianity, and Islam on the one side, and the other major world religions on the other. But it is no secret that these three monotheistic faiths disagree with each other, and do so over a matter that lies at their very heart. If, then, we are to understand their special characteristics, we must now examine what this fundamental difference is.

But first let us emphasise what they have in common. To start with, all three are monotheistic, that is, they believe in the One True God; and they attribute the creation of the world and of humankind to him.

Christians gladly acknowledge their huge debt to Judaism. They accept the Old Testament—called by the Jews *Tanak*, an acronym for the Hebrew words *Torah* (Law), *N^ebi'im* (Prophets), *K^ethubim* (Writings)—as the inspired word of God. The Christian New Testament, moreover, is a Jewish book; and above all, the one whom Christians worship as the Messiah, the Son of God, and Redeemer, was a Jew. Christians in fact believe that he was the one whose coming the Old Testament prophets predicted.

Islam's holy book, the Qur'an, commands Muslims to honour the *Tawret*, the *Zabur* and the *Injil*, i.e. the Pentateuch of Moses, the Psalms of David, and the Gospel of Jesus. (Qur'an, *Sura* 10. 94; 5. 44–46; 4. 163). The Qur'an believes in the virgin birth of Jesus (*Sura* 3. 45–47; 19. 16–21); accepts that Jesus is the Messiah (*Sura* 3. 45), is (in some sense) the Word of God (*Sura* 4. 171) and is the Spirit, or, Soul of God (*Sura* 4. 171) and believes that Jesus is now alive in heaven (*Sura* 4. 157–158).[8]

But when it comes to the question how, and on what terms, humankind can be released from the guilt of sin and have peace with God, then both Judaism and Islam disagree most resolutely with Christianity.

---

[8] As in any comparison of religions, we must take care to understand how the adherents of one faith define both their own terms and those of the faith with which they are claiming to agree.

The Christian doctrine of salvation

The Christian gospel presents Jesus not only as a prophet, or teacher, or Messiah, but as Saviour and Redeemer. The classic statement of the gospel runs like this:

> Now I would remind you, brothers, of the gospel I preached to you, which you received, in which you stand, and by which you are being saved . . . that Christ died for our sins in accordance with the Scriptures, that he was buried, that he was raised on the third day in accordance with the Scriptures. (1 Cor 15:1–4)

According to Christianity, then, human salvation depends on Christ. Christ's death on the cross was the God-appointed sacrifice for the sins of the world: he was 'the Lamb of God, who takes away the sin of the world' (John 1:29). His resurrection and ascension were God's way of declaring that the sacrifice of Christ paid the penalty imposed on human sin by God's justice, and that in consequence God can in full justice pardon and accept all those who in true repentance put their faith in Jesus (Rom 3:23–28; 4:24–25). That means that people are forgiven and saved not by their own sufferings (as in Hinduism), but by the suffering of Christ on their behalf; not on the basis of their meritorious deeds (as in so many religions), but on the basis of the work of redemption that Christ accomplished for them by his death and resurrection (1 Pet 3:18; Titus 3:3–7; Eph 2:1–10). The resultant peace and confidence that this gives in view of the final judgment, is then expressed like this:

> But as it is, he has appeared once for all at the end of the ages to put away sin by the sacrifice of himself. And just as it is appointed for man to die once, and after that comes judgment, so Christ, having been offered once to bear the sins of many, will appear a second time, not to deal with sin but to save those who are eagerly waiting for him. (Heb 9:26–28)

Or as the Christian Apostle Paul puts it:

> You see, at just the right time, when we were still powerless, Christ died for the ungodly. Very rarely will anyone die for a righteous person, though for a good person someone might possibly dare

to die. But God demonstrates his own love for us in this: while we were still sinners, Christ died for us.

Since we have now been justified by his blood, how much more shall we be saved from God's wrath through him! For if, when we were God's enemies, we were reconciled to him through the death of his Son, how much more, having been reconciled, shall we be saved through his life! Not only is this so, but we also boast in God through our Lord Jesus Christ, through whom we have now received reconciliation. (Rom 5:6–11 NIV)

Islam's doctrine of salvation

Its difference from Christianity

Islam denies the deity of the Lord Jesus. Though it regards him as the Messiah, as the Word and the Spirit of God, it denies that he is God incarnate. Moreover, though it believes that John the Baptist, the forerunner of Christ, was a prophet—and John, according to the New Testament officially announced Jesus as the Lamb of God who takes away the sin of the world (John 1:29)—nevertheless Islam denies that Jesus died on the cross. At the last moment, so the Qur'an teaches, before he was crucified, God snatched him alive up to heaven, and someone else—perhaps Barabbas, or a look-alike, none can be sure who—was substituted for him (see *Sura* 4. 156–158).

Islam's own doctrine of salvation

Islam teaches the reality of heaven (e.g. *Sura* 2. 59; 7. 40) and hell (e.g. *Sura* 81. 12; 82. 14–16; 83. 16; 85. 10), and urges the need for belief in the One True God and for the performance of good works to gain heaven and avoid hell. It takes seriously the final judgment, and emphasizes its justice:

> Just balances will we set up for the day of resurrection, neither shall any soul be wronged in aught; though, were a work but the weight of a grain of mustard seed, we would bring it forth *to be weighed*: and our reckoning will suffice. (*Sura* 21. 48, Rodwell trans.)

But Islam has no Saviour—the Prophet Muhammad never claimed to be one—and no atoning sacrifice on the basis of which God grants salvation. Hope of salvation in the end, therefore, depends on a person's good works outweighing the bad in the scales of God's justice. As to forgiveness the Qur'an states:

> Verily, God will not forgive the union of other gods with himself! But other than this will He forgive to whom He pleaseth (*Sura* 4. 48 Rodwell trans., cf. 4. 116).

> But believers and doers of good works, for them is mercy, and a great reward! (*Sura* 35. 7, Rodwell trans.)

None then can be sure in advance that his good works will outweigh his bad deeds. And, even if they did, how could a holy God be content with any admixture of evil with good? If, moreover, forgiveness depends on God's arbitrary decision—'He will forgive to whom He pleases' (*Sura* 4. 48)—no one can ever be sure in this life that he or she will be forgiven.

Judaism's doctrine of salvation

Unlike Islam, Judaism does not deny that Jesus died on the cross; but it does deny his resurrection and ascension into heaven, and along with that it denies that by that resurrection God vindicated Jesus' claim to be the Son of God. It follows that Judaism denies that Jesus is mankind's Redeemer and that his death was the God-appointed sacrifice for the sins of the world.

This all means that Judaism nowadays has no atoning sacrifice for sin. In Judaism, as in Islam, final salvation depends on the quality of a person's works, though again the hope has to be that in arriving at his verdict God will be merciful and generous.

Historically, this was not always so in Israel. According to their own holy Scriptures, God's forgiveness was connected with the offering in the temple of sacrifices for sin. No serious thinkers in Israel imagined that the death of the animals concerned compensated God for their sins, or paid him—still less bribed him—to forgive their sins. These sacrifices were an expression and constant reminder of God's justice. As the moral governor of the universe he could not simply agree to forget sin and create the impression that in the end sin does not really matter. Justice demanded that God's wrath and displeasure at sin must be expressed, and the penalty of sin paid. Hence the sacrifices.

In the light of that, it is significant that one of Israel's most famous prophets, who eventually foretold the coming of God's Servant, proclaimed that God would lay on this Servant the iniquity of us all, and that he would be wounded for our transgressions. Thus he would be the real sacrifice for sin, of which Israel's animal sacrifices were but foreshadowings (Isa 53).

Israel, then, continued the practice of offering sacrifices for sin right up to the time of Jesus. He claimed to be the fulfilment of those sacrifices, the Lamb of God who takes away the sin of the world. The majority in Israel were not convinced, and continued with their animal sacrifices until in AD 70 the Romans destroyed their temple, the only place on earth where according to their Scriptures those sacrifices were allowed to be offered. Still today Orthodox Judaism observes the yearly Day of Atonement—Yom Kippur—and confesses its sins according to the Old Testament's prescriptions. But the sacrifices which the Old Testament prescribed, it cannot offer; and it has no substitute.

But to sum up the central difference between Judaism and Islam on the one side and Christianity on the other: Islam denies that Jesus died; Judaism denies that he rose from the dead. But these are matters of history, and it is to history that we now turn.

CHAPTER 2

THE HISTORICITY
OF THE NEW TESTAMENT

If you remove the person of Jesus Christ from
the Christian gospel, you have destroyed it.
Its truths are primarily truths about him—his
life and teaching about himself, his death, his
resurrection and ascension; in the first place
these are facts of history, though the message
they convey is spiritual and everlasting.

THE HISTORICAL NATURE
OF THE CHRISTIAN GOSPEL

A reader of the New Testament will almost immediately be struck with its strong historical tones. For example, the author of the Third Gospel, Luke, gives us this introduction to his work:

> Many have undertaken to draw up an account of the things that have been fulfilled among us, just as they were handed down to us by those who from the first were eyewitnesses and servants of the word. With this in mind, since I myself have carefully investigated everything from the beginning, I too decided to write an orderly account for you, most excellent Theophilus, so that you may know the certainty of the things you have been taught. (Luke 1:1–4 NIV)

So Luke claims to be writing about events that happened over a period of time, the report of which was traceable back to eyewitnesses. He also claims that he had personally conducted his own research in order to prepare an orderly account for a highly-positioned Roman called Theophilus, with the object of showing him the certainty of these events.

It, therefore, belongs to his objectives to anchor his account of the life of Christ firmly in its setting in contemporary history. So he starts his account proper with the statement: 'In the time of Herod king of Judaea' (1:5 NIV). He dates the events surrounding the birth of Christ in more detail: 'In those days Caesar Augustus issued a decree that a census should be taken of the entire Roman world. (This was the first census that took place while Quirinius was governor of Syria)' (2:1 NIV). When he comes to the start of the public life of Christ he gives even more dating information:

> In the fifteenth year of the reign of Tiberius Caesar—when Pontius Pilate was governor of Judaea, Herod tetrarch of Galilee,

his brother Philip tetrarch of Iturea and Traconitis, and Lysanias tetrarch of Abilene—during the high priesthood of Annas and Caiaphas . . . (3:1–2 NIV)

This kind of detail and method of dating is characteristic of serious ancient historians who wish to mark important events. Luke does not content himself with the 'sometime, somewhere' of mythology; he pins down the event accurately to its historical context with checkable information, which shows his readers that he intends them to take what he is recounting as serious history.

Luke's credibility as a historian is a separate issue, which we shall discuss later. At the moment we wish simply to stress that the New Testament claims to be firmly anchored in history. This shows that the Christian message does not, like mathematics or philosophy, consist simply of a set of timeless ideas and truths, where the important thing is their content, and not so much when, or where, or by whom, they were first enunciated. Nor is it a set of religious ideas like Buddhism, in which it is the teaching that is important, not so much the person who gave it. The Christian gospel is based on the historical person of Jesus Christ and on the historical events surrounding him. If you remove the person of Jesus Christ from the Christian gospel, you have destroyed it. Its truths are primarily truths about him—his life and teaching about himself, his death, his resurrection and ascension; in the first place these are facts of history, though the message they convey is spiritual and everlasting.

> The Christian message does not, like mathematics or philosophy, consist simply of a set of timeless ideas and truths, where the important thing is their content, and not so much when, or where, or by whom, they were first enunciated.

Two samples of early Christian preaching

From its very beginning Christian preaching was marked by its constant emphasis on these major themes. We see that in the very first public statement of the Christian gospel, given by Peter in Jerusalem on the day of Pentecost, a mere fifty days after the resurrection of Christ (Acts 2). Again and again we find these same statements recurring in the examples of early Christian preaching given in the Acts of the Apostles. Here, as a sample, is part of the speech the Apostle Paul made in the synagogue at Antioch of Pisidia:

> After the reading from the Law and the Prophets, the rulers of the synagogue sent a message to them, saying, 'Brothers, if you have any word of encouragement for the people, say it.' So Paul stood up, and motioning with his hand said:
>
> 'Men of Israel and you who fear God, listen. The God of this people Israel chose our fathers and made the people great during their stay in the land of Egypt, and with uplifted arm he led them out of it. And for about forty years he put up with them in the wilderness. And after destroying seven nations in the land of Canaan, he gave them their land as an inheritance. All this took about 450 years. And after that he gave them judges until Samuel the prophet. Then they asked for a king, and God gave them Saul the son of Kish, a man of the tribe of Benjamin, for forty years. And when he had removed him, he raised up David to be their king, of whom he testified and said, "I have found in David the son of Jesse, a man after my heart, who will do all my will." Of this man's offspring God has brought to Israel a Saviour, Jesus, as he promised. Before his coming, John had proclaimed a baptism of repentance to all the people of Israel. And as John was finishing his course, he said, "Who do you suppose that I am? I am not he. No, but behold, after me one is coming, the sandals of whose feet I am not worthy to untie."
>
> 'Brothers, sons of the family of Abraham, and those among you who fear God, to us has been sent the message of this salvation. For those who live in Jerusalem and their rulers, because they did not recognize him nor understand the utterances of the prophets, which are read every Sabbath, fulfilled them by condemning him. And though they found in him no guilt worthy of death, they asked Pilate to have him executed. And when they had carried out all that was written of him, they took him down from the tree and laid him in a tomb. But God raised him from the dead, and for many days he appeared to those who had come up with him from Galilee to Jerusalem, who are now his witnesses to the people. And we bring you the good news that

what God promised to the fathers, this he has fulfilled to us their children by raising Jesus, as also it is written in the second Psalm, "You are my Son, today I have begotten you." And as for the fact that he raised him from the dead, no more to return to corruption, he has spoken in this way, "I will give you the holy and sure blessings of David." Therefore he says also in another psalm, "You will not let your Holy One see corruption." For David, after he had served the purpose of God in his own generation, fell asleep and was laid with his fathers and saw corruption, but he whom God raised up did not see corruption. Let it be known to you therefore, brothers, that through this man forgiveness of sins is proclaimed to you, and by him everyone who believes is freed from everything from which you could not be freed by the law of Moses. Beware, therefore, lest what is said in the Prophets should come about: "Look, you scoffers, be astounded and perish; for I am doing a work in your days, a work that you will not believe, even if one tells it to you."'

As they went out, the people begged that these things might be told them the next Sabbath. (Acts 13:15–42)

This passage gives us a fascinating glimpse into what the early Christians preached. Let us list the elements.

1. Paul gives a summary of Israel's history, from its inception to the time of King David.
2. Jesus is introduced as a historical descendant of David, whose unique divine character was announced to Israel by the historical person known as John the Baptist.
3. In spite of that, Jesus was rejected by the leaders in Jerusalem and executed (by crucifixion) by the historical Roman procurator Pilate.
4. Jesus was buried.
5. But Jesus rose from the dead and was seen alive by eyewitnesses over a lengthy period of time.
6. All this happened in precise fulfilment of what the Hebrew prophets had predicted.
7. On the basis of these facts, forgiveness of sins is offered to all, through faith in Jesus as Saviour.

The constant emphasis on the historical dimension is unmistakable.

Or take another famous summary of the Christian gospel, again from the pen of the Apostle Paul:

> Now I would remind you, brothers, of the gospel I preached to you, which you received, in which you stand, and by which you are being saved, if you hold fast to the word I preached to you— unless you believed in vain.
>
> For I delivered to you as of first importance what I also received: that Christ died for our sins in accordance with the Scriptures, that he was buried, that he was raised on the third day in accordance with the Scriptures, and that he appeared to Cephas, then to the twelve. Then he appeared to more than five hundred brothers at one time, most of whom are still alive, though some have fallen asleep. Then he appeared to James, then to all the apostles. Last of all, as to one untimely born, he appeared also to me. For I am the least of the apostles, unworthy to be called an apostle, because I persecuted the church of God. (1 Cor 15:1–9)

Here Paul is writing mainly to non-Jews, and so we do not have any mention of the history of Israel; but we once more see the same strong historical assertions as before:

1. Christ died for our sins.
2. He was buried.
3. He rose the third day.
4. This all fulfils the Hebrew prophetic Scriptures.
5. There are many witnesses who saw Jesus alive after his resurrection.
6. Most of these witnesses are themselves still alive (and, therefore, are accessible for questioning).
7. Paul is one of the witnesses, who, far from being prejudiced in favour of Christ, started off completely hostile to the Christian church.

Of course, what claims to be historical is open to historical criticism, and so we must presently attend to the matter of historical method.

THE RELIABILITY OF THE HISTORICAL SOURCES

Historical method

History and natural science are two very different disciplines. Whereas one of the fundamental tools in the natural sciences is repeatable experimentation, history by definition deals with unrepeatable past events. The battle of Waterloo cannot be re-run, in order for us to observe what really happened! Therefore, the historian is more like a lawyer than a natural scientist, in that he or she must rely on evidence from historical sources, determine how reliable and authentic those sources are, and then make as reasonable an inference as possible to the best coherent explanation of the evidence.

Historians will want to ask a number of questions, including the following:

1. What is the evidence that the things claimed in the New Testament actually happened?
2. What are the sources for the information contained in the New Testament?
3. How near in time are the sources to those events?
4. How near in time to the events were the accounts written?
5. How reliable is the documentary evidence?
6. What archaeological, and what independent contemporary historical, evidence is there?

The earliest datable written sources

Perhaps the first important thing to notice is that the order in which the books appear in the New Testament is not chronological. The first four books, the Gospels, which are biographies of Jesus, were written after almost all of the letters of Paul. Paul's letters, which take up more than half of the New Testament, date from the late 40s AD onwards, most of them appearing during the 50s.

For many years, the standard dating for the Gospels was, Mark in the 70s, Matthew and Luke in the 80s, and John in the 90s; although there were arguments for placing John earlier. Some will disagree, but the scholarly consensus has moved towards earlier dates for all of the

Gospels, and it is quite probable that all but John were written before AD 70.

The book of Acts ends with Paul under house arrest in Rome, so we do not learn his fate (execution by Nero, in AD 62) from the book of Acts. This strongly suggests that Acts was written before Paul died—hence before 62.

Thus, most of the New Testament was written within the lifetime of many eyewitnesses of the events; and it was from the reports of these eyewitnesses that the New Testament writers compiled their records. This also means that the New Testament was written at a time when any hostile eyewitnesses could easily have objected to inaccurate reporting, or to the overlaying of the historical facts with legendary material.

> Most of the New Testament was written within the lifetime of many eyewitnesses of the events.

It is useful at this point to have some kind of comparison with other historical documents. For example, the two earliest biographies of Alexander the Great, by Arrian and Plutarch, were written more than 400 years after Alexander's death in 323 BC; yet historians consider them to be generally reliable. Interestingly, legendary material did begin to develop around the story of Alexander, but not until the centuries after Arrian and Plutarch. Thus, the amount of time between the events depicted in the Gospels and Acts, and their being written down, is practically negligible by comparison; so that the question of legendary additions is essentially a non-starter.

However, for the earliest information, we turn first to Paul and ask if there are indications that even earlier sources were available for use by him. The answer is clearly in the affirmative, since Paul incorporates in his writings some very early creeds, which go back to the very beginning of the Church.

The most important of these creeds is probably the one cited just above, from 1 Corinthians 15, which was written by Paul about AD 55. Consider its historical significance. Paul's conversion took place about AD 32. Immediately after his conversion he went to Damascus and met with Ananias and some other Christian disciples; his first meeting with the apostles would have been about AD 35 in Jerusalem. In AD 55, after preaching the Christian gospel himself in Asia and in Europe, he then wrote down in credal form what he had been preaching for the last 20 years. When we look at his writing, we find it contains the same major themes as the very first sermon preached by Peter on the day of Pentecost.

This extremely short time-gap between the events and the sources reporting them refutes the all-too-common notion, that the resurrection of Jesus was a legendary concept added in later centuries to enhance his status among his followers.

The Roman historian, A. N. Sherwin-White, who has studied the way in which myth and legend get added to history in the ancient world, concludes:

> Herodotus enables us to test the tempo of myth-making, and the tests suggest that even two generations are too short a span to allow the mythical tendency to prevail over the hard historic core of the oral tradition.[1]

Luke's credibility as a historian: the confirmation of archaeology

Historical and archaeological research has confirmed Luke's status as a historian again and again. For example, we quoted above his dating of the beginning of Christ's public life as occurring when Lysanias was tetrarch of Abilene (Luke 3:1). For a long time this was cited as evidence that Luke could not be taken seriously as a historian, since it was said to be common knowledge that Lysanias was not a tetrarch, but the ruler of Chalcis half a century earlier. Then, an inscription was found from the time of Tiberius (AD 14–37), naming a Lysanias as tetrarch in Abila near Damascus—precisely as Luke had said!

Similarly, Luke was thought by critics to be mistaken, when he refers in his history of the early Christian church, the book of Acts, to city officials in Thessalonica as 'politarchs' (Acts 17:6), since there was no evidence from other contemporary Roman documents that such a term was used. Yet subsequently, archaeologists have found over 35 inscriptions referring to politarchs, some of them in Thessalonica, dating from the very same period to which Luke was referring.

An earlier generation of scholars felt that the mention of non-Jewish 'God-fearers' in the book of Acts (see, e.g. Acts 17:17) showed that Luke

---

[1] *Roman Society and Roman Law in the New Testament*, 190.

could not be taken as a serious historian, since the existence of such a category of Gentiles was doubtful. However, the ancient historian, Irina Levinskaya, of the Russian Academy of Sciences and St Petersburg University, impressively demonstrates in her book,[2] that Luke's account has been vindicated by archaeological research. Inscriptions have been found, indicating the existence of precisely such a class of Gentiles. They are, in fact, listed on one Greek inscription from Aphrodisias, under a separate heading from the members of the Jewish community. She writes:

> The importance of this inscription for the historical controversy about Gentile sympathisers with Judaism lies in the fact that, once and for all, it has tipped the balance and shifted the onus of proof from those who believe in the existence of Luke's God-fearers to those who have either denied or had doubts about it.[3]

The eminent historian Sir William Ramsay spent over twenty years' archaeological research in the areas about which Luke wrote, and showed that, in his references to thirty-two countries, fifty-four cities and nine islands, Luke made no mistakes.[4]

In his magisterial work Colin Hemer details many areas in which Luke displays very accurate knowledge.[5] We can give only a very few examples:

1. Acts 13:7 shows Cyprus correctly as a proconsular (senatorial) province at the time, with the proconsul resident at Paphos;
2. 14:11 shows correctly that Lycaonian was (unusually) spoken in Lystra, at the time;
3. 14:12 reflects local interest in, and concepts of, the gods Zeus and Hermes;
4. 16:12: Philippi is correctly identified as a Roman colony, and its seaport is correctly named Neapolis;
5. 16:14: Thyatira is identified as a centre of dyeing, confirmed by at least seven inscriptions in the city;

---

[2] *The Book of Acts in its First Century Setting*, 5:51–82.
[3] *The Book of Acts in its First Century Setting*, 80.
[4] *St. Paul the Traveller and the Roman Citizen*.
[5] *The Book of Acts in the Setting of Hellenistic History*, 107–155.

6. 17:1 rightly shows Amphipolis and Apollonia as stations on the Egnatian Way from Philippi to Thessalonica;

7. 17:16–18 shows accurate knowledge of Athens: its abundance of idols, its interest in philosophical debate, and its Stoic and Epicurean philosophers and their teachings;

8. chs. 27–28 show detailed accurate knowledge of the geography and navigational details of the voyage to Rome.

All this accurately recorded detail, and much more besides, supports Roman historian A. N. Sherwin-White's verdict: 'For Acts the confirmation of historicity is overwhelming . . . any attempt to reject its basic historicity even in matters of detail must now appear absurd.'[6] Thus Luke has proved to be a first-rate historian, and we have no reason to doubt his record.

The accuracy of oral tradition upon which the Gospels depend

Jesus wrote nothing himself so that it was left to his followers to provide us with records of what he said and did. This is felt by some to be a weakness in the evidence for the authenticity of the New Testament documents. This reaction betrays the fact that most of us today live in cultures where oral tradition does not play a significant role and memorising is not part of everyday scholarly life.

In New Testament times it was very different. Historical research has established that oral tradition played an important part in many ancient societies, including Israel; and was therefore preserved with astonishing accuracy. Some rabbis were famed for having memorised all of the Old Testament, which is very much bigger than the New Testament; and so there really is no difficulty in believing that Jesus' disciples were capable of memorising the teaching of Jesus and passing it on accurately.

Oral tradition often passed direct from grandfather to grandson, thus spanning the generations accurately and rapidly. Being often retold at any given time in history, it was constantly subject to checking by knowledgeable and critical audiences—much in the same way as children often insist we tell them a story again, in exactly the same words

---

6 *Roman Society*, 189.

as we told it before; and, as most parents know, they will notice at once if we make any alterations.

Now if you (at some point in the future) tell your grandson something you clearly recall your grandfather saying, you will find that it is very easy to bridge more than 120 years! Many of us who are already older have total vivid recall of important events and conversations of forty years ago.

Moreover, it is conceivable—even probable—that some of Christ's disciples made written notes of his teaching as he gave it; just as many students in the schools of the first two centuries AD made notes of what their lecturers said. Matthew, the author of the first Gospel, was a former tax collector; such people in the ancient world are known to have been accustomed to taking notes and keeping records. It is quite possible, therefore, that Matthew did what we know that first century authors did: he used his notes in order to produce the final version of his Gospel.[7]

The accuracy and consistency of the Four Gospels

It is often alleged that the Four Gospels, with their distinctive accounts of the life, death and resurrection of Christ, cannot be regarded as historical, since they contain contradictory material. There are a number of aspects to this question.

The first is that, if each of the Gospels simply repeated word for word what the other said, then the charge would be made that the writers had simply conspired among themselves to produce one common testimony instead of four. That charge would certainly invalidate them as independent witnesses and make us suspicious as to why four accounts were necessary.

If, indeed, the Gospels are largely independent works, written by four different people from four different points of view, to give us a rounded and comprehensive account, then it is highly likely there will appear in them what, at least at first sight, appear to us as discrepancies in the accounts. We have already seen that the writer, Luke, has again and again been proved right where critics formerly thought him

---

[7] See Millard, *Reading and Writing in the Time of Jesus*. See also Powers, *The Progressive Publication of Matthew*.

wrong, because they did not have adequate knowledge. So we ought at least to be cautious before we automatically assume that an apparent discrepancy between the accounts invalidates them.

For example, Craig Blomberg, an authority on the Gospels, points out that some of the differences can be accounted for by the fact that studies of cultures with oral traditions have shown that 'there was freedom to vary how much of the story was told on any given occasion—what was included, what was left out, what was paraphrased, what was explained, and so forth.'[8] Blomberg goes on to say that, if we make allowance for this, 'the Gospels are extremely consistent with each other by ancient standards, which are the only standards by which it's fair to judge them.'[9]

As an example of this kind of thing, we find Matthew saying about a certain incident that a certain centurion came to ask Jesus to heal his servant; whereas Luke says that the centurion sent the elders to ask Jesus (Matt 8:5). For the people of the time there is no contradiction here, since it was acceptable, common practice that actions were often attributed to people in authority, even if those actions were actually carried out by their subordinates. Indeed, the same occurs today. We all know that when a news report says 'The president said today . . .', it may well be that the speech was written by a speechwriter, given by a press secretary, and simply checked by the president.[10]

EVIDENCES FROM NON-CHRISTIAN SOURCES

Tacitus

Tacitus (c. AD 56–c.120) is one of the most important Roman historians of the period, and is regarded as one of the more accurate ancient historians. In his account of the Great Fire of Rome, he refers to the fact that the emperor Nero had been blamed for the fire, and had used the Christians as scapegoats:

[8] Interviewed by Lee Strobel, *The Case for Christ*, 43.
[9] *The Case for Christ*, 45.
[10] For a fuller discussion of this passage from Matthew and the related issues, see Poythress, *Inerrancy and the Gospels*.

Consequently, to get rid of the report, Nero fastened the guilt, and inflicted the most exquisite tortures, on a class hated for their abominations, called Christians by the populace. Christus, from whom the name had its origin, suffered the extreme penalty during the reign of Tiberius at the hands of one of our procurators, Pontius Pilatus, and a most mischievous superstition, thus checked for the moment, again broke out not only in Judea, the first source of the evil, but even in Rome. . . Accordingly, an arrest was first made of all who pleaded guilty; then, upon their information, an immense multitude was convicted, not so much of the crime of firing the city, as of hatred against mankind.[11]

Suetonius

Suetonius (born *c.* AD 69), the chief secretary to the Roman emperor Hadrian (AD 117–138), wrote the following two important passages:

(*a*) 'The Jews he expelled from Rome, since they were constantly in rebellion, at the instigation of Chrestus.'[12]

(*b*) After the great fire of Rome 'punishments were imposed on the Christians—adherents of a new and dangerous superstition.'[13]

Again, we see that the texts establish the historical existence of Christ. The disturbances at Rome related to Christ (but, of course, were not directly caused by him: Suetonius was probably in no position, and had no interest, to check out the detail). Interestingly, Suetonius, in mentioning the expulsion of Jews from Rome by Claudius, confirms Luke's account of the same event, in Acts 18:2.

Josephus

More evidence comes from the historian, Flavius Josephus (AD 37/38–97), a Jewish revolutionary, who changed over his allegiance to the Romans. In his famous book, *Antiquities of the Jews*, he mentions how a high priest, named Ananias, took advantage of the death of the

---

[11] *Annals*, xv.44; online at Perseus, http://data.perseus.org/citations/urn:cts:latinLit:phi1351 .phi005.perseus-eng1:15.44.

[12] *Claudius*, 25.

[13] *Nero*, 16.

Roman governor, Festus, in order to have James killed. Now, Ananias and Festus are both mentioned in the New Testament; as also is James, whom Josephus describes as 'the brother of Jesus, who was called Christ';[14] thus confirming the New Testament's claim as to the existence of Jesus called Christ and his brother James. But Josephus' most famous quotation is: 'Now there was about this time Jesus, a wise man, if it be lawful to call him a man; for he was a doer of wonderful works . . . he appeared to them alive again the third day; as the divine prophets had foretold these and ten thousand other wonderful things concerning him.'[15]

The consensus of Jewish and Christian scholarly opinion about this text is that, in general, it is authentic, although there may well be interpolations, possibly supplied by later Christian copyists. For example, there is good reason to think that the mention of Jesus is not an interpolation. Christians would not normally refer to him as a 'wise man'. On the other hand, Christians might well have added, 'if it be lawful to call him a man'. In addition, the reference to Jesus in *Antiquities* xx.9, mentioned above, arguably presupposes an earlier reference to Jesus in the book.

Pliny

The Roman author and administrator Pliny the Younger, who was governor of Bithynia, in what is now northwestern Turkey, gives an interesting and important description of early Christian worship in his famous correspondence with his friend the emperor Trajan (*c.* AD 112), in which he describes the trial and punishment of Christians:

> I have asked them in person if they are Christians, and if they admit it, I repeat the question a second and third time, with a warning of the punishment awaiting them. If they persist, I order them to be led away for execution; for, whatever the nature of their admission, I am convinced that their stubbornness and unshakeable obstinacy ought not to go unpunished. . . . They also declared that the sum total of their guilt or error amounted to no

---

[14] *Antiquities*, xx.9.
[15] *Antiquities*, xviii.3.

more than this: they had met regularly before dawn on a fixed day to chant verses [of a hymn] amongst themselves in honour of Christ as if to a god, and also to bind themselves by oath, not for any criminal purpose, but to abstain from theft, robbery, and adultery, to commit no breach of trust and not to deny a deposit when called upon to restore it. After this ceremony it had been their custom to disperse and reassemble later to take food of an ordinary, harmless kind.[16]

This is a striking confirmation of the New Testament claim that the early Christians worshipped Jesus as God, and that they were committed to live lives of exemplary purity. The meal referred to is the 'Lord's Supper' or 'Communion', which, according to the New Testament, was instigated by Christ himself (see, e.g. Luke 22:7–20 and 1 Cor 11:23–26).

Pliny's letter also attests to the rapid spread of Christianity, not only geographically (he is writing from Bithynia), but also socially; for, elsewhere in the letter, he mentions having Christian slave-women tortured, and having Roman citizens among the Christians sent to Rome for trial. It was a criminal offence for Roman governors to torture Roman citizens.

All this shows that Bertrand Russell was talking in sheer igno-rance of the facts, when he wrote: 'Historically it is quite doubtful whether Christ ever existed at all, and if He did we know nothing about Him.'[17]

THE MANUSCRIPTS OF THE NEW TESTAMENT

The number of the manuscripts

It is the fact that no original manuscripts of the New Testament survive today: all we have are copies. This leads many people to feel that, if all we possess is the result of a multiple-copying-process over centuries, how can we have any hope today that what we read bears any resem-blance to the original text?

---

[16] *Letters*, xx.96.
[17] *Why I am Not a Christian*, 16.

This difficulty is generally felt by people who are not aware of how overwhelmingly strong the evidence for the original text of the New Testament actually is. First, there is the sheer number of the manuscripts. There are 5,664 partial or complete manuscripts of the New Testament in the original Greek language which have been catalogued; and over 9,000, in early translations into Latin, Syriac, Coptic, Arabic, etc. Added to this, there are 38,289 quotations of the New Testament by the early Church Fathers, who wrote between the second and fourth centuries AD. If, then, we lost all the New Testament manuscripts, from these quotations we could reconstruct the entire New Testament (except for eleven verses).

In order to get some idea of the significance of this manuscript evidence, we can compare it with the documentary evidence available for other ancient works of literature. Take, for example, *The Annals of Imperial Rome*, which was written by the Roman historian Tacitus in about AD 116. The first six books of the *Annals* survive in only one manuscript, which was copied in about AD 850. Books XI to XVI are in another single manuscript, dated to the eleventh century. Thus, not only is the manuscript evidence extremely scanty, but the time gap between original compilation and the earliest manuscripts is over 700 years.

The ancient secular work with the most documentary support is Homer's *Iliad* (c.800 BC) . . . the time gap between the original and the earliest surviving manuscripts is a thousand years.

Or consider *The Jewish War*, written in Greek by the first-century historian Josephus. The surviving documentary evidence for it consists of nine manuscripts, copied in the tenth to twelfth centuries AD, a Latin translation from the fourth century, and some Russian versions from the eleventh and twelfth centuries.

The ancient secular work with the most documentary support is Homer's *Iliad* (c.800 BC), of which there are 643 manuscript copies, dated from the second and later centuries AD. Thus, in this case, the time gap between the original and the earliest surviving manuscripts is a thousand years.

The very important point to note here is that, in spite of the paucity of the number of manuscripts and their late dates, scholars have confidence in treating these documents as authentic representations of the originals.

In comparison, the New Testament is, in fact, the best-attested document from the ancient world.

The age of the manuscripts

We have mentioned the time lapse between the date of certain ancient manuscripts, and the originals of which they are copies. Now, we must consider the same question, in relation to the New Testament. Here, once more, the evidence for the text of the New Testament is simply overwhelming.

Some of the New Testament manuscripts are of a very great age. The Bodmer Papyri (in the Bodmer Collection, Culagny, Switzerland) contain about two-thirds of the Gospel of John, in one papyrus dated to about AD 200. Another third-century papyrus has parts of Luke and John. Perhaps the most important manuscripts are the Chester Beatty Papyri, which were discovered in 1930 and are now housed in the Chester Beatty Museum in Dublin, Ireland. Papyrus 1 comes from the third century and contains parts of the Four gospels and Acts. Papyrus 2 contains substantial portions of eight of Paul's letters, plus parts of the Letter to the Hebrews, and is dated to around AD 200. Papyrus 3 has a large part of the book of Revelation and is dated to the third century.

Some fragments are even earlier. The famous Rylands fragment (Rylands Library Papyrus P52 held in the John Rylands Library in Manchester, England), which consists of five verses from the Gospel of John, is dated by some to the time of the emperor Hadrian, AD 117–138; and by others even to the reign of Trajan, AD 98–117. This refutes the influential view of sceptical nineteenth-century German scholars that John's Gospel could not have been written before AD 160.

The earliest surviving manuscripts containing all the books of the New Testament were written around AD 325–350. Incidentally, it was in AD 325 that the Council of Nicaea decreed that the Bible could be freely copied. The most important of these manuscripts are the Codex Vaticanus and the Codex Sinaiticus, which are called uncial manuscripts, because they are written in Greek capital letters. The Codex Vaticanus was catalogued by the Vatican Library (hence its name) in 1475; but for 400 years after that, scholars were forbidden to study it—rather odd, in light of the original decision of the Council of Nicaea!

The Codex Sinaiticus was found by Tischendorf (1815–44) in the Monastery of St. Catherine on Mount Sinai in Arabia, and is now in the British Museum in London. It is regarded as one of the most important witnesses to the text of the New Testament because of its antiquity, accuracy and lack of omissions.

Mistakes in the copying process

We can now readily see that the objection that the New Testament cannot be reliable, because it has been copied out so many times, is completely unfounded. Take, for example, a manuscript that was written about AD 200, and is therefore now some 1800 years old. How old was the manuscript from which it was originally copied? We do not know, of course; but it could very easily have been 140 years old at the time it was copied. If that were so, then that manuscript was written out when many of the authors of the New Testament were still alive. Thus, we get from New Testament times to the modern day in just *two* steps!

Furthermore, whereas there are copying mistakes in most manuscripts (it is virtually impossible to copy out a lengthy document by hand without making some mistakes), no two manuscripts contain exactly the same mistakes. Therefore, by comparing all these manuscripts with each other, it is possible to reconstruct the original text to a point where expert opinion holds that less than two per cent of that text is uncertain, with a large part of that two per cent involving small linguistic features that make no difference to the general meaning. Moreover, since no New Testament doctrine depends solely on one verse or one passage, no New Testament doctrine is put in doubt by these minor uncertainties.[18]

Summing up the situation, Sir Frederic Kenyon, former Director of the British Museum, and a leading authority on ancient manuscripts wrote:

The number of manuscripts of the New Testament, of early translations from it, and of quotations from it in the oldest writers of the Church, is so large that it is practically certain that the true

---

[18] See Wallace, 'The Majority Text and the Original Text: Are They Identical?'. See also Geisler and Nix, *A General Introduction to the Bible.*

reading of every doubtful passage is preserved in some one or other of these ancient authorities. This can be said of no other ancient book in the world.[19]

This verdict was approved by Bruce Metzger, formerly Professor Emeritus of New Testament at Princeton Theological Seminary:

> We can have great confidence in the fidelity with which this material has come down to us, especially compared with any other ancient literary work.[20]

On this basis, then, we may have every confidence that, when today we read the New Testament, we have for all practical purposes what its original authors intended us to have.

THE CANON OF THE NEW TESTAMENT

Granted, then, that there is overwhelming manuscript evidence establishing the text of the New Testament, why does the New Testament contain just these twenty-seven books and no others? For example, there are four Gospels in the New Testament canon; but other documents exist which claim to be gospels: for example, the Gospels of Barnabas, Nicodemus, Philip, Peter, Thomas, the *Gospel of the Egyptians*, and the *Gospel of the Nativity of Mary*, and many others. Why should Matthew, Mark, Luke and John be included and these excluded?

The question arises, therefore: who decided which books should be included in, and which excluded from, the canon; and by what criteria was the question settled? Bruce Metzger says: 'the canon is a list of authoritative books more than it is an authoritative list of books.' He goes on to explain what he means:

> These documents didn't derive their authority from being selected; each one was authoritative before anyone gathered them together. The early church merely listened and sensed that these were authoritative accounts. For somebody now to say that

---

[19] *Our Bible and the Ancient Manuscripts*, 23.
[20] Interview recorded by Lee Strobel, *The Case for Christ*, 63. Metzger was the author of *The Text of the New Testament, Its Transmission, Corruption and Restoration*. Until his death in 2007, he was one of the world's most eminent New Testament scholars.

the canon emerged only after councils and synods made these pronouncements would be like saying, 'Let's get several academies of musicians to make a pronouncement that the music of Bach and Beethoven is wonderful.' . . . 'We knew that before the pronouncement was made.' We know it because of sensitivity to what is good music and what is not. The same with the canon.[21]

The general considerations which moved the early church was a combination of the following:

Apostolic authority. Any book that was written by an apostle, or by people close to the apostles, was included.

Conformity to the rule of faith. Books were only recognised as canonical if they were consistent with the basic doctrines of Christianity, as taught from the beginning by Christ and his apostles.

Most of the books, of what is now the New Testament, were accepted very rapidly. In a few countries, there were one or two books which were not accepted in all quarters until the fourth century. After that, there was no dispute for centuries.

Spurious gospels

Metzger says of the 'Gospels' that are not regarded as canonical: 'They're written later than the four Gospels, in the second, third, fourth, fifth, even sixth century, long after Jesus, and they're generally quite banal. They carry names—like the *Gospel of Peter* and the *Gospel of Mary*— that are unrelated to their real authorship.'[22] They also include material completely alien to the canonical Gospels. For example, in the *Gospel of Thomas*, Jesus is alleged to say, 'Split wood; I am there. Lift up a stone and you will find me there.'[23] This is pantheism. At the end of the Gospel, we read, 'Let Mary go away from us because women are not worthy of life.'[24] Such a statement is completely incongruous with the Jesus of the canonical Gospels, who treated women with a courtesy and dignity uncommon in ancient society. It is easy to see why the church rejected the *Gospel of Thomas*.

---

[21] Interviewed by Strobel, *The Case for Christ*, 69.
[22] Strobel, *The Case for Christ*, 67.
[23] Strobel, *The Case for Christ*, 68.
[24] Strobel, *The Case for Christ*, 68.

The Gospel of Barnabas

An interesting test case is the so-called *Gospel of Barnabas*, which is supposed to be written by Barnabas, who was the companion of Paul (Acts 13:1–3). Incidentally, it is important not to confuse the *Gospel of Barnabas* with the first-century *Epistle of (Pseudo-)Barnabas*, which is a completely different book, also not in the canon. The question is: why should we not accept the *Gospel of Barnabas'* account, along with that of the canonical Gospels?

In their introduction to the text of the *The Gospel of Barnabas*, Lonsdale and Laura Ragg point out that the book evidences:

1. 'an obvious and primary dependence on the Christian Bible and especially on the four canonical Gospels';
2. frequent and voluminous insertions of Jewish and Islamic material; and
3. traces of mediaeval materials.[25]

The Raggs make the important observation that the first point once-for-all disposes of the *Gospel of Barnabas'* claim to be an authentic and independent Gospel. Other major reasons for rejecting the book as canonical are:

The lack of early manuscript evidence. The Raggs say of the *Gospel of Barnabas* that the earliest form of it known to us is in an Italian manuscript. This has been closely analysed by scholars and is judged to belong to the fifteenth or sixteenth century AD, i.e. 1400 years after the time of Barnabas.[26] Moreover, from the first to the fifteenth century, no teacher of the Christian church ever quoted from it; which is hardly likely to be the case, if it had ever been regarded as authentic.

The presence of anachronisms. For example, it uses the text from the Latin Vulgate version of the Bible (fourth century), even though it is supposed to have been written by Barnabas in the first century AD. It contains descriptions of mediaeval European life and customs, which reveal that it could scarcely have been written before the fourteenth century. For example, it refers to the year of jubilee only coming once every one hundred years, instead of the biblical fifty; and we know that

---

25 *The Gospel of Barnabas*, ix.
26 *The Gospel of Barnabas*, xxxvii.

there was a papal decree in AD 1343, which changed it to every one hundred years.

The presence of factual errors. There are clear and serious historical errors, such as the assertion that Jesus was born when Pilate was Governor of Judea; when, in fact, Pilate did not become governor until AD 26/7. There are glaring geographical errors, such as the assertion that Jesus sailed to Nazareth—a town which is not even on the seashore! There are even mistakes in citing the books of the Bible: the book of Proverbs is called 'David', and Isaiah is called 'Ezekiel'!

The *Gospel of Barnabas* is also well known for its contradiction of the canonical Gospels, in that it claims (sect. 217) that Jesus did not die on the cross; but that Judas Iscariot was substituted for him. From the fifteenth or sixteenth centuries onwards, many Muslims have cited the *Gospel of Barnabas* to support their conviction—which they express with considerable vigour—that Christians have changed the New Testament, in order to make it say that Jesus died on the cross, when originally it said that he did not. The use of the *Gospel of Barnabas* to support this view is very strange, in light of the fact that in other respects the *Gospel of Barnabas* contradicts the Qur'an. For example, the *Gospel of Barnabas* says that Jesus said that he was not the Messiah, but that he was the forerunner of Muhammad, who is named and referred to as the Messiah. It even asserts that the name 'Muhammad' was written on the left thumbnail of Adam before the creation of Eve.

Academician Professor Sir Norman Anderson, former Professor of Oriental Laws, and Director of the Institute of Advanced Legal Studies in London University, writes:

> It is intrinsically unlikely, moreover, that the Barnabas of the first century should have predicted by name the coming of Muḥammed and should (contrary to the Qur'ān as well as the Bible) have referred to him, rather than Jesus, as the Messiah. It is very strange that orthodox Muslims should accept a book which flatly, and repeatedly, contradicts the clear Quranic statement 'O Mary, Allāh giveth thee tidings of a word from Himself whose name is the Messiah, Jesus, son of Mary . . .' (*Sura* 3. 40). The Qur'ān never gives this title to Muḥammed.[27]

---

[27] *Islam in the Modern World*, 234.

In any case, the assertion that Jesus did not die is refuted, not only by the thousands of manuscripts of the four Gospels which we have, but also by the evidence from the non-biblical sources cited above, that clearly attest the death of Jesus by crucifixion. The sheer weight of textual evidence means that it is simply contrary to the plain historical facts to suggest on the basis of one mediaeval document that the New Testament documents have been changed from their supposed original agreement with the *Gospel of Barnabas*. The extreme improbability of this position is further seen if one reflects that, if it were true, it would force one to assume that the non-biblical sources had also been tampered with in this way.

Moreover, we have seen that the very earliest datable sources go back to the apostles themselves, to a very few years after the events which they are describing. Those sources are unanimous in making the death of Jesus central to their message. In light of all of this, to suggest that all the manuscripts attesting to the historical death of Jesus have been corrupted and changed, is simply incredible.

CHAPTER 3

THE FIGURE OF CHRIST: FICTION, MYTH, OR REALITY?

If Jesus is the Son of God, then these records of what he said and did on earth do, in fact, come to us with his authority. But if we are prepared to read them, then it is up to him to convince us that he is the truth. He is on record as inviting his contemporaries to use their critical judgment on the moral character of his word and actions.

INTRODUCTION

In the preceding chapter we discovered that the Christian gospel is firmly rooted in history. We saw, for example, that the prologue to Luke's Gospel clearly shows that his intention was to write history, and that, in order to do so, he thoroughly researched all possible sources, both oral and written (Luke 1:1–4). He carefully places both the birth of Christ and the beginning of his public ministry in the context of contemporary political history (Luke 2:1–2; 3:1). Furthermore, in the Acts—his account of the rise and initial spread of Christianity from Jerusalem outwards—Luke has proved to be extremely accurate in his use of background terminology: geographical, political, social, nautical, etc.

However, as we all well know, a modern writer of a historical novel will research the background for the novel meticulously, so that all the detailed historical, geographical, social and technical details are authentic. But that background accuracy is, of course, no guarantee that the novelist has not been very imaginative and given rein to exaggeration in his or her depiction of the central characters of the narrative, or even invented them.

The question arises, therefore, as to whether the same is true of the New Testament Gospel writers. We may well believe that the historical background is accurate, but the writers make extraordinary claims for their central figure, Jesus of Nazareth. In particular, they record him as saying that he was the Son of God. How do we know in particular that the figure of Christ, as depicted in the New Testament, was not invented? His biographers were obviously fervid and loyal disciples: could it not be that their devotion to him has led them to polish or exaggerate their account of him?

It is precisely this issue that is being discussed between the literary editor Berlioz and the poet Bezdomny in the opening scene of Bulgakov's literary masterpiece, *The Master and Margarita*. Berlioz has commissioned Bezdomny to write an anti-religious poem for his journal; but the result represents Jesus as far too lifelike for Berlioz's taste. 'Now Berlioz wanted to prove to the poet that the main thing was not how Jesus was, good or bad, but that this same Jesus, as a person, simply never existed in the world, and all the stories about him were mere fiction, the most ordinary mythology.'[1] A foreign-looking man (who later turns out to be the devil in disguise) breaks in on their conversation:

> 'Unless I heard wrong, you were pleased to say that Jesus never existed?' the foreigner asked, turning his left green eye to Berlioz.
>
> 'No, you did not hear wrong,' Berlioz replied courteously, 'that is precisely what I was saying.' . . .
>
> 'And you were agreeing with your interlocutor?' inquired the stranger, turning to Homeless [Bezdomny] on his right.
>
> 'A hundred percent!' confirmed the man, who was fond of whimsical and figurative expressions. . . .
>
> 'In our country atheism does not surprise anyone,' Berlioz said with diplomatic politeness. 'The majority of our population consciously and long ago ceased believing in the fairy tales about God.'[2]

All of this, then, leads us to ask if Berlioz and Bezdomny are right. Is the figure of Christ a literary fiction, a religious myth or a historical reality?

IS THE FIGURE OF JESUS IN THE GOSPELS AN INVENTION?

The achievement of the Gospel writers

For the sake of the argument, let us suppose that the authors of the Gospels did not simply describe a Jesus who actually lived, but invented this character, taking as their raw material, perhaps, some peasant 'wise man' and freely reconstructing, adding to, shaping and exaggerating it, so that the result was an ideal, more than human, but fictional, character, who as such

---

[1] *The Master and Margarita*, 9.
[2] *The Master and Margarita*, 11–12.

never existed. Let us suppose that this was how it was, and then let us work out the implications of this theory.

The first thing to say about it would be that, if the character of Jesus is a literary fiction, then what we have in the Gospels is a near-miracle. Literature is full of fictional characters; but comparatively few of them have attained worldwide fame. To have created the character of Jesus, and to have invented and put into his mouth parables that are in themselves literary masterpieces, would have required literary genius of the highest order. But in the Gospels we have apparently four such geniuses, all flowering at once. Who were these men? What kind of men were they? Were they brilliant men, coming from the very top rank of the educated literary elite? Hardly. According to the New Testament, Matthew was a low-level tax official, John a fisherman, and about Mark we have very little information. Luke, the physician, was probably the only one who had any significant education. It is, therefore, scarcely credible that all four just happened simultaneously to be literary geniuses of world rank.

But there is more to be said. Even the most brilliant, most lifelike, fictional characters remain for their readers simply that: fictional characters. They do not rise up out of the page, so to speak, take on an independent existence, and become for their readers a real living person, whom they can know in the way one knows a living person, and with whom they can have a personal relationship. Understandably not! Yet that is what has happened to this supposedly fictional character, Jesus Christ. For millions of people over twenty centuries, he has become a real, living person, with whom they would claim to have a personal relationship: a person whom they love, to the point of being prepared to die for him, as thousands actually have. Now, some people may, of course, think them seriously misguided for feeling this way about Jesus, but that does not alter the undeniable fact that they do. And our point is this: if Jesus was merely a fictional character invented by the authors of the Gospels, then, in creating a character who for millions has become a living person worthy of love, devotion and sacrifice, those authors have achieved a literary feat unparalleled in the whole of world literature. Miracle would not be too strong a word for it.

There are, of course, some (though remarkably few) characters in literature that strike us as real persons, whom we can know and recognise. One of them is Plato's Socrates. Plato's dialogues are not only philosophical works; they are works of world-ranking literature. Yet, the Socrates who appears in them has struck generation after generation of readers as a real person, whose character traits they would recognise anywhere; so much so that, if they were presented with a depiction of Socrates in some apocryphal, second-rate work, they would say at once, 'No, that was not how the real Socrates would have reacted, or spoken.'

But the reason why the Socrates of Plato's dialogues strikes us like that is precisely because Plato did not invent him. He was a real, historical person, who actually lived. Plato's picture of Socrates may be highly polished, but the person and character of Socrates were no invention of Plato's. It was the other way round. It was the impact of Socrates' character that helped to 'create' the philosopher and literary artist, Plato. So it is with Jesus Christ.

Jesus: nobody's idea of a hero

We stay for a moment longer with the hypothesis that someone invented the character of Jesus and presented this fiction to the world, where it immediately appealed to people of widely different cultures and was taken over as their religious ideal.

But this hypothesis falls at the very first historical hurdle. The more we know about the leading cultures of the time, the more it becomes clear that, if the character of Jesus had not been a historical reality, nobody would have invented it—even if they could. The Jesus of the Gospels fitted nobody's concept of a hero. Greek, Roman and Jew—all found him the very opposite of their ideal.

Not the Jewish ideal

Take, first, the Jews. Not merely the Jews who were, and continued to be, hostile to Jesus, but the comparatively few who were at first his friends. They themselves tell us—and they certainly did not invent this bit—that when he first announced to them that he would go to Jerusalem, be rejected by the leaders of the nation and be killed, they were so shocked that they tried very hard to dissuade him (Matt 16:21–23). The reason for this reaction was that, if this announcement was true, Jesus was turning out to be utterly contrary to what they looked for in a hero. Their concept of a hero was a messianic figure like the Maccabee—a strong, military type, fired with religious ideals, and prepared to fight (with the help of angelic assistance, so popular fervour believed) the imperialist Romans, who had subjugated the country. At least some of the popular following that Jesus enjoyed must be attributed to the fact that there were many in Israel who looked for such a messiah.

The Jesus of the Gospels fitted nobody's concept of a hero. Greek, Roman and Jew— all found him the very opposite of their ideal.

But when matters came to a head between Jesus and the authorities, and they came to arrest him, Jesus refused to fight, or to let his disciples fight either, and deliberately allowed himself to be arrested; at which point, all his followers abandoned him for a time (Matt 26:47–56). Such non-resistance to evil simply was not a Jewish ideal. Many Jews today feel similarly. A Jewish friend of one of the authors, who only just managed to escape Hitler's gas chambers, used to say, 'This Jesus of yours is a weakling. He won't do as a messiah for me. My philosophy is that if someone hits you on the nose, you hit him back!' That is how Jesus' first disciples originally thought. Indeed, the historian Luke records a conversation that took place between the risen Jesus and two of his disciples on the road between Emmaus and Jerusalem. Not recognising who Jesus was at first, the travellers discussed with him the events that had just happened at Jerusalem, and said concerning Jesus, 'We had hoped that he was the one who would liberate Israel' (Luke 24:21 own trans.). They were clearly expecting a powerful military liberator to lead them to political freedom: they were certainly not expecting him to be crucified. Jesus had to explain to them that their preconceived ideas about the Messiah were false. In the end, they tell us, it was his explanation of the Old Testament Scriptures that radically changed their ideas of what the Messiah should be and do, and led them to believe that he had risen from the dead.

Not the Greek ideal

Contemporary Greeks admired various kinds of character. Some favoured the ideal Epicurean, who, as far as possible, carefully avoided all pains and pleasure that could disturb his tranquillity. Others favoured the ideal Stoic, who, following a rigid rationality, subdued his emotions and met suffering and death with undisturbed self-possession. Plato's followers would have looked back with admiration to Socrates, who, we remember, drank the poisoned cup with unflinching cheerfulness and equanimity.

In the form of the eyewitness testimony by Phaedo of Elis to a group of philosophers, including one, Echecrates, Plato gives us this information—we break into his account, as the prison official hands the cup of poison to Socrates:

> As he spoke he handed the cup to Socrates, who received it quite cheerfully, Echecrates, without a tremor, without any change of colour or expression, and said, looking up under his brows with his usual steady gaze, 'What do you say about pouring a libation from this drink? Is it permitted, or not?'
>
> 'We only prepare what we regard as the normal dose, Socrates,' he replied.
>
> 'I see,' said Socrates. 'But I suppose I am allowed, or rather bound, to pray the gods that my removal from this world to the other may be prosperous. This is my prayer, then; and I hope that it may be granted.' With these words, quite calmly and with no sign of distaste, he drained the cup in one breath.[3]

How completely different is the Jesus of the Gospels. Tormented with anguish and agony in Gethsemane, until his sweat rolled down like heavy drops of blood, he pleaded with God to let him off drinking the cup that was presented to him; and on the cross he cried out publicly: 'My God, my God, why have you forsaken me?' (Matt 27:46). He certainly was no one that a Greek would have recognised as a hero, no one that a Greek philosopher would have invented as an ideal to look up to.

Not the Roman ideal

As for the Romans, the philosophically minded tended to prefer Stoicism (cf. Cicero and Seneca). Christ would not have fitted their ideal. Pilate, the military and political man, seems to have found Christ unworldly and impractical,[4] and King Herod mocked him, and his

---

[3] Plato, *Phaedo* 117B–C; see *The Last Days of Socrates*, 182.
[4] See Ch. 8—'Truth on Trial', in Book 3: *Questioning Our Knowledge*.

soldiers considered a 'king' like Jesus to be fair game for the crudest of practical jokes (Luke 23:11).

The plain fact is that, in the end, Jesus ran counter to everybody's concept of an ideal hero—political, philosophical, or religious. Nobody invented him, and nobody (even if they had invented him) would have considered for a moment that here was an ideal that would instantly appeal to the public.

The cross: nobody's idea of a philosophy

This is also very much the case, when it comes to what the early Christians preached. Even some years after the resurrection of Christ, the great Christian preacher and missionary, Paul, confesses in his writings that the preaching of the cross of Christ constantly struck the Jews as scandalous, and the Greeks as sheer folly (1 Cor 1:20–25). It is important that we understand why that was.

The scandalous folly of the Christian gospel

In the ancient Roman world, crucifixion was the most opprobrious form of punishment one could possibly imagine, so that it was not even regarded as a subject suitable for polite conversation. Martin Hengel, former Professor of New Testament and Ancient Judaism at the University of Tübingen, writes:

> It should be further noted that we find very few descriptions of crucifixion from antiquity. Mark 15:20–39 and the parallel account of the other three gospels are by far the most extensive of these. Ancient authors generally considered it far too unsavoury a subject. If it was mentioned at all, the mere indication *that* someone had been crucified sufficed; for *this reason* other details were not mentioned.[5]

The famous orator Marcus Tullius Cicero wrote: 'Even the mere word, cross, must remain far, not only from the lips of the citizens of Rome, but also from their thoughts, their eyes, their ears.'[6] In light of this, the early Christian preaching of the cross of Christ seemed highly

---

[5] *Studies in Early Christology*, 48.
[6] *Pro Rabirio*, v.16.

distasteful and foolish to the sophisticated Graeco-Roman world—how could a crucified man be the ultimate solution to the world's problems and the key to the enigma of the universe?

For the Jews it was even worse. To preach that someone who had recently been crucified was God's Messiah and the Redeemer of humankind, sounded hideously blasphemous. The reason for that was simple. In Jewish law, in the worst cases of capital crime, the criminal was stoned to death, and then his body was hung for a short time on a tree as a public example:

> If a man has committed a crime punishable by death and he is put to death, and you hang him on a tree, his body shall not remain all night on the tree, but you shall bury him the same day, for a hanged man is cursed by God. (Deut 21:22–23)

To the Jews, therefore, the fact that God had allowed Jesus Christ to be hung on a cross was evidence that God's curse was on him. To suggest to them that someone whom God had cursed was their Messiah, Son of God, and the Saviour of the world, was not only absurd, but also unspeakably blasphemous.

The source of the message of the cross

It is obvious, then, that the disciples of Christ did not invent the story of the crucifixion. Where, then, did the idea behind their message come from? Was it that, after the crucifixion, the Christians did their best to salvage their faith in Jesus as the Messiah by inventing the idea that his death was a sacrifice for the sins of the world? The answer to that is an emphatic, No. The idea goes back to Christ himself, who, before the cross, announced: 'the Son of Man did not come to be served, but to serve, and to give his life as a ransom for many' (Matt 20:28 NIV).

Furthermore, the night before his crucifixion he instituted a ceremony by which his followers should thereafter remember him. It is very instructive to notice the nature of that ceremony. When his followers met together, he did not ask that they should recite the story of one of his spectacular miracles: that would have suggested that the main thing about his ministry was that he was a miracle-worker. Nor did he ask that they should select and recite a portion of his moral teaching: that would have suggested that the main purpose of his life was to be a philosopher-teacher. He asked that they should take bread and wine to represent his body and blood, and eat and drink them in memory of the fact that on the cross he gave his body, and shed his blood, to secure for them forgiveness of sins (Matt 26:26–28).

Thus, according to Christ, the message of the cross, that seemed so scandalous and foolish to the world, was actually the very heart of the Christian gospel of forgiveness of sins. What is more, he pointed out that it had its roots even further back in the Old Testament prophetic tradition. In the conversation recorded in Luke 24 between the two disciples on the road to Emmaus and the risen Christ, that we referred to above, Jesus chided them for their failure to see from the Old Testament that the Messiah (Christ in Greek), whoever he was, had to suffer:

> 'How foolish you are, and how slow to believe all that the prophets have spoken! Did not the Messiah have to suffer these things and then enter his glory?' And beginning with Moses and all the Prophets, he explained to them what was said in all the Scriptures concerning himself. (Luke 24:25–27 NIV)

In talking about his death as a ransom for the forgiveness of sins, Christ was echoing words written by the Hebrew prophet Isaiah about seven centuries before the crucifixion:

> Surely he has borne our griefs
>   and carried our sorrows;
> yet we esteemed him stricken,
>   smitten by God, and afflicted.
> But he was wounded for our transgressions;
>   he was crushed for our iniquities;
> upon him was the chastisement that brought us peace,
>   and with his stripes we are healed.
> All we like sheep have gone astray;
>   we have turned—every one—to his own way;
> and the LORD has laid on him
>   the iniquity of us all.
>
> He was oppressed, and he was afflicted,
>   yet he opened not his mouth;

like a lamb that is led to the slaughter,
and like a sheep that before its shearers is silent,
so he opened not his mouth. (Isa 53:4–7)

Again in this connection, much is made in the Gospels of the fact that John the Baptist, the forerunner of Christ, was a fulfilment of another one of the prophet Isaiah's predictions, in chapter 40 (see Matt 3:1–3, Mark 1:1–4, Luke 3:1–20, John 4:19–28). It was John, who—not after the cross, but at the beginning of Christ's ministry—heralded him as 'the Lamb of God, who takes away the sin of the world' (John 1:29); and the term he used, 'the Lamb of God', would have been understood by all his hearers. They were accustomed to lambs being sacrificed as offerings for sin, particularly at the Jewish ceremony of Passover; and so they clearly understood that John was saying that Jesus had come in order to die as such a sacrifice.

And the early Christians understood all of this very clearly. The records show that, from the very beginning, they began to meet on the first day of the week (Acts 20:7), to do what Christ had commanded them to do: eat bread and drink wine, to recall his sacrificial death on the cross for their forgiveness. This understanding of his death, therefore, was not a later theological interpretation, put upon it by subsequent theologians.

The early preaching of the cross

In their preaching in the synagogues, the Christians were not slow to explain to their Jewish hearers that the death of Christ had fulfilled the Old Testament prophecies (see, for example, Acts 13:13–52). But then they would make the further telling point—it was not the Christians who had organised the crucifixion of Christ, so as to bring it about that he would appear to have fulfilled those Old Testament prophecies—it was the Jewish authorities, themselves hostile to Christ, who had acted in collusion with Pilate to get Christ crucified, in order to put an end to his claim that he was the Messiah. As the Christians acutely observed:

For those who live in Jerusalem and their rulers, because they did not recognize him nor understand the utterances of the prophets, which are read every Sabbath, *fulfilled them by condemning him.* And though they found in him no guilt worthy of death, they asked Pilate to have him executed. And when they had carried out all that was written of him, they took him down from the tree and laid him in a tomb. (Acts 13:27–29, emph. added)

It remains to be said that this story of the cross of Christ, as God's provision for forgiveness and reconciliation of man to God, is unique in all the history of religion, and it is not disrespectful of any other religion to take from the hands of Christ what no other religion or philosophy offers.

WHAT IS THE EVIDENCE THAT JESUS CLAIMED TO BE THE SON OF GOD?

Alternative explanations

There are three very common reactions to the Christian claim that Jesus is the Son of God:

1. to suggest that Jesus himself never claimed it, but that the whole idea is the product of primitive superstition;
2. to suggest that it arose from a subsequent misunderstanding, when the sayings of Christ were in later decades translated from their original language (Aramaic) into Hellenistic Greek;
3. to suggest that the term 'Son of God' is the language of Christian mythology.

Let us look at these three suggestions in turn:

First suggestion: a primitive superstition

Since the ancient world was full of stories of gods visiting earth in the form of exceptional human beings, the suggestion here is that it is likely that the Gospels were written under the influence of these superstitions. Now, it is true that the nations in the ancient world believed that there were many gods, and that those gods did visit earth from time to time. That is, all the nations did, with one notable exception. That one exception was the Jewish nation, to which, almost to a man, the writers of the New Testament belonged. The Jews in the time of Christ were strict monotheists. They despised the other nations for their absurd polytheism, and for making gods out of their kings and heroes. For them, to claim divine honours for anybody other than God the Creator was a blasphemy so serious that, according to their law, it was punishable by death. For centuries, in every home in the land, as the fundamental tenet of their faith, they had been taught to recite in their daily religious devotions: 'Hear, O Israel: the LORD our God is one LORD' (Deut 6:4 ESV mg.). This was the last nation and culture on earth, therefore, where one would expect to find the claim that a man was the Son of God. Yet, in that land, according to the Gospels, Jesus did make that claim.

Second suggestion: a translation error

The suggestion here is that the idea that Jesus was the Son of God arose, not among the original disciples of Christ, but only decades later among Hellenistic Christians, and was occasioned by a misunderstanding of the translation of the original words of Jesus from Aramaic into Greek. In Aramaic, the term *Son of God* could be used as an honorific, and applied to a king (see, for example, the elevated way in which the king is addressed in Psalm 45). It is argued that, when the gospel spread into Greek-speaking countries and the Aramaic of Jesus' speech was translated in Greek, Greek speakers misunderstood it, taking the term *Son of God* to mean that he was really the Son of God in an ontological sense.

Furthermore, it is noticed by some that this emphasis on Christ's deity occurs particularly in the Gospel of John, in which Christ is entitled *the Word* (*Logos*) of God (John 1:1). Older critics pointed out that the term *Logos* was commonplace in Hellenistic philosophy, as, for instance, in the writings of Philo of Alexandria, the Hellenistic Jewish religious philosopher. They argued, therefore, that the Gospel of John was a late production, made under the influence of Hellenistic thought. The result was a reinterpretation and upgrading of the figure of Christ.

Historical research, however, has shown that these ideas are unfounded. Martin Hengel[7] pointed out that Palestine in the time of

---

[7] *Judaism and Hellenism.*

Christ had already been thoroughly Hellenized for two or three centuries. Greek was widely known and spoken, and, of course, the ten cities founded by Alexander the Great (the Decapolis) were Greek cities. It is even possible that on occasion Christ himself spoke Greek. There is no evidence, therefore, that the use of the term *Logos* for Christ indicates later Hellenistic interpretation.

There is another consideration that reinforces this view. The fact is, as we now know, that the literature of the Dead Sea Scrolls (which is contemporary with Christ, and written in Aramaic) already used the Aramaic word, *memra* (= word), to denote the Word of God, by which God made the universe. When, therefore, the Gospel of John styles the Lord Jesus as the Word of God, through whom God made the universe (John 1:1–3), he is certainly using a Greek word that would have been *understood* by the Greeks (as the rational mind behind the universe); but that does not prove that he *derived* this term from Hellenistic philosophy, and was reinterpreting the nature of Christ in the light of that philosophy.

Third suggestion: a mythological term

The third suggestion is that such terms as *Son of God* are part of the mythological vocabulary, by which the apostles struggled to express the impact that Christ had had upon them. Having experienced the impact of the person and teaching of Christ, the early Christians used the only kind of language available to them to express that experience, namely, mythological language; but in our day, when we decode what they wrote into straightforward theological language, we must abandon their mythological language, thus leaving us with a Jesus who was certainly a remarkable teacher about God, but still no more than human. However, on inspection, this view is shown to be inadequate by the fact that the claim that Jesus was, in the fullest ontological sense, the Son of God, goes back to Christ himself during his life on earth.

Christ's explicit statements

There are two strands to the argument here. Firstly, the explicit statements Christ made. Here are some examples of the ways in which Jesus made his claim to be God incarnate, as recorded by the Apostle John. He said to his contemporaries: 'I am from above. . . . I am not of this world. . . . unless you believe that I am he[8] you will die in your sins' (John 8:23–24). He also claimed that he existed before Abraham: 'Before Abraham was born, I am' (John 8:58 NIV).

In other places he claimed oneness with the Father: 'I and the Father are one', he said (John 10:30), and then in addition he claimed to be the exact representation of the Father: 'Whoever has seen me has seen the Father' (John 14:9).

> It is not for a good work that we are going to stone you but for blasphemy, because you, being a man, make yourself God.
> —John 10:33

It is quite obvious from the Gospels that this is what the contemporary Jews understood him to be saying. On one occasion, when they accused him of breaking the Sabbath, he replied by saying: 'My Father is working until now, and I am working'—they objected very strongly to this statement—'This was why the Jews were seeking all the more to kill him, because not only was he breaking the Sabbath, but he was even calling God his own Father, making himself equal with God' (John 5:17–18). Somewhat later there was another attempt to kill him, on the same grounds: 'It is not for a good work that we are going to stone you but for blasphemy, because you, being a man, make yourself God' (John 10:33).

And when eventually they brought him before the Roman procurator, they urged their case upon Pilate to have him crucified, arguing: 'We have a law, and according to that law he ought to die because he has made himself the Son of God' (John 19:7).

As a matter of history, therefore, there can be no doubt that Jesus made the claim to be God incarnate, and gave his life for it. What is more, Christ put having faith in himself in the same category as having faith in God. He said to his disciples, 'You believe in God, believe also in me' (John 14:1 ESV mg.). He also accepted divine honours from his fellow human beings. Indeed, as we shall presently see, he claimed that the Father had committed all judgment unto him, with the explicitly stated purpose that 'all may honour the Son, just as they honour the Father' (John 5:22–23). And when, according to the Apostle John, in one of Jesus' resurrection appearances in Jerusalem, the disciple Thomas addressed him as 'My Lord and my God', Jesus did not rebuke

---

[8] We should remember that, in Exod 3:14, God expressed his name as, 'I am that I am'. It was because Jesus used this kind of language about himself that people picked up stones to stone him to death (John 8:59).

him but approved of his worship, responding: 'Because you have seen me, you have believed' (John 20:28–29 NIV).

The implicit claims of Christ

The second strand of the argument is equally important, and concerns claims to deity *implicit* in Christ's statements. On several occasions (and not only in the Gospel of John) his contemporaries were staggered to hear him forgive sins (Mark 2:1–12). The record bears all the hallmarks of a contemporary statement of Christ's that was not invented by the apostles. C. S. Lewis analyses it as follows:

> Now it is quite natural for a man to forgive something you do to *him*. Thus if somebody cheats *me* out of £5 it is quite possible and reasonable for me to say, 'Well, I forgive him, we will say no more about it.' What on earth would you say if somebody had done *you* out of £5 and *I* said, 'That is all right, I forgive him'?[9]

The only person who has the right to forgive sins is God, because, in the last analysis, all sin is sin against him and his law. It was for this reason, when Jesus claimed to forgive the sins of the paralytic man, that the teachers of the law said, 'Who can forgive sins but God alone?' (Mark 2:7). They correctly understood that his action in forgiving the man, without reference to the person he had sinned against, directly implied a claim to divinity.

In the Sermon on the Mount Christ makes himself the centre of morality. He ends the series of his famous Beatitudes ('Blessed are the poor in spirit', etc.) by pronouncing a blessing on those who are perse-cuted for his sake: 'Blessed are you when others revile you and persecute you and utter all kinds of evil against you falsely on my account' (Matt 5:11). And then he repeatedly takes precepts from the Old Testament, and comments on them in such a way as to imply that he has the same authority as the God who was originally said to have given them: 'You have heard that it was said to those of old, "You shall not murder; and whoever murders will be liable to judgment." But I say to you that everyone who is angry with his brother will be liable to judgment' (Matt 5:21–22). Or again, 'You have heard that it was said, "You shall love your neighbour and hate your enemy." But I say to you, Love your enemies

---

9 *God in the Dock*, 167.

and pray for those who persecute you, so that you may be sons of your Father who is in heaven' (Matt 5:43–44).

Not only that, but Christ makes himself and his teaching the criterion of the final judgment:

> On that day many will say to me, 'Lord, Lord, did we not prophesy in your name, and cast out demons in your name, and do many mighty works in your name?' And then will I declare to them, 'I never knew you; depart from me, you workers of lawlessness.'
>
> Everyone then who hears these words of mine and does them will be like a wise man who built his house on the rock. And the rain fell, and the floods came, and the winds blew and beat on that house, but it did not fall, because it had been founded on the rock. And everyone who hears these words of mine and does not do them will be like a foolish man who built his house on the sand. And the rain fell, and the floods came, and the winds blew and beat against that house, and it fell, and great was the fall of it. (Matt 7:22–27)

Such implicit claims to divine authority had a breathtaking effect on those who heard them. It is no wonder, as Matthew finally records, that 'the crowds were astonished at his teaching, for he was teaching them as one who had authority, and not as their scribes' (Matt 7:28–29).

C. S. Lewis sums up the situation as follows:

> The historical difficulty of giving for the life, sayings and influence of Jesus any explanation that is not harder than the Christian explanation is very great. The discrepancy between the depth and sanity and (let me add) *shrewdness* of his moral teaching and the rampant megalomania which must lie behind his theological teaching unless he is indeed God, has never been satisfactorily got over. Hence the non-Christian hypotheses succeed one another with the restless fertility of bewilderment.[10]

Incidentally, Christ's claim is without parallel in other religions. Again, C. S. Lewis writes,

---

[10] *Miracles*, 174–5, emphasis in original.

If you had gone to Buddha and asked him, 'Are you the son of Bramah?' he would have said, 'My son, you are still in the vale of illusion.' If you had gone to Socrates and asked, 'Are you Zeus?' he would have laughed at you. If you had gone to Mohammed and asked, 'Are you Allah?' he would first have rent his clothes and then cut your head off. If you had asked Confucius, 'Are you Heaven?' I think he would probably have replied, 'Remarks which are not in accordance with nature are in bad taste.' The idea of a great moral teacher saying what Christ said is out of the question.[11]

In the light of that evidence, that Christ's claim to be the Son of God was no invention of the early Christians but stemmed from himself, we next ask: Was he, then, a deliberate liar?

Was Christ a fraud?

If Christ was a deliberate deceiver, we run at once into a major moral difficulty. To enable us to grasp it, just imagine that we wanted an opinion about some question to do with music. We should not consult just anybody. We should not even consult a top medical doctor, since possessing the highest qualifications in medicine says nothing at all about a person's ability as a musician. We should consult the best teachers of music we could get hold of. If we could resurrect Bach, we would naturally consult him.

Now suppose we wanted to know not about music, but about morality. Once more we would consult the highest world-ranking experts we could find. And that would lead us, of course, directly to Jesus Christ. None ever taught a higher, purer morality. His Sermon on the Mount remains an unsurpassed standard—as anyone can easily verify by trying to live according to its precepts even for a week.

But with this, we come to the point of this discussion. Throughout the New Testament, when we come alongside Jesus of Nazareth, we find that his teaching on morality and his personal holiness of life expose us to ourselves as the sinners we are. We need no external proof that he is true at this level: we know it instinctively. But then comes the striking fact: it was this Jesus Christ—whose

---

[11] *God in the Dock*, 168.

moral teaching was flawless, and whose life matched his teaching—that claimed to be equal with God. As the above quote from C. S. Lewis shows, no other great moral teacher has ever claimed anything like it. This unique circumstance surely means that, if his claim is false, then Jesus was a fraud of the most despicable moral and religious kind in that, having taught morality, he deliberately deceived others on such a scale. Thus the view that Jesus was a fraud makes no moral sense whatsoever.

Could Jesus have been mistaken in his claim?

It will, however, be argued by some that Jesus could have been genuinely mistaken, without being a deliberate fraud. He may have made the claim to be the Son of God, without realising that it was false. However, the logical implications of this view surely rule it out very quickly. People who mistakenly think they are God are suffering from serious megalomania, and clearly are deeply mentally disturbed. Are we to conclude, then, that Jesus Christ was suffering from mental illness? One is tempted to say that, if this is the case, very few people have ever been sane.

As for megalomania, it is impossible to study the behaviour and words of Christ as described in the New Testament and come to any such conclusion. The Jesus who could say with conviction, 'Come to me, all who labour and are heavy laden, and I will give you rest. Take my yoke upon you, and learn from me, for I am gentle and lowly in heart' (Matt 11:28–29), was no Hitler or Mussolini. In fact, one might well think that, if he really was a megalomaniac, the world could do with more like him; for it is a simple matter of fact, that Jesus Christ has been responsible for more mental health and stability than anyone else in the world. Reading his words has brought peace to millions. Faith in him and in his sacrifice has given millions release from the torture of a guilty conscience.

It was Jesus Christ, of course, who taught us that God is love. If we believe in God at all, we probably take it for granted that he is love. We might even suppose that anyone in any century could have seen that God is love. And yet, for example, if we consider the rich store of ancient Greek and Latin literature, there is, so far as we know, not one writer or philosopher who claimed that God was love. All-powerful, yes. Good, in a detached, absolute sense, approving man's good behaviour, and disapproving his evil acts. But not love in the sense of positive, warm-hearted, involved, caring, sacrificing love for mankind.[12] No one ever thought it or taught it like Jesus Christ did: 'Are not five sparrows sold for two pennies? And not one of them is forgotten before God. Why, even the hairs of your head are all numbered. Fear not; you are of more value than many sparrows' (Luke 12:6–7). These are scarcely the words of a deluded megalomaniac.

WHERE DOES THE EVIDENCE ULTIMATELY COME FROM, THAT JESUS IS THE SON OF GOD?

A circular argument?

The answer to our question is: it comes from Jesus himself! Now we admit at once that this looks as if it involves the following circular argument:

1. Jesus claims to be the Son of God.
2. How do I know that he is speaking the truth?
3. I know it because it is he who claims it.

To which you might object: but you are assuming what you want to prove! Well, in a sense you are right. The reasoning is circular, but it is not a vicious circle.

To see that, let us begin with God. Now, of course, you may not believe in God. But, for the sake of the argument, it is important to realise that if there is a God, then, in the last analysis, he must supply his own evidence. Since he is the Creator of all things, then by defini-tion everything is dependent on him: nothing and no one is, or can be, independent of him. In the nature of things, there can be no source of evidence for God's existence independent of God himself. Indeed, if we were ultimately dependent for evidence for God on something independent of God, then that something would inevitably be of greater authority than God—which is absurd.

---

[12] See the concepts of God discussed in connection with Hinduism, Aristotle and Plotinus in Book 2: *Finding Ultimate Reality*.

In light of this, it is instructive to see how Christ himself referred to the source of the evidence that he is the Son of God. John, the writer of the Fourth Gospel, records in detail an incident that took place at the Pool of Bethesda near the Sheep Gate in Jerusalem, when Jesus healed a man who had been diseased for thirty-eight years (John 5). Some of the Jews present were angry with Jesus because he did this on the Sabbath day, in apparent contravention of their laws on Sabbath observance. Jesus replied to them, 'My Father is working until now, and I am working.' But his claim to have a uniquely special relationship with God incensed them even more: 'This was why the Jews were seeking all the more to kill him, because not only was he breaking the Sabbath, but he was even calling God his own Father, making himself equal with God' (John 5:17–18). Notice that, in reply to their objection, Jesus did not say, 'You have mistaken me; I didn't mean to claim equality with God.' Instead, he proceeded to make a series of statements, emphasising his equality with God even further.

We summarise it in propositional form:

1. *The Son does exactly what the Father does and does it in the very same way as the Father:* 'Truly, truly, I say to you, the Son can do nothing of his own accord, but only what he sees the Father doing. For whatever the Father does, that the Son does *likewise*' (John 5:19, emph. added).

Christ then spells out the implications of this statement:

2. *The Son is the source of life, just as the Father is:* 'For as the Father has life in himself, so he has granted the Son also to have life in himself' (John 5:26).

3. *The Son, of his own volition, raises the dead, as does the Father:* 'For as the Father raises the dead and gives them life, so also the Son gives life to whom he will. . . . an hour is coming when all who are in the tombs will hear his voice and come out' (John 5:21, 28–29).

4. *The Son, not the Father, is the final judge:* 'The Father judges no one, but has given all judgment to the Son, that all may honour the Son, *just as they honour the Father*. Whoever does not honour the Son does not honour the Father who sent him' (John 5:22–23, emph. added).

The claim that he should be honoured as the Father is honoured would be the height of blasphemy, if Jesus was merely a human being and not equal to the Father.

The question arises: what was the source of the evidence for such a tremendous claim?

The source of the evidence submitted by Christ

Christ first cites the evidence of the prophet John the Baptist, whose role as the forerunner of Messiah was predicted in the Old Testament (see, for example, Mark 1:1–3; Luke 3:1–6); and who in that role had clearly pointed the Jewish nation to Jesus as the Messiah, as we have just seen above. But after citing John as witness, Christ then significantly adds, 'But it is not from a human being that I receive evidence' (John 5:34 own trans.). Here he is stating the principle to which we alluded earlier: as God incarnate he must ultimately be the source of his own evidence. There can be no evidence independent of him.

John the Baptist was a very great witness—according to Christ 'a burning and shining lamp' (John 5:35). However, if Jesus is the Word of God incarnate, as he claimed to be, then he was behind the witness of John—he was ultimately responsible for arranging it. And so it is with every other human witness to God throughout the ages: ultimately it all depends on God himself. Take, for example the phenomenon of Old Testament prophecy. It was, says the Apostle Peter, the Spirit of Christ in the prophets that 'predicted the sufferings of Christ and the subsequent glories' (1 Pet 1:11). There are no sources of witness independent of God.[13]

Next, Christ invited his hearers to consider as a witness, the works which he did:

> But the testimony that I have is greater than that of John. For the works that the Father has given me to accomplish, the very works that I am doing, bear witness about me that the Father has sent me. (John 5:36)

But here, once more, the works are not a source of evidence independent of God. It is the Father dwelling in Christ who does them:

---

[13] We note that it is the same with creation. By its design, creation points to God. But then, creation actually comes from the pre-incarnate Word and Son of God, so it is not an independent source of evidence either: 'All things were made through him' (John 1:3).

Do you not believe that I am in the Father and the Father is in me? The words that I say to you I do not speak on my own authority, but the Father who dwells in me does his works. Believe me that I am in the Father and the Father is in me, or else believe on account of the works themselves. (John 14:10–11)

Because the Father lives and works through him, his evidence is the Father's evidence—it comes directly from God himself. It is interesting and important to note that Christ is fully aware of the fact that he must be his own evidence. If he had not been aware of it, but had relied only on the evidence of the men around him, it would have given ground to thinking that his claim was false.

The implications for our approach to the New Testament

This fact that, in the end, Christ must be his own evidence, has important implications for the kind of attitude we bring to the reading of the narratives in the Gospels. The persuasive power of those narratives, if they have any persuasive power, must ultimately derive from Christ himself. Of course, we cannot know the facts about Christ if we do not read the New Testament; but many people seem to find a difficulty here. They feel that if they are going to believe that Jesus is the Son of God, they must first believe that the New Testament is true. However, since they do not themselves grant the supposition that the New Testament is true, they feel it is pointless to read what the Gospels say about Jesus.

But the objection is not valid. You don't have first to believe that the Gospels are true before you read them, any more than you have to believe that the newspapers are true before you read them. Indeed, when it comes to newspapers, we know that much in them is not true, and we certainly do not decide, before we read them, to believe whatever they say. But, of course, that doesn't stop us reading them. We usually have confidence enough in our own judgment to read what they say, reflect on it, and make up our own mind whether it's true or not. Therefore, it is not unreasonable to treat the New Testament in the same way; although, of course, the New Testament claims higher authority than our newspapers. But you don't have to grant this before you start reading it.

If Jesus is the Son of God, then these records of what he said and did on earth do, in fact, come to us with his authority. But if we are prepared to read them, then it is up to him to convince us that he is the truth. He is on record as inviting his contemporaries to use their critical judgment on the moral character of his word and actions: 'Do not judge by appearances, but judge with right judgment' (John 7:24). If we are thus prepared to use our moral judgment and think seriously about Christ's words and works, then Christ himself says that God will show us personally whether Christ's claims are true or not—on one condition. The condition is this: 'If anyone's will is to do God's will'—that is, when he discovers what God's will is—'he will know whether the teaching is from God or whether I am speaking on my own authority' (John 7:17). He will find out because, as he reads, studies and thinks about what Jesus taught, God will speak to his heart, and show him that what Jesus says is true.

> If Jesus is the Son of God, then these records of what he said and did on earth do, in fact, come to us with his authority. But if we are prepared to read them, then it is up to him to convince us that he is the truth.

The trouble sometimes lies in the fact that many people find this condition to be stringent and difficult. Some people sense that, if God did show them, it would carry far-reaching implications for their way of life that they might not wish to face. So they would prefer to approach the whole thing impersonally, like they approach experiments in physics or chemistry, without committing themselves in advance to any practical implications. But it is not possible to treat God like that, precisely because he is God. Clearly, we cannot come to the Almighty, and virtually say to him, 'Please show me if Jesus is your Son or not; but I want you to know in advance that, if you do show me that he is your Son, I am not necessarily willing to accept the implications of it.' God has no time for spiritual dilettantes.

Seeing and believing

But someone else will object, by saying, 'If I read the Gospels in that frame of mind, might I not very easily persuade myself that I have had some kind of spiritual enlightenment, when all the time my experience is only the result of wish fulfilment or autosuggestion? After all, we can persuade ourselves to believe all sorts of things, can't we?'

Perhaps an answer to that difficulty is to be found, to some extent, in the story of one of Christ's miracles, as recorded in John 9. We do not stop to argue the case for miracles at this point (for that, see the next chapter), since all we wish to do at this juncture is to appeal to the account solely as an illustration.

The story goes like this: Jesus once came across a man who had been born blind, and asked him if he would like to be given sight. Now it is clear that it would be extremely difficult to try to explain to someone born blind what sight is, or what colour is like; or even to convince him that there are such things as light and colour. Therefore, we could have well understood it, if the blind man had replied to Jesus that he didn't know what sight was, and considered all claims that there was such a thing as sight to be nonsense. That, at least, is the way many people react nowadays, when they hear Jesus Christ say that he can give them spiritual sight: that he can give them eternal life, which is the faculty of knowing God personally (John 17:3).

So Jesus Christ suggested to the man that, if he was willing, there was an experiment he could perform; and he guaranteed that if he performed it, he would receive sight. Now the experiment Christ laid down seemed very odd. First he spat on the ground and made clay with the spittle. Then he put the clay on the man's eyes and told him to go to the Pool of Siloam and wash himself.

Now to suggest that physical sight could be given to him this way probably seemed completely absurd. But now the man had to make up his mind about Jesus. Was he a crank or a charlatan? Certainly, the nature of the experiment arguably pointed in that direction. And suppose he went and did what Christ asked, and it didn't work—would he not look a fool, as well as being very disillusioned and disappointed? Even if he did have some kind of experience (after all, he didn't know what 'seeing' meant), might that not simply be the result of autosuggestion or wish fulfilment, and be of little value to him? On the other hand, he had evidence around him of other people who claimed to have experienced the power of Christ. So what was he to do? And anyway, he had nothing to lose, and possibly everything to gain, by making the experiment. So he made his way to the Pool of Siloam, washed his eyes, and recovered his physical sight at once.

Thereafter it is interesting to see how he eventually came to the conclusion that Jesus is the Son of God. He did not see that at once. The text shows that he had a keen mind, and, in argument with his neighbours and the Pharisees, he worked through all the suggested alternative explanations that they made to him about Jesus, and came to the conclusion that the only explanation that fitted all the facts was that Jesus actually was the Son of God. But we note that, if the man had not originally been prepared to do the experiment, he would never have found out whether or not Christ could give him sight as he claimed; and he would never have discovered whether or not Jesus was the Son of God.

The double purpose of the evidence

The story of the blind man is one among many pieces and kinds of evidence for the deity of Christ that John includes in his Gospel. Towards the end of his Gospel, he formally states the purpose that he has had in mind in presenting the evidence:

> Now Jesus did many other signs in the presence of the disciples, which are not written in this book; but these are written so that you may believe that Jesus is the Christ, the Son of God, and that by believing you may have life in his name. (John 20:30–31)

We notice that there are, not just one, but two objectives stated here. The second describes a personal faith-commitment to Christ: it is belief *in* him as the only way of having that spiritual experience called 'receiving eternal life'; and it is the only way of discovering the full reality of Christ. After all, a man and woman cannot fully experience what marriage is, unless and until they commit themselves one to the other and get married. So it is with believing in Christ 'that you may have life in his name'.

But that faith-commitment is not, as many imagine it, a leap in the dark—an act of blind faith, an arbitrary, irrational step, taken without any evidence. It is only the second step of a double process; the first step is to consider the evidence, the massive evidence, for the truth of the proposition that Jesus is, in fact, the Christ, the Son of God. And it is to the cornerstone of that evidence that we turn next: the resurrection of Christ.

CHAPTER 4

THE RESURRECTION OF CHRIST AND THE QUESTION OF MIRACLES

A miracle is a violation of the laws of nature;
and as a firm and unalterable experience has established these laws, the proof
against a miracle, from the very nature of
the fact, is as entire as any argument from
experience as possibly can be imagined.

—David Hume,
An Enquiry Concerning Human Understanding

THE PRIME MIRACLE

The Christian gospel is based squarely on a miracle. It was the miracle of the resurrection of Christ that started it going, and that same miracle is its central message. Indeed the basic qualification of a Christian apostle was to be an eyewitness of the resurrection (Acts 1:22). C. S. Lewis expresses the situation precisely:

> The first fact in the history of Christendom is a number of people who say they have seen the Resurrection. If they had died without making anyone else believe this 'gospel', no gospels would ever have been written.[1]

According to the early Christians, then, without the resurrection there simply is no Christian message. Paul writes: 'If Christ has not been raised, our preaching is useless and so is your faith' (1 Cor 15:14 NIV).

DAVID HUME AND MIRACLES

It is here that the Christian gospel conflicts with the widely held view that miracles are impossible. One of the thinkers who was most influential in spreading the view that science has made it impossible to believe in miracles was the Enlightenment Scottish philosopher David Hume (1711–76). He was a sceptical naturalist philosopher. In his famous essay *An Enquiry Concerning Human Understanding* (EHU), he wrote:

> A miracle is a violation of the laws of nature; and as a firm and unalterable experience has established these laws, the proof against a miracle, from the very nature of the fact, is as entire as any argument from experience as possibly can be imagined. . . .

---

[1] *Miracles*, 235.

It is no miracle that a man, seemingly in good health, should die on a sudden: because such a kind of death, though more unusual than any other, has yet been frequently observed to happen. But it is a miracle, that a dead man should come to life; because that has never been observed, in any age or country. There must, therefore, be a uniform experience against every miraculous event, otherwise the event would not merit that appellation.[2]

We notice that there are essentially two arguments here, although they overlap.

First, there is an argument from the uniformity of nature:

1. Miracles are violations of the laws of nature.
2. These laws have been established by 'firm and unalterable' experience.
3. Therefore, the argument against miracle is as good as any argument from experience can be.

Second, there is the argument from the uniformity of experience:

1. Unusual, yet frequently observed, events are not miracles— like a healthy person suddenly dropping dead.
2. A resurrection would be a miracle because it has never been observed anywhere at any time.
3. There is uniform experience against every miraculous event, otherwise it would not be called miraculous.

The argument from the uniformity of nature

In this instance, Hume holds a self-contradictory position. Hume denies miracle because, as he says, miracles would go against the uniform laws of nature. But elsewhere he denies the uniformity of nature! He famously argues that, just because the sun has been observed to rise in the morning for thousands of years, that does not mean that we can be sure that it will rise tomorrow.[3] On the basis of past experience you cannot predict the future, says Hume. But if that were true, see what it implies in particular.

---

[2] EHU 10.12; Dover edn, 73.
[3] EHU 4.2; Dover edn, 14. This is an example of the so-called Problem of Induction which we discuss under 'Induction' in the Appendix to this book: 'The Scientific Endeavour'.

Suppose that Hume is right that no dead man has ever risen up from the grave through the whole of earth's history so far; then, by his own argument, he still couldn't be sure that a dead man will not rise up tomorrow. That being so he cannot rule out miracle. What now has become of Hume's insistence on the laws of nature and the uniformity of nature? He has exploded the very basis on which he denies the possibility of miracle.

The same argument would work just as well backwards in time, as well as forwards. For instance, the fact that no one has been observed to rise from the dead in the past thousand years, is no guarantee that there was no resurrection before that. Let us illustrate this with the following analogy. Uniform experience over the past three hundred years shows that kings of England are not decapitated. If you knew this, and were faced with the claim that King Charles I was decapitated, you might refuse to believe it because it went against uniform experience. You would be wrong! He was beheaded. Uniformity is one thing; absolute uniformity another.

> Hume denies miracle because, as he says, miracles would go against the uniform laws of nature. But elsewhere he denies the uniformity of nature!

In any case, if, according to Hume, we can infer no regularities, it would be impossible even to speak of a 'law of nature', let alone the uniformity of nature with respect to those laws. And if nature is not uniform, then using the uniformity of nature as an argument against miracles is simply absurd.

In spite of this fundamental inconsistency, Hume's argument has been, in large part, responsible for the widespread contemporary view (at least in the western world), that we have a straightforward choice between mutually exclusive alternatives. Either we believe in miracles, or we believe in the scientific understanding of the laws of nature, but not both. The latter, of course, being the only option for the intelligent person.

It cannot, however, be quite as simple as that; if only for the fact that there are highly intelligent, eminent, scientists, like Professor William Phillips (Physics Nobel Prizewinner 1997), Professor John Polkinghorne FRS (Quantum Physicist, Cambridge), and the former Director of the Human Genome Project, Francis Collins (to name just three), who, though well aware of Hume's argument, nevertheless publicly affirm their belief in the resurrection of Jesus. This means, at the very least, that it is clearly no necessary part of being a scientist that one should reject the resurrection. In that connection, it is important that we discuss Hume's definition of miracles as 'violations of the laws of nature'.

MIRACLES AND THE LAWS OF NATURE

It has been one of the impressive achievements of science, not only to describe what goes on in the universe, but to discover the laws which govern its workings. Since Hume defines miracles to be violations of those laws, it will be important for us here, both to understand, and indeed to grant, what scientists claim about their nature.

Scientific laws are not simply descriptions of what happens, although they are at least that. They arise from our perception of the essential processes involved in any given phenomenon. That is, the laws are giving us insight into the internal logic of a system in terms of the cause and effect relationships of its constituent parts.

It is just here that we meet another self-contradictory element in Hume's position. For Hume denies the very cause and effect relationships which are involved in formulating these laws. He says: 'All events seem entirely loose and separate. One event follows another; but we never can observe any tie between them. They seem *conjoined*, but never *connected*.'[4] Hume then gives the example of someone watching a moving billiard ball collide with a stationary one. He sees the second ball begin to move but, according to Hume, the first time he saw such a thing,

> he could not pronounce that the one event was *connected* but only that it was *conjoined* with the other. After he has observed several instances of this nature, he then pronounces them to be *connected*. What alteration has happened to give rise to this new idea of *connection*? Nothing, but that he now *feels* these events to be *connected* in his imagination, and can readily foretell the existence of one from the appearance of the other.

---

[4] EHU 7.26; Dover edn, 47.

When we say, therefore, that one object is connected with another, we mean only that they have acquired a connection in our thought . . .[5]

We have underlined the last sentence to emphasise the fact that Hume explicitly denies the idea of necessary connection. He would thus undermine a great deal of modern science, since scientific laws involve precisely what Hume denies—cause-effect descriptions of the workings of a system. For example, Hume would admit that there are many cases of smoking being associated with lung cancer, but he would deny any causal relationship. But this, if true, would undermine the scientifically established relationship between smoking and lung cancer. And just think of what would be left of atomic physics if we were not allowed to infer the existence of elementary particles from the tracks we observe in a bubble-chamber!

In a famous attack on Hume's theory of causation, the eminent mathematician and philosopher Sir Alfred North Whitehead pointed out that we all have many everyday experiences in which we are directly aware of cause and effect connections; for example, the reflex action in which a person in a dark room blinks when an electric light is turned on. Obviously, the person is aware that the light flash causes the blink. Research shows that the photon stream from the bulb impinges on the eye, stimulates activity in the optic nerve and excites certain parts of the brain. This scientifically demonstrates that there is a complex causal chain.[6]

We now have two reasons for concluding that Hume's view of miracles is deeply flawed and inadequate:

1. Since he denies that the uniformity of nature can be established, he cannot turn round and use it to disprove miracle.
2. Since he denies necessary causation, he cannot regard nature as described by laws embodying necessary relationships that would preclude miracle.

However, not all who regard miracles as violations of the laws of nature would argue like Hume, and so we must consider this issue

---

[5] EHU 7.28; Dover edn, 48. Emphasis in italics in original. The underlined sentence has been emphasised by the authors.
[6] *Process and Reality.*

from the perspective of modern science and its thinking about the laws of nature. For the modern scientist, it is precisely because scientific laws embody cause-effect relationships that they do not only describe what happened in the past. Provided we are not working at the quantum level, such laws can successfully predict what will happen in the future with such accuracy that, for example, the orbits of communication satellites can be precisely calculated, and moon and Mars landings are possible.

It is understandable, therefore, that many scientists resent the idea that some god could arbitrarily intervene and alter, suspend, reverse, or otherwise 'violate', these laws of nature. For that would seem to them to contradict the immutability of those laws, and thus overturn the very basis of the scientific understanding of the universe. As a corollary to this, many such scientists would advance two arguments.

Argument 1—Belief arose from ignorance

This argument says that belief in miracles in general, and in the New Testament miracles in particular, arose in a primitive, pre-scientific culture where people were ignorant of the laws of nature and so readily accepted miracle stories.

Hume endorses this view when he says that accounts of miracles 'are observed chiefly to abound among ignorant and barbarous nations'.[7] Yet, however plausible this explanation may seem at first sight, it is in fact nonsense when applied to the New Testament miracles. For a moment's thought will show us that, in order to recognise some event as a miracle, there must be some perceived regularity to which that event is an apparent exception. You cannot recognise something that is abnormal if you do not know what is normal.

Take, for instance, the New Testament story that Jesus was born of a virgin without a human father. To say that the early Christians believed this miracle because they did not understand the laws of nature governing the conception and birth of children is frankly ridiculous. They knew well enough about these fixed laws. If they had not known of those laws, they might well have imagined that children could be born without a father or without a mother; but in that case they would not

---

[7] EHU 10.20; Dover edn, 77.

have regarded the story of the birth of Jesus from a virgin as a miracle at all. The very fact that they report it as a miracle shows that they understood perfectly the normal laws governing childbirth. Indeed unless one has first understood that there are laws which normally govern events, how would one ever conclude that a miracle had taken place?

In fact, when Joseph, who was betrothed to Mary, first heard from her that she was pregnant, he proposed to divorce her; he was well enough acquainted with human biology to know where babies come from. He simply did not believe her story of divine intervention. He was not a gullible man. When he was finally persuaded to accept her story, he did so precisely because he came to see that God had performed a miracle (see Matt 1:18–24).

Or take another incident: Luke, who was a doctor trained in the medical science of his day, begins his biography of Christ by raising this very matter (Luke 1:5–25). He tells the story of a man, Zechariah, and of his wife, Elizabeth, who for many years had prayed for a son because she was barren. When, in his old age, an angel appeared to him and told him that his former prayers were about

> Unless one has first understood that there are laws which normally govern events, how would one ever conclude that a miracle had taken place?

to be answered and that his wife would conceive and bear a son, he very politely but firmly refused to believe it. The reason he gave was that he was now old and his wife's body decrepit. For him and his wife to have a child at this stage would run counter to all that he knew of the laws of nature. The interesting thing about him is this: he was no atheist; he was a priest who believed in God, in the existence of angels, and in the value of prayer. But if the promised fulfilment of his prayer was going to involve a reversal of the laws of nature, he was not prepared to believe it.

But it shows this, at least: the early Christians were not a credulous bunch, unaware of the laws of nature, and therefore prepared to believe any miraculous story, however absurd. They felt the difficulty in believing the story of such a miracle, just like anyone else. If in the end they believed, it was because they were forced to, by the sheer weight of the evidence before their very eyes, that a miracle had taken place.

Similarly, in his account of the rise of Christianity, Luke shows us that the first opposition to the Christian message of the resurrection of Jesus Christ came not from atheists, but from the Sadducean high priests in Judaism (Acts 4:1–21). They were highly religious men. They believed in God. They said their prayers and conducted the services in the temple. But that did not mean that the first time they heard the claim that Jesus had risen from the dead they believed it. They did not believe it; for they had embraced a worldview which denied the possibility of bodily resurrection of any one at all, let alone that of Jesus Christ (Acts 23:8).

To suppose, then, that Christianity was born in a pre-scientific, credulous and ignorant world, is simply false to the facts. The ancient world knew as well as we do the law of nature, that dead bodies do not get up out of graves. Christianity won its way by dint of the sheer weight of evidence that one man had actually risen from the dead.

Argument 2—Knowledge makes belief impossible

Those who would argue against the idea of divine intervention in nature would further argue that, now that we know the laws of nature, belief in miracles is impossible.

However, this idea that miracles are 'violations' of the laws of nature, involves another fallacy, which C. S. Lewis illustrated by the following analogy.

> If I put six pennies into a drawer on Monday and six more on Tuesday, the laws decree that—other things being equal—I shall find twelve pennies there on Wednesday. But if the drawer has been robbed I may in fact find only two. Something will have been broken (the lock of the drawer or the laws of England) but the laws of arithmetic will not have been broken. The new situation created by the thief will illustrate the laws of arithmetic just as well as the original situation. [8]

The analogy also helps point out that the scientific use of the word 'law' is not the same as the legal use, where we often think of a law as constraining someone's actions. There is no sense in which the laws of arithmetic constrain or pressurise the thief in our story! Suppose we make an experiment. Let's drop an apple. Newton's Law of Gravitation

---

[8] *Miracles*, 92.

tells me that if I drop an apple it will fall towards the centre of the earth. But that law does not prevent someone intervening, and catching the apple as it descends. In other words, the law predicts what will happen, provided there is no change in the conditions under which the experiment is conducted.

Thus, from the theistic perspective, the laws of nature predict what is bound to happen if God does not intervene; though, of course, it is no act of theft, if the Creator intervenes in his own creation. To argue that the laws of nature make it impossible for us to believe in the existence of God, and the possibility of his intervention in the universe, is plainly fallacious. It would be like claiming that an understanding of the laws of the internal combustion engine makes it impossible to believe that the designer of a motor car, or one of his mechanics, could or would intervene and remove the cylinder head. Of course they could intervene. Moreover, this intervention would not destroy those laws. The very same laws that explained why the engine worked with the cylinder head on would now explain why it does not work with the head removed.

It is, therefore, inaccurate and misleading to say with Hume that miracles 'violate' the laws of nature. It is rather, that God feeds new events into the system from time to time. There is no alteration to or suspension of the laws themselves. As C. S. Lewis expresses it:

> If God annihilates or creates or deflects a unit of matter He has created a new situation at that point. Immediately all Nature domiciles this new situation, makes it at home in her realm, adapts all other events to it. It finds itself conforming to all the laws. If God creates a miraculous spermatozoon in the body of a virgin, it does not proceed to break any laws. The laws at once take it over. Nature is ready. Pregnancy follows, according to all the normal laws, and nine months later a child is born.[9]

To put this another way: one might say that it is a law of nature that human beings do not rise again from the dead by some natural mechanism. But Christians are not claiming that Christ rose from the dead by such a mechanism. They are claiming that he rose from the dead by supernatural power. By themselves, the laws of nature cannot rule

---

[9] *Miracles*, 94.

out that possibility. When a miracle takes place, it is the laws of nature that alert us to the fact that it is a miracle. It is important to grasp that Christians do not deny the laws of nature, as Hume implies they do. It is an essential part of the Christian position to believe in the laws of nature as descriptions of those regularities and cause-effect relationships built into the universe by its Creator and according to which it normally operates. If we did not know them, we should never recognise a miracle if we saw one.

EVIDENCE FOR THE HISTORICAL FACT
OF THE RESURRECTION

Hume's argument from the uniformity of experience

In anybody's book, miracles, by definition, are exceptions to what normally happens. If miracles were normal, they wouldn't be called miracles! What, then, does Hume mean by 'uniform experience'? It is one thing to say 'Experience shows that such and such normally happens, but there may be exceptions, although none has been observed, that is, the experience *we have had* has been uniform.' It is an entirely different thing to say 'This is what we normally experience, and we must always experience it, for there can be and are no exceptions.'

Hume appears to favour the second definition. For him, a miracle is something that has never been experienced before, for if it had been experienced before, you could no longer call it a miracle. But that is a very arbitrary statement. Why can there not have been a succession of miracles in the past, as well as the particular one we may be discussing at the moment? What Hume does is to assume what he wants to prove, namely that there have never been any miracles in the past, and so there is uniform experience against this present instance being a miracle. But here his argument runs into very serious trouble. How does he know? In order to know that experience against miracles is absolutely uniform, he would need to have total access to every event in the universe at all times and places, which is, self-evidently, impossible. It would seem that Hume has forgotten that humans have only ever observed a tiny fraction of the sum total of events that have occurred in the universe; and that, in any case, very few of the total of all human observations have been written down. Therefore, Hume cannot know that miracles have never occurred. He is simply assuming what he wants to prove—that nature is uniform, and no miracles have taken place. Hume is begging the question.

The only real alternative to Hume's circular argument, of course, is to be open to the possibility that miracles have occurred. That is a historical question, and not a philosophical one, and depends on witness and evidence. But Hume does not appear willing to consider the question of whether there is any valid historical evidence that a miracle or miracles have taken place. He simply denies it, claiming that experience against miracles is 'firm and unalterable'. But, we repeat, his claim has no substance unless he has demonstrated that all reports of miracles are false. He singularly fails even to attempt to do this, so there is simply no way in which he can know the answer.

In particular, he simply says that no resurrection has ever been observed, without making the slightest attempt to discuss the actual historical evidence for the resurrection of Jesus—evidence which, in the estimate of the eminent nineteenth-century Oxford historian Thomas Arnold, is overwhelming.

> I have been used for many years to study the histories of other times, and to examine and weigh the evidence of those who have written about them; and I know of no one fact in the history of mankind, which is proved by better and fuller evidence of every sort to the understanding of a fair inquirer than the great sign which God hath given us, that Christ died and rose again from the dead.[10]

We must, therefore, now discuss that evidence.

Hume's criteria for evidence, and the credibility of witnesses

Hume notes that 'a wise man . . . proportions his belief to the evidence.'[11] That is, the strength of his belief depends upon the strength of the evidence that supports the belief. It means that, when faced with, say,

---

[10] *Christian Life*, 11–12.
[11] EHU 10.4; Dover edn, 71.

the report of a miracle, the wise person will weigh up all the evidence for the miracle on the one side, and all the evidence against it on the other, and then come to his decision. Hume adds a further criterion to aid this process:

> No testimony is sufficient to establish a miracle, unless the testimony be of such a kind, that its falsehood would be more miraculous, than the fact, which it endeavours to establish . . . When anyone tells me, that he saw a dead man restored to life, I immediately consider with myself, whether it be more probable, that this person should either deceive or be deceived, or that the fact, which he relates, should really have happened. I weigh the one miracle against the other; and according to the superiority, which I discover, I pronounce my decision, and always reject the greater miracle. If the falsehood of his testimony would be more miraculous, than the event which he relates; then, and not until then, can he pretend to command my belief or opinion.[12]

Let us examine what Hume means by 'falsehood'. Here is someone who tells you that a miracle has happened. You have to decide whether it is true or false. If the character of the witness is dubious, you would be likely to dismiss his story out of hand. However, if the witness is of known moral integrity, you turn next to the actual thing that is claimed. Hume's view is that you must reject it as false, unless believing in its falsity would land you in such an impossible situation, and have such totally inexplicable implications in history, that you would need an even bigger miracle to explain them.

Hume's criteria applied to the idea that the disciples were fraudsters

But this criterion of Hume's is precisely the argument that Christians will use. Academician Professor Sir Norman Anderson, formerly Director of the Institute of Advanced Legal Studies in the University of London, writes in the opening words of his book *The Evidence for the Resurrection*:

> Easter is not primarily a comfort, but a challenge. Its message is either the supreme fact in history or else a gigantic hoax. . . . If it

---

[12] EHU 10.13; Dover edn, 75.

is true, then it is the supreme fact of history; and to fail to adjust one's life to its implications means irreparable loss. But if it is not true, if Christ be not risen, then the whole of Christianity is a fraud, foisted on the world by a company of consummate liars, or, at best, deluded simpletons. St. Paul himself realised this when he wrote: 'If Christ be not risen, then our preaching is meaningless, and your faith worthless. More, we are found to be false witnesses.'[13]

Centuries before Hume, then, the Christian Apostle Paul saw the issue clearly: either Christ is risen from the dead, or he and the other apostles are deliberate perpetrators of fraud (1 Cor 15:15). But then, the question cannot be avoided, is it possible to believe that Christ's apostles were the kind of men who would concoct a lie, foist it somehow upon their followers, and not only watch them go to their deaths for it, but themselves pay for their deliberate lie with prison, constant harassment and suffering, and eventually with their lives?

We must remember that, at the very beginning of Christianity, Peter and John were imprisoned twice by the authorities for preaching the resurrection (Acts 4:3; 5:18). Not long afterwards, John's brother, James, was murdered by Herod. Can we imagine that John would have been prepared to have that happen, if he knew his brother was dying for a lie? By the time John died as an old man, exiled for his faith on the island of Patmos, many people had given their lives in the name of the risen Christ. John, so he tells us, was not prepared to condone a lie even in a good cause. His reason was that 'no lie comes from the truth' (1 John 2:21 NIV). Was he the kind of man who would nevertheless watch his brother, and others as well, die for a lie that he himself had concocted? And what about Peter? Historical tradition tells us that he was eventually martyred—as Jesus had indicated to him (John 21:18). Was he martyred for what he knew to be a lie?

In any case, is it reasonable to suppose that none of the disciples, who perpetrated such a fraud, would never have broken under torture and confessed that it was a fraud? No. It is frankly impossible to believe that they were deliberate liars. Hence, according to Hume's criterion, if believing that the disciples were deliberate liars would

---

[13] p. 1.

involve a totally inexplicable historical and moral contradiction, then we must accept their testimony, as millions have over the last twenty centuries.

Hume's criteria applied to the cause of the rise of Christianity

The existence of the Christian church throughout the world is an indisputable fact. In the spirit of Hume's criterion we ask: what explanation is adequate to explain the transformation of the early disciples? From a frightened group of men and women, who were utterly depressed and disillusioned at what, to them, was the calamity that had befallen their movement when their leader was crucified, there suddenly exploded a powerful, international movement that rapidly established itself all over the Roman Empire, and ultimately all over the world. And the striking thing is, that the early disciples were all Jews. Their religion was not noted for its enthusiasm in making converts from other nations. What could have been powerful enough to set all of this going?

If we ask the early church, they will answer at once that what set them going was the resurrection. Moreover, they maintained that the very reason and purpose for their existence was to be a witness to the resurrection of Christ. That is, they came into existence, not to promulgate some political programme or campaign for moral renovation; but to bear witness to the fact that God had intervened in history, raised Christ from the dead, and that forgiveness of sins could be received in his name. This message would, of course, ultimately have major moral implications for society, but it was the message of the resurrection itself that was central.

If we reject the early Christians' own explanation for their existence on the basis that it involves too big a miracle, what are we going to put in its place that will not involve an even greater strain on our capacity for belief? To deny the resurrection simply leaves the church without a raison d'être, which is historically and psychologically absurd.

Professor C. F. D. Moule of Cambridge writes:

> If the coming into existence of the Nazarenes, a phenomenon undeniably attested by the New Testament, rips a great hole in history, a hole of the size and shape of Resurrection, what does the secular historian propose to stop it up with? . . . the birth and rapid rise of the Christian Church . . . *remain an unsolved enigma*

for any historian who refuses to take seriously the only explanation offered by the Church itself. [14]

Problems with holding Hume's position on miracles

So far, Hume's criterion makes good sense. But then he goes on to show that he is not content to let the matter rest with an even-handed assessment of evidence to decide whether a miracle has happened or not. He has determined the verdict against miracles in advance without allowing any trial to take place.

After stating that, 'No testimony is sufficient to establish a miracle, unless the testimony be of such a kind, that its falsehood would be more miraculous, than the fact, which it endeavours to establish' he tries to create an escape from an unwelcome conclusion. In his very next paragraph, he says that he has been far too liberal in imagining that the 'testimony, upon which a miracle is founded, may possibly amount to an entire proof', since 'there never was a miraculous event established on so full an evidence'.[15] But this is precisely what Christians will dispute, especially on the basis of the evidence for the resurrection of Christ, which Hume never seems to have considered.

Hume's logic, then, looks something like this:

1. The laws of nature describe regularities.
2. Miracles are singularities, exceptions to the regular course of nature and so are exceedingly rare.
3. Evidence for what is regular and repeatable must always be more than evidence for what is singular and unrepeatable.
4. The wise man bases his belief on the weight of evidence.
5. Therefore no wise man can ever believe in a miracle.

In other words, although Hume seems at first to be open to the theoretical possibility of a miracle having occurred, provided the evidence is strong enough; he eventually reveals that he is completely convinced from the beginning that there never can be enough evidence that would convince a rational person that a miracle has happened, because rational people know that miracles cannot happen. Hume lays himself open to the charge of begging the question.

---

[14] *The Phenomenon of the New Testament*, 3, 13 (italics in original).
[15] EHU 10.13; Dover edn, 75.

The idea that evidence for what is regular and repeatable must always be more than evidence for what is singular and unrepeatable (point 3 above) was, for many years, emphasised heavily by the philosopher Antony Flew in his modern defence of Hume's argument.[16] Flew, one of the world's leading authorities on Hume, argued that 'the proposition reporting the (alleged) occurrence of the miracle will be singular, particular and in the past tense'. He deduced that, since in any case, propositions of this sort cannot be tested directly, the evidence for them will always be immeasurably weaker in logical strength, than the evidence for general and repeatable propositions.[17]

In more recent years, Flew has revised his own assessment of Hume and has gone so far as to warn those who would agree with his previous positions that his own book needed to be rewritten:

> One matter in particular calls for extensive corrections. The three chapters 'The Idea of Necessary Connection', 'Liberty and Necessity', and 'Miracles and Methodology' all need to be rewritten in the light of my new-found awareness that Hume was utterly wrong to maintain that we have no experience, and hence no genuine ideas, of making things happen and preventing things from happening, of physical necessity and of physical impossibility. Generations of Humeans have in consequence been misled into offering analyses of causation and of natural law that have been far too weak because they had no basis for accepting the existence of either cause and effect or natural laws. Meanwhile, in 'Of Liberty and Necessity' and 'Of Miracles', Hume himself was hankering after (even when he was not actually employing) notions of causes bringing about effects that were stronger than any that he was prepared to admit as legitimate ... Hume's scepticism about cause and effect and his agnosticism about the external world are of course jettisoned the moment he leaves his study.[18]

---

[16] See his article 'Miracles' in *The Encyclopaedia of Philosophy*; and his essay, 'Neo-Humean Arguments about the Miraculous'.

[17] *Encyclopaedia of Philosophy*, 252.

[18] *There is a God*, 57–58. In this book, Flew discusses his own reasons for moving away from his previously held (and much celebrated) atheism and embracing theism instead.

Quite apart from the question of miracle, this argument is inimical to science; the classic example being the origin of the universe. The so-called 'Big Bang' is a singularity in the past, an unrepeatable event; so, if Flew's original argument had been valid, no scientist should be prepared to believe in the Big Bang. Indeed, when scientists began to talk of the universe having a beginning in a singularity, they met strong objections from fellow scientists who held strong uniformitarian views. However, it was studying the data supplied to them, not theoretical arguments on what was or what was not possible on the basis of an assumed uniformity, that convinced them that the Big Bang was a plausible explanation. It is very important, therefore, to realise that, even when scientists speak of the uniformity of nature, they do not mean absolute uniformity—especially if they believe in singularities like the Big Bang.

> What Hume seems to have overlooked is that it is simply inadequate to judge the likelihood of the occurrence of the resurrection of Jesus on the basis of the observed very high probability of dead people remaining dead.

Turning to the question of the resurrection of Christ, what Hume seems to have overlooked is that it is simply inadequate to judge the likelihood of the occurrence of the resurrection of Jesus on the basis of the observed very high probability of dead people remaining dead. What he should have done (but did not do) was to weigh the probability of the resurrection of Jesus against the probability of the tomb of Jesus being empty *on any other hypothesis* than the resurrection. We shall do this in our next chapter.[19]

Hume is, of course, aware that there are situations where people have understandable difficulty in accepting something because it is outside their experience, but which is nonetheless true. He relates a story of an Indian prince who refused to believe what he was told about the effects of frost.[20] Hume's point is that, although what he was told was not contrary to his experience, it was not conformable with it.

However, even here, Hume is not on safe ground. For, in modern science, especially the theories of relativity and quantum mechanics,

---

[19] Another defect in the Hume-Flew view is that it does not appear to be falsifiable in the sense that neither Hume nor Flew appear to be able to conceive of an observation that would prove it false (see the section on Falsifiablity in the Appendix: 'The Scientific Endeavour').
[20] EHU 10.10; Dover edn, 73.

there are key ideas which do appear contrary to our experience. A strict application of Hume's principles might well have rejected such ideas, and thus have impeded the progress of science. It is often the counter-intuitive anomaly, the contrary fact, the exception to past repeated observation and experience, that turns out to be the key to the discovery of a new scientific paradigm. But the crucial thing here is that the exception is a *fact*, however improbable it may be on the basis of past repeated experience. Wise people, particularly if they are scientists, are concerned with facts, not simply with probabilities; even if those facts do not appear to fit into their uniformitarian schemes.

Excluding the possibility of miracle, and making Nature and its processes an absolute in the name of science, ends up by removing all ground for trusting in the rationality of science in the first place.

We agree, of course, that miracles are inherently improbable. We should certainly demand strong evidence for their happening in any particular case (see Hume's point 5 above). But this is not the real problem with miracles of the sort found in the New Testament. The real problem is that they threaten the foundations of naturalism, which is clearly Hume's basic worldview at this point. That is, he regards it as axiomatic that nature is all that there is and that there is nothing and no one outside nature that could from time to time intervene in nature. It is this that he means when he claims that nature is uniform. His axiom, of course, is simply a belief, and not a consequence of scientific investigation.

Ironically enough, Christians will argue that it is only belief in a Creator that gives us a satisfactory ground for believing in the uniformity of nature in the first place. In denying that there is a Creator the atheists are kicking away the basis of their own argument! As C. S. Lewis puts it:

If all that exists is Nature, the great mindless interlocking event, if our own deepest convictions are merely the by-products of an irrational process, then clearly there is not the slightest ground for supposing that our sense of fitness and our consequent faith in uniformity tell us anything about a reality external to ourselves. Our convictions are simply a fact *about us*—like the colour of our hair. If Naturalism is true we have no reason to trust our conviction that Nature is uniform. It can be trusted only if quite a different Metaphysic is true. If the deepest thing in reality, the Fact which is the source of all other facthood, is a thing in some degree like ourselves—if it is a Rational Spirit and we derive our rational spirituality from It—then indeed our conviction can be trusted. Our repugnance to disorder is derived from Nature's Creator and ours.[21]

Thus, excluding the possibility of miracle, and making Nature and its processes an absolute in the name of science, ends up by removing all ground for trusting in the rationality of science in the first place. On the other hand, regarding nature as only part of a greater reality, which includes nature's intelligent Creator God, gives a rational justification for belief in the orderliness of nature (a view which led to the rise of modern science).[22]

Secondly, however, if, in order to account for the uniformity of nature, one admits the existence of a Creator, that inevitably opens the door for the possibility of a miracle in which that same Creator intervenes in the course of nature. There is no such thing as a tame Creator who cannot, or must not, or dare not intervene in the universe he has created. So, miracles may occur.

Our conclusions so far

There is a sense, of course, in which Christians can agree with Hume, that 'uniform experience' shows that resurrection *by means of a natural mechanism* is extremely improbable, and we may rule it out. But Christians do not claim that Jesus rose by some natural mechanism. They claim something totally different—that God raised him from the dead. And if there is a God, why should that be judged impossible?

In this chapter we have so far been considering essentially a priori reasons[23] for which Hume and others have rejected miracles. However,

---

[21] *Miracles*, 167–8.
[22] For further discussion of this point, see John Lennox's book *God's Undertaker*, 20–23.
[23] Those reasons that have to do with the convictions, beliefs, and principles we already have, before we bring them to bear on a situation are 'a priori' reasons. For more detailed discussion of different kinds of reasons and the ways in which we can know anything, see Book 4: *Questioning Our Knowledge*.

we have seen that it is not science that rules out miracle. Surely, then, the open-minded attitude demanded by reason is now to proceed to investigate the evidence, to establish the facts, and be prepared to follow where that process leads, even if it entails alterations to our a priori views. We shall never know whether or not there is a mouse in the attic unless we actually go and look!

CHAPTER 5

THE EVIDENCE FOR
THE RESURRECTION

If several witnesses to an event make
statements in court which agree in every
detail word-for-word, any judge would
be likely to deduce that the testimonies
were not independent; and, worse still,
that there had possibly been collusion
to mislead the court.

DID HE RISE AGAIN?

For centuries, Christians have greeted each other at Easter time with the words 'Christ is risen! Indeed he is risen.' We must now proceed to look at the evidence that he did in fact rise. The evidence is cumulative. That is, we need to put together evidence from four major areas:

1. The death of Jesus
2. The burial of Jesus
3. The fact of the empty tomb
4. Eyewitnesses of the appearances of Christ

THE DEATH OF JESUS

Why it is important to establish the fact of Christ's death

It is self-evident, if we are going to claim that Christ rose from the dead, that he must have died in the first place. For, if Christ did not really die on the cross, there could not be a resurrection. That is why it is important first of all to establish the fact of his death, a fact claimed by Paul in his very early credal summary of the Christian faith (1 Cor 15:3–4).

Christ's death disputed

Some have seriously suggested that Christ did not really die on the cross, but only swooned and then revived in the cool air of the tomb. Although very weak, he managed to get out of the tomb and was seen by some of his disciples, looking (not surprisingly) pale like a ghost. They imagined that a resurrection had occurred and spread the story around; but, in fact, Christ probably simply wandered off and perished in some obscure, unknown place.

However, in the light of two major pieces of evidence, this theory, as has repeatedly been pointed out, is seen to be absurd. First, the extent of the injuries suffered by Christ on the cross; and, second, the fact that his body was wrapped up in grave clothes, covered in a great weight of spices and placed in a sealed tomb.

The evidence that Christ really died and was dead before he was buried

Before Jesus was crucified, he was flogged and had a crown of thorns pressed on to his head (Matt 27:26–31). Such flogging, as practised by the Romans, involved the use of a brutal instrument called a *flagrum*, which was like a whip with pieces of metal and bone attached to it, to bite deep into human flesh. As a result, the victim sometimes died under its use. In Jesus' case, he was so weak as a result of the flogging that he was not able to carry the cross as far as the place of execution (see Matt 27:32).

Jesus was then crucified. This meant nailing him to a rough wooden structure in the shape of a cross, with an upright pole and a crosspiece: one large nail through both feet, fastening them to the upright, and other nails through the outstretched wrists, fastening them to the crosspiece. This arrangement was maximally cruel because the nails through the feet meant that the legs could give support as the victim struggled to raise his body up so as to be able to breathe a bit easier; this merely prolonged the agony of death, sometimes for several days.

However, the Jewish Sabbath was approaching and, according to John's eyewitness account (John 19:31 ff.), the Jewish authorities did not want the bodies, which they regarded as defiling, to remain on the crosses on the Sabbath. They therefore asked permission from Pilate to have death hastened by the expedient of breaking the legs of the three crucified men (see again John 19:31–37). This would have the effect of removing support for the upper body, which would then hang with a dead weight and render the breathing action of the ribcage very difficult, thereby hastening death, if it had not already occurred. The permission was granted. However, when the soldiers came to Jesus they found he was dead already, so they did not break his legs. This means that they were absolutely sure he was dead—these men knew a dead body when they saw one. However, presumably to make doubly sure, one of the soldiers pierced his side with a spear.

John tells us that the spear thrust produced a flow of blood and water (John 19:34). This supplies us with medical evidence of death, as it indicates that massive blood clotting had taken place in the main arteries; and that in turn shows that Jesus had died even before the spear thrust. Since John could not have known of the pathological signifi-cance of this, it is a powerful piece of circumstantial detail establish-ing the Christian claim that Christ really died. Medical experts have frequently drawn attention to it. For example, Dr William Edwards writes:

> Clearly the weight of historical and medical evidence indicates that Jesus was dead before the wound to his side was inflicted.[1]

Pilate's concern to establish the fact of Christ's death

When the Sanhedrin councillor Joseph of Arimathea subsequently came to Pilate to request the body for burial (for the details, see below), Pilate, ever a cautious man, was not willing to take any risks, not even for such a prominent person. In the very earliest of the Gospel accounts, Mark records that Pilate was surprised to hear that Jesus was already dead (recall the fact mentioned above, that crucified people often lived in agony for some days); so he took the precaution of checking with the duty centurion that Jesus was actually dead. Only when he had received this assurance did Pilate release the corpse of Jesus for burial (Mark 15:44–45).

All the evidence, then, goes to show that Jesus died upon the cross.

THE BURIAL OF JESUS

Who buried him?

All four Gospels tell us that a rich man, Joseph, from the town of Arimathea, went to the Roman procurator Pilate and requested the

---

[1] 'On the Physical Death of Jesus Christ', 1463.

body of Jesus for burial in a tomb which belonged to Joseph (Matt 27:57–60; Mark 15:42–46; Luke 23:50–53; John 19:38–42). Presumably, he was able to get access to Pilate because of his status as a member of the Jewish Sanhedrin Council.

His motivation was clear: he had become a follower of Jesus, and wanted to ensure that he had a decent burial. But in all probability he had another motive: by his action he wanted to show that he had no part in the Sanhedrin's decision to execute Jesus, and was protesting against it. He had not joined the Sanhedrin in condemning him (Luke 23:50–51). Indeed, it might well be that, by burying the body of Jesus as he did, he was effectively handing in his resignation from the Sanhedrin. In light of his action, it is very unlikely that the Sanhedrin would have tolerated his membership any longer.

From John's account of the trial of Jesus, we have already deduced that Pilate had nothing but contempt for the Sanhedrin: he had seen that their case against Jesus was pathetically thin, and had acceded to their request to crucify Jesus only because they had blackmailed him.[2] It may be, therefore, that in Joseph he was glad to see at least one member of the Sanhedrin who had disagreed with the general verdict; and in giving the body to Joseph he may well have felt a slight easing of his conscience.

This account of Pilate's acceding to Joseph's request for the body bears all the hallmarks of authentic history. Bearing in mind the antagonism of the Sanhedrin to Christ and his followers, it is highly improbable that those same followers would have invented the story of a member of the Sanhedrin being prepared to stand with Jesus by ensuring he had an honourable burial, while many of the disciples themselves had run off in fear! In addition, if the story were false, it would have been fatal for the Christian version of events for the Gospel writers to name someone with such a high public profile as Joseph. It would have been so easy for opponents to check the details afterwards and prove the story untrue.[3]

---

[2] See Ch. 8 in Book 3: *Questioning our Knowledge*.
[3] We are assuming here, in the light of the evidence amassed in Ch. 2, that the Gospels are not late compilations.

The place of the burial

According to the record, Joseph, together with another member of the Sanhedrin, Nicodemus (see John 7:50–52; 19:39–42), buried the body of Jesus in a private tomb belonging to Joseph (Matt 27:50). In addition, other witnesses saw where the tomb was: the women from Galilee saw it (Luke 23:55), as did the two Marys (Matt 27:61; Mark 15:47).

Implication of burial in a tomb

The fact of Jesus' burial in a tomb plays an important role in the evidence for the resurrection. If Jesus' corpse had simply been thrown into a common grave—as often happened to criminals—the determination of whether a specific body was no longer there would have been made very difficult, if not impossible. And not only was Jesus buried in a tomb; it was a new tomb in which no one had ever been laid before, so there was no question of his body being accidentally confused with that of someone else (Luke 23:53). Moreover, since, as we have just noticed, some of the women believers followed Joseph, and saw the tomb in which Christ's body was laid (Mark 15:47; Luke 23:55), it makes it extremely unlikely that, when the women came early on the first day of the week while it was still dark, they mistook the tomb, as some scholars have suggested.

Indeed, it is likely that one of those women was Joanna, the wife of Chuza, the steward or manager of Herod's household. Luke tells us that she was a follower of Jesus from Galilee (Luke 8:3), and that these women from Galilee not only witnessed the crucifixion, but also the burial (Luke 23:49–55). As a member of the upper crust of society, and as a follower of Jesus, she would have been well known to Joseph of Arimathea and Nicodemus. With such prominent people involved, it is inconceivable that a mistake could have been made regarding the location of the tomb, especially in light of the additional information that John gives us, to the effect that the tomb was in Joseph's private garden, near to the place where Jesus was crucified (John 19:41–42).

The manner of the burial

Together with Nicodemus, Joseph wrapped the body in linen cloths interlaced with spices (John 19:39). They were following a time-honoured custom for the burial of an important person; and in the process they would have used a mixture of myrrh and aloes—about 25 kg in all. As wealthy people, in all probability they would have had a store of such spices readily available at home. It is possible that they were helped in this by the well-off women from Galilee (Luke 23:55–56). In any case, between them they had enough spices for the preliminary embalming. The rest could wait till the Sabbath was over.

The other women, being less well-off, had no such spices available, and they had to wait until the shops reopened after the Sabbath in order to buy them (Mark 16:1).

Implication of the preparation of the body

One thing is very clear from all of this: they were not expecting a resurrection. If you expect a body to rise from the dead, you do not embalm it in this way! Indeed, when the women arrived the next morning (Sunday), they were only concerned with the problem of gaining access to the tomb in order to continue the embalming (Mark 16:1–3). This is clear evidence once more that they were not expecting a resurrection.

> If you expect a body to rise from the dead, you do not embalm it in this way!

It is also to be noted that the weight of the spices, and the way in which the grave-clothes would have been tightly bound around the body, render incredible the theory mentioned earlier—that Christ swooned on the cross, revived in the tomb, and then managed to escape.

The stone at the tomb entrance

The body was placed in a tomb, which had been hewn out of the rock, not in a grave dug in the earth. The tomb must have been of considerable size, since Peter and John were later able to go right into it (John 20:3–9). In such tombs the body was usually placed in an alcove on a rock ledge, the ledge having an elevated part at one end where the head could rest slightly higher than the body. The tomb was then secured by Joseph with a large disc-shaped stone that fitted into a downward-slanting groove at the entrance to the tomb; though easily rolled into place, it would have required several men to move it away

(Mark 15:46; Matt 27:60). In addition, acting on the authority of Pilate, the next day the Jewish leaders had the stone officially sealed, so that no one could break that seal without incurring the wrath of officialdom (Matt 27:62, 65–66).

The guard at the tomb

Moreover, at the request of the Pharisees and with Pilate's permission, guards were placed around the tomb. Matthew tells us that this was to prevent the disciples coming, removing the body of Jesus, and fraudulently announcing a 'resurrection'. Here are the details of his account:

> The next day, that is, after the day of Preparation, the chief priests and the Pharisees gathered before Pilate and said, 'Sir, we remember how that impostor said, while he was still alive, "After three days I will rise." Therefore order the tomb to be made secure until the third day, lest his disciples go and steal him away and tell the people, "He has risen from the dead", and the last fraud will be worse than the first.' Pilate said to them, 'You have a guard of soldiers. Go, make it as secure as you can.' So they went and made the tomb secure by sealing the stone and setting a guard. (Matt 27:62–66)

Although some have questioned the authenticity of the story about the guards, there is strong evidence of its truth. First of all, it is not hard to imagine the unease and nervousness of the priests as they recalled Christ's prediction of his resurrection. They could not afford to run any risk of a deception here, so that it was in their interests to get the tomb guarded. In addition to this, the story is confirmed by its sequel, as we shall see in a moment. Here, however, we should notice in passing that it was not until the day after the burial that the priests posted the guard. The women, who had gone home immediately after the burial, would have known nothing about the guard. This accounts for the fact that, as they were going to the tomb the next (Sunday) morning, they questioned among themselves, 'Who will roll away the stone for us?' The stone had in fact been rolled away by angelic intervention (Mark 16:3–5).

THE FACT OF THE EMPTY TOMB

It is the constant and unvarying testimony of the Gospels that, when early in the morning of the first day of the week the Christian women went to the tomb to complete the task of encasing the body of Jesus in spices, the tomb was found to be empty; and when the apostles went to investigate the women's report, they likewise found the tomb empty.

It is impossible to exaggerate the significance of this fact, for it shows us what the early Christians mean when they testify to the resurrection of Jesus. They mean that the same body of Jesus that they buried in the tomb, knowing it to be dead, was raised from the dead and vacated the tomb. However much that body was changed (and the descriptions of what that body was like, when they eventually saw and handled it alive, will indicate some of these changes), they insist that it was the same body that had been laid in the tomb. It was not another, new, body, unconnected with the original body of Jesus. It was a genuine resurrection of the original body, not the substitution of a new body in place of the original.

This fact is very important, because, in the last roughly two centuries, some theologians have argued that the testimony of the early Christians to the bodily resurrection of Christ was never more than a mythical way of expressing their faith that Christ's spirit had survived death; and, therefore, it would not have made any difference to their claim that Christ had risen from the dead, if it could have been demonstrated to them that his body was still in the tomb.

But this is a comparatively modern, and indeed a modernist, theory. It cannot be made to square with the insistent emphasis that the early witnesses lay on the fact that the tomb was empty. When they explain that fact by saying that Christ had risen from the dead, they mean by that the literal resurrection of his body.

The evidence for the fact that the tomb was found empty

The Jewish authorities: the first witnesses to the fact of the empty tomb

According to the Gospel of Matthew, the first people to tell the world that the tomb of Jesus was empty were the Jewish authorities, and not the Christians at all! They started a story circulating in Jerusalem to the effect that the disciples had stolen the body while the guards slept:

> Some of the guard went into the city and told the chief priests all that had taken place. And when they had assembled with the elders and taken counsel, they gave a sufficient sum of money to the soldiers and said, 'Tell people, "His disciples came by night and stole him away while we were asleep." And if this comes to the governor's ears, we will satisfy him and keep you out of trouble.' So they took the money and did as they were directed. And this story has been spread among the Jews to this day. (Matt 28:11–15)

The question arises: is Matthew's story authentic? Some have suggested that it is a late myth, invented long after the event. But that explanation is unlikely. Matthew's Gospel, in which the story is related, is by common consent the most Jewish Gospel in the New Testament. It bears every mark of having been written for circulation among Jews. It was published, as we earlier saw, probably in the late 60s AD. By that time the facts about the crucifixion and burial of Christ would have been widely circulated in Jewish synagogues in that part of the Middle East. If the story were a late invention, concocted by Matthew, it would immediately have been seen as a recent fiction. Matthew certainly would not have risked telling such a story to Jewish communities.

There is, therefore, no reason to suppose that this story is not true. The question now arises: why would the Jewish authorities have put their money into circulating such a story? The only reason could have been to achieve a pre-emptive strike. They knew from the guards that the tomb was empty; and they immediately foresaw that the Christians would publish this, and as an explanation they would say that Jesus was risen from the dead. So the authorities decided to strike first, tell the story that the tomb was empty, and give their explanation of it to counter the force of the inevitable Christian explanation. The very fact, however, that they circulated such a story, is proof that the tomb was empty.

Therefore, it must have been much to their embarrassment, when (contrary to their logical expectation) the Christians did not say anything publicly for another seven weeks.[4] During those seven weeks

---

[4]   The reasons for this are clear. Firstly, the disciples were at first afraid of the Jewish authorities, as is evidenced by the fact that for some time afterwards they met behind closed doors (John 20:19,

of Christian silence, however, the rumour of the empty tomb would have been filling Jerusalem.

It is not hard to imagine that many in Jerusalem perceived how thin the guards' story was. It was scarcely conceivable that the Jewish authorities would entrust such a highly sensitive mission to the kind of men who would fall asleep. In any case, if they were asleep, how did they know what had happened, let alone identify the disciples as the culprits? The story was evidently a product of bewilderment and desperation. As propaganda coming from the enemies of Christ, the circulation of this story is historical evidence of the highest quality that *the empty tomb of Jesus was a fact.*

> It is not hard to imagine that many in Jerusalem perceived how thin the guards' story was. It was scarcely conceivable that the Jewish authorities would entrust such a highly sensitive mission to the kind of men who would fall asleep.

Furthermore, if the tomb had not been empty, the authorities would have had no difficulty in producing the body of Jesus, demonstrating conclusively that no resurrection had happened, with the result that, when the apostles subsequently proclaimed that he had risen, they would have met with nothing but derision, and Christianity could never have got started.

Alternatively, if they had had the slightest evidence that the tomb was empty because the disciples had removed the body, they had the authority and the forces to hunt down the disciples, arrest them and charge them with grave robbing, which at the time was a very serious offence.

An interesting sidelight is thrown on all of this by an inscription, found in the nineteenth century, dating to AD 30–40. It contains the so-called Edict of Nazareth, and warns that robbery from, or desecration of, graves was an offence carrying the death penalty. Historians think that something very unusual must have happened around that time to cause such a severe edict to be issued—the most likely thing being the circumstances surrounding Joseph's empty tomb.[5]

---

26). Secondly, Jesus met with them on various occasions during the time after the resurrection, and told them to wait until the day of Pentecost before they told the nation that he had risen (Acts 1:4–5).

[5] See Ethelbert Stauber, *Jesus—Gestalt und Geschichte*, 163–4.

The Christian disciples: their explanation of the empty tomb

We are now at the point in our investigation where we have an empty tomb to be explained. The disciples claimed that Jesus had risen, but could they have been deceived about that? What if somebody had stolen the body away without the disciples' knowledge, and now had deceived them into thinking that there had been a resurrection? But who would have been interested in doing that? In our discussion of the moral character of the disciples in the previous chapter, we have seen why it could not have been any one of the friends of Christ; and the last thing the enemies of Christ wanted was that anything should happen that could lead people to believe in a resurrection. After all, it was for this very reason that they had ensured that the tomb was guarded. The idea, then, that the disciples were deceived has no explanatory power whatsoever, especially when it comes to the evidence that they advanced for positively believing that Jesus had risen; and this we must now consider.

The dramatis personae

But, first of all, we must consider the historical characters in this narrative. It is clear from the gospel records that the events at the cross and tomb of Jesus involved several groups of women.

Matthew says:

> There were also many women there, looking on from a distance, who had followed Jesus from Galilee, ministering to him, among whom were Mary Magdalene and Mary the mother of James and Joseph and the mother of the sons of Zebedee. (Matt 27:55–56)

Mark says:

> There were also women looking on from a distance, among whom were Mary Magdalene, and Mary the mother of James the younger and of Joses, and Salome. When he was in Galilee, they followed him and ministered to him, and there were also many other women who came up with him to Jerusalem. (Mark 15:40–41)

John specifically records that the mother of Jesus and three other women were standing by the cross—Jesus' mother's sister, Mary the wife of Clopas, and Mary Magdalene (John 19:25).

It is natural to presume that the three woman specially distinguished in the descriptions were the same in each case, having come to support Mary the mother of Jesus in her hour of acute distress. John Wenham, in his detailed study of the events surrounding the resurrection,[6] points out that this would mean that Jesus' mother's sister was called Salome, and was the wife of Zebedee and mother of James and John (the author of the Fourth Gospel). Mary the wife of Clopas was the mother of James the Younger and of Joses (or Joseph).[7]

From this, we see that between these women there are family relationships, which become important for our purposes when we remember that it was Passover time at Jerusalem. The city would be crowded with pilgrims who would naturally lodge with relatives wherever possible. One very important detail here is the fact that, from the cross, Jesus explicitly instructed John to look after his mother, Mary; and we read that he took her at once to his own home (John 19:27). In all probability this home was in Jerusalem, possibly not far from the house of the high priest, Caiaphas. Presumably John's mother, Salome, and her husband, Zebedee, were staying there also, along with Peter, who, as John records, accompanied John to the tomb on Easter morning (John 20:3).

But clearly other women were involved as well; and in all probability one of them was Joanna (see Luke 24:10), the wife of Chuza,

---

[6] *Easter Enigma: Are the Resurrection Accounts in Conflict?*, 34.

[7] There is no further information about Joses, but in the lists of the Apostles (see, e.g., Matt 10:3 ff., Mark 3:13 ff.) there are two men with the same name, James: James the son of Zebedee, and James the son of Alphaeus. Alphaeus and Clopas could well be versions of the same Aramaic name, which is usually transliterated *Chalphai*. The reason for this is that the first letter of the name in Aramaic is a guttural, which can either be transliterated as a *k*, thus yielding Clopas (or *Cleopas*, in its nearest Greek equivalent, according to Wenham, *Easter Enigma*, 37); or as an *h*. The latter is represented in Greek by a small sign called a rough breathing, and it was commonly dropped both in speaking or writing, so yielding the Greek *Alphaios*, which is Latinized as *Alphaeus*. It is also of interest that the historian Eusebius in his *Ecclesiastical History*, written towards the beginning of the fourth century, mentions that Clopas was the brother of Joseph (that is, Joseph, the husband of Mary, Jesus' mother).

Herod's steward (Luke 8:3). She was a wealthy woman who, as the wife of a very senior civil servant in Herod's Court, would have been living in the Hasmonean palace in Jerusalem, where Herod and his retinue stayed on their visits to the city. In Luke 8:3 Joanna's name is linked with that of Susanna; and it is possible that she, too, was one of the unnamed women in the crucifixion narrative.

But what about the other apostles? Where were they? Just before the Feast of Passover they had been staying in Bethany (John 12:1). This was a village just over the Mount of Olives, about 3 km from Jerusalem and therefore within walking distance. The arrest of Christ took place in a garden at the foot of the Mount of Olives: a garden that may well have belonged to the family of John Mark, the author of the Second Gospel. After the arrest of Christ we read that all the disciples forsook him and fled (Matt 26:56; Mark 14:50).[8] The most likely place for them to flee to was back up over the Mount of Olives to the comparative safety of Bethany. As far as we know, John and Peter were the only two to remain in the city.

We see, therefore, that there were different groups of people staying in a variety of locations: some in Jerusalem, and some outside the city. These facts assume great importance when we come to study the events of Easter morning, as detailed in the Gospel narratives. The narratives are often compressed; and one might be tempted to think that they contain contradictory elements, if unaware of the complexities of the situation, and the fact that there were different groups of people going to and coming from the tomb of Christ, not only from different directions and by different routes, but also at different times. Matthew's brief account has telescoped these features, as we shall later see.

Physical evidence found at the tomb: the grave-clothes of Christ

The Gospel accounts tell us that a number of women disciples of Christ came early to the tomb, to embalm his body more thoroughly than Joseph and Nicodemus had done (Mark 16:1; Luke 23:56–24:1).

---

[8] It is thought by many that the young man who was in the garden at the time of Jesus' arrest, and who just managed to escape the arrest party, may well have been Mark himself (Mark 14:51–52).

Incidentally, their intention shows again that resurrection was the last thing they were expecting.[9]

According to Mark (16:1), Mary Magdalene, the 'other Mary' (the mother of James the younger and Joseph), and Salome, had bought spices the previous evening at sundown ('when the Sabbath was past'). Wenham makes the very plausible suggestion that Mark's account is told from the perspective of these three women; whereas Luke's account, which records how certain women returned from the burial and prepared spices and ointments and then rested on the Sabbath, is most likely to have been written from the perspective of Joanna, the wife of Herod's steward.[10] As a wealthy Jewess she would have had her own store of spices and ointments, and so would not have had to wait, as the other groups of women did, until the Sabbath ended for the shops to open to enable her to buy them.

As Wenham says, it is likely that these two groups of women arrived at the tomb separately. The first group—Mary Magdalene, the 'other Mary', and Salome—arrived at the tomb first. To their astonishment, they found the stone rolled away from the tomb, and the tomb empty! One of them, Mary (perhaps without entering the tomb), ran at once to tell the apostles Peter and John. Mary did not speak of a resurrection, but simply presumed that the body of Jesus had been removed (John 20:2). Archaeologists point out that grave-robbing was a very common activity in the ancient world—in ancient Egypt, for example. Thieves would show particular interest in the tombs of the wealthy, as the cloths in which the corpse was wrapped and the spices used for embalming were valuable, resellable items; to say nothing of the jewellery and other possessions that might accompany the corpse. Now Jesus was not wealthy, but Joseph was; so Mary may have thought that grave-robbers had been active.

Peter and John ran to the tomb. John got there first, stooped, and looked inside. Immediately he noticed something strange: the linen grave-clothes that had been wrapped around the body of Jesus were still there. Stranger still, they were lying just as they had been

---

[9] It is interesting to note that, although Jesus had told his disciples he would die and rise again (for example, Matt 16:21), it had clearly not sunk in. The psychological reason for this is clear: it ran counter to all they hoped that Jesus, being the Messiah, would do (see Luke 24, which we discuss below, for an instance of this). The Jewish authorities, however, had noticed Jesus' predictions, which was their reason for guarding the tomb (Matt 27:62–65).

[10] *Easter Enigma*, 68–69.

when his body was in them, but the body had gone. Peter caught up with John, who must therefore have been the faster runner (one of those little details that give the narrative the ring of eyewitness writing). Both of them went into the tomb and saw what was possibly the strangest sight of all: the cloths which had been wrapped around Jesus' head were lying on the slightly elevated part of the ledge within the tomb; and, though his head was no longer in them, they were still wrapped round as if it had been, except that they had probably collapsed flat. The effect on John was powerful: 'he saw and believed' (John 20:3–8). This does not merely mean that he now believed what Mary had said for, from his first glimpse into the tomb, it was obvious that the body was missing. Now he believed that something very mysterious indeed must have happened. It looked as if in some way the body of Jesus had come right through the grave-clothes and left them exactly where they were when the body was inside. John had no doubt that he was seeing the evidence of a miracle!

> How could any grave-robber have removed the stone when the guard was there? The noise would have been considerable.

What was it about the grave-clothes that carried such convincing power? The obvious question for him, or for anyone else, to ask is, how did they get to be like that? Grave-robbers would not have taken the corpse and left the valuable linen and spices. And even if, for some unfathomable reason, they had wanted only the corpse, they would have had no reason whatever for wrapping all the cloths round again as if they were still round a body, except, perhaps, to give the impression that the tomb had not been disturbed. But if they wanted to give that impression they would surely have done better to roll the stone back into its place! But here we meet another matter: how could any grave-robber have removed the stone when the guard was there? The noise would have been considerable. The rolled-away stone was a complete giveaway that the tomb had been disturbed. It was an open invitation to come and have a look inside.

If it wasn't grave-robbers, then, who could it have been? Perhaps misguided followers of Jesus, trying to get the body away from under the noses of the authorities to a safer place? But if they had done that, they would not have kept it secret from the other apostles. They would have reburied him reverently (as Mary was intending to do—see John 20:15), and eventually all the Christians would have come to know where his tomb was. In any case, we are still left with the noisy problem of rolling away the stone within earshot of the guard.

The way in which the grave-clothes were lying convinced John of a miracle. So, could someone have taken the body and rewound the cloths deliberately to give the impression that a miracle had happened? But who could this have been? It was morally impossible for the followers of Christ to have done it.[11] It was also psychologically impossible, since they were not expecting a resurrection. And it was practically impossible, because of the guards.

Finally, it would be absurd to think of the authorities doing anything remotely suggestive of a resurrection. After all, it was they who had ensured that the tomb was guarded, to avoid anything like that.

For John and Peter, it was an electrifying discovery. They had ruled out impossible explanations, so they were left with only one alternative: that the body had come through the grave-clothes. But what did that mean? And where was Jesus now?

So they left the tomb. They thought there was nothing more to be gained by remaining there. However, as events proved, they were wrong.

EYEWITNESSES OF THE APPEARANCES OF CHRIST

The empty tomb is important: if it were not empty, you could not speak of resurrection. But we need to be clear that the early Christians did not simply assert that the tomb was empty. Far more important for them was the fact that they had subsequently met the risen Christ intermittently over a period of forty days culminating in his ascension (Acts 1:3). They had actually seen him, talked with him, touched him and eaten with him. It was nothing less than this that galvanised them into action and gave them the courage to confront the world with the message of the Christian gospel. And what is more, when the apostles began to preach the gospel publicly, this fact that they had personally witnessed these appearances of the risen Christ formed an integral part of that gospel. So, for instance:

---

[11] See Ch. 5 for the evidence for this point about the disciples' moral character.

Peter in Jerusalem (1):   On the day of Pentecost, in the first public announcement of the resurrection of Jesus in Jerusalem, Peter says: 'This Jesus God raised up, and of that we all are witnesses' (Acts 2:32).

Peter in Jerusalem (2):   Shortly after Pentecost, in the second major speech recorded by Luke, Peter says: 'and you killed the Author of life, whom God raised from the dead. To this we are witnesses' (Acts 3:15).

Peter in Caesarea: In the first major announcement of the Christian message to non-Jews, Peter says to Cornelius, the Roman centurion, that he and others 'ate and drank with him after he rose from the dead' (Acts 10:41).

Paul at Pisidian Antioch: In a major speech in a synagogue, Paul says of Christ: 'And when they had carried out all that was written of him, they took him down from the tree and laid him in a tomb. But God raised him from the dead, and for many days he appeared to those who had come up with him from Galilee to Jerusalem, who are now his witnesses to the people' (Acts 13:29–31).

And when Paul eventually comes to write down a brief, but definitive, statement of the gospel, he includes a selection of Christ's appearances to various witnesses as an essential part of that statement:

I made known to you the gospel . . .
how that Christ died for our sins according to the Scriptures; and
    that he was buried;
and that he has been raised the third day according to the
    Scriptures;
and that he appeared to Cephas, then to the twelve;

then . . . to more than five hundred brothers at once, of whom the
    greater part remain until now,
but some have fallen asleep;
then . . . to James, then to all the apostles;
and last of all . . . to me also. (1 Cor 15:1–8 own trans.)[12]

Hume's criteria for witnesses

Hume, as we saw in our last chapter, lists several criteria that he
regards as important for assessing the strength of evidence for an
alleged occurrence, particularly the number and character of the
witnesses, and the way in which they deliver their testimony. In that
chapter in response to Hume we spoke about the character and integrity of the apostles as witnesses; now we shall look at other aspects
of the witnesses.

Criterion 1 — The number and variety of witnesses

As to the number of witnesses we gather from Paul's list in 1 Corinthians
15, and from the Gospels and the Acts, that there were originally well
over five hundred people who at different times witnessed appearances
of the risen Christ during the forty days between his resurrection and
ascension. Twenty years later, in the mid-fifties AD when Paul was writing 1 Corinthians, over two hundred and fifty of them were still alive
(i.e. the 'greater part' of the 'five hundred brothers'), and presumably,
if need be, available for questioning. There was, then, no shortage of
eyewitnesses to the bodily resurrection of Christ during the early phase
of the growth of the Christian church.

But it is not only the number of eyewitnesses who actually saw the
risen Christ that is significant; it is also the widely divergent characters
of those eyewitnesses and the different places and situations in which
Christ appeared to them: to some, for instance, in a group of eleven
in a room, to one by herself in a garden, to a group of fishermen by
the sea, to two travelling along a road, to others on a mountain. It is
this variety of character and place that refutes the so-called hallucination theories.

---

[12] A full list of references to the appearances is: Matt 28:1–10, 16–20; Mark 16:9 ff.; Luke 24:13–31,
34, 36–49; John 20:11–18, 19–23, 24–29; 21:1–23; Acts 1:1–3, 6–11; 9:1–9; 22:3–11; 26:12–18; 1 Cor
15:5–9.

The inadequacy of hallucination theories

It has often been suggested that the so-called resurrection 'appearances' were actually psychological occurrences, like hallucinations; that the disciples 'saw' something, but that something was not objectively real, rather something going on inside their brain. However, psychological medicine itself witnesses against this explanation.

1. *Hallucinations usually occur to people of a certain temperament, with a vivid imagination.* The disciples were of very different temperaments: Matthew was a hard-headed, shrewd tax collector; Peter and some of the others, tough fishermen; Thomas, a dyed-in-the-wool sceptic; etc. They were not the sort of people one normally associates with susceptibility to hallucinations.

2. *Hallucinations tend to be of expected events.* Philosopher William Lane Craig points out that 'Hallucinations, as projections of the mind, can contain nothing new.'[13] But none of the disciples was expecting to meet Jesus again. The expectation of Jesus' resurrection was not in their minds at all. Instead, there was fear, doubt and uncertainty—exactly the wrong psychological preconditions for a hallucination.

3. *Hallucinations usually recur over a relatively long period, either increasing or decreasing.* But the appearances of Christ occurred frequently, over a period of forty days, and then abruptly ceased. None of the disciples involved ever claimed a similar experience again. The only exception was Paul, who records having once met the risen Christ, as the last to do so (Acts 9:3–5). This pattern is not, therefore, consistent with hallucinatory experiences.

4. *It is difficult to imagine that the five hundred people who saw him at once (1 Cor 15:6) were suffering from collective hallucination.*

5. *Hallucinations would not have led to belief in the resurrection.* Hallucination theories are severely limited in their explanatory scope: they only attempt to explain the appearances. They have nothing whatsoever to say about the empty tomb. However many hallucinations the disciples had, they could never have preached the resurrection in Jerusalem, if the nearby tomb had not been empty!

C. S. Lewis perceptively adds another reason that the theory is implausible when he writes:

---

[13] *Reasonable Faith*, 394.

Any theory of hallucination breaks down on the fact (and if it is an invention it is the oddest invention that ever entered the mind of man) that on three separate occasions this hallucination was not immediately recognised as Jesus. (Luke 24:13–31; John 20:15; 21:4)[14]

Criterion 2—The consistency of the testimony

If several witnesses to an event make statements in court which agree in every detail word-for-word, any judge would be likely to deduce that the testimonies were not independent; and, worse still, that there had possibly been collusion to mislead the court. On the other hand, testimonies of independent witnesses, which were hopelessly in disagreement on all the main points, would be of no use to a court either. What is looked for in independent testimonies is agreement on all the main facts, with just that amount of difference which can be accounted for by different perspectives. There may even be what appear to be minor discrepancies or inconsistencies in the secondary details, which can either be harmonised with one another in a natural way when more background information is available, or else must be left hanging for the time being, in the hope that further information will clear them up; but which are of such a nature that none of the primary details is affected.

Historians proceed in a similar way to lawyers. No historian would dismiss multiple versions of an event just because there were discrepancies in the secondary details. Indeed, that is true, even if some of the details are irreconcilable; as is the case, for example, with the two versions of Hannibal's journey across the Alps to attack Rome. Although they differ in many details, no scholar doubts the truth of the core-story, that Hannibal did indeed cross the Alps in his campaign against Rome.

When we apply these criteria to the records of the resurrection, we find that the Gospel narratives have the same primary details. There is a clear core-story: Joseph of Arimathea puts the body of Jesus in his tomb; a small group, or groups, of women disciples visit the tomb early on the first day of the week, and find the tomb

---

[14] *Miracles*, 241.

empty. They, and the apostles, subsequently meet Jesus on a number of occasions.

In the secondary details there are some apparent discrepancies. For example, Matthew says that Mary Magdalene came to the tomb 'towards the dawn' (Matt 28:1); whereas John says 'while it was still dark' Mary went to the tomb (John 20:1). Such statements are easily harmonised: Mary may well have set out while it was still dark and got to the tomb as dawn broke.

In addition, in any attempt at a detailed reconstruction of events, it is important to be aware, as we pointed out above, that there were different groups of women associated with the death and resurrection of Christ. The group consisting of Mary Magdalene, the 'other Mary', and Salome arrived at the tomb first. On approaching the tomb they saw the tomb opened and Mary ran back into the city to tell Peter and John. While she was gone, Joanna (and possibly Susanna), who had set out from the Hasmonean Palace, arrive by a different route. They would have come through a different gate of the city, and so they did not meet Mary Magdalene. The four women now went into the tomb, where they are told to go back into the city and tell the disciples. As there are many routes through the narrow streets of Jerusalem, they did not meet Peter and John running towards the tomb, followed by Mary Magdalene. John and Peter, on arriving at the tomb, saw the evidence of the grave-clothes that indicated to them that Jesus had risen. They left the tomb. Mary Magdalene lingered, and it was at this point that she saw Jesus (John 20:11–18). She then returned to the others at the house in Jerusalem.

> What is looked for in independent testimonies is agreement on all the main facts, with just that amount of difference which can be accounted for by different perspectives.

Now the women had been told to tell the disciples. So far, only two of them knew—John and Peter. The other nine, who had presumably spent the night in Bethany, had to be told. At this point, then, Wenham argues,[15] a group of women (probably including 'the other' Mary and Salome) set out for Bethany, and on the way they too met Jesus (Matt 28:9).

---

[15] *Easter Enigma*, 76–89.

Another apparent discrepancy lies in the fact that in Luke 24:33 ff., Jesus is described as appearing to 'the eleven', whereas John's description of what appears to be the same event (John 20:19–25) says that Thomas was not present on that occasion. Thus, in fact, only ten disciples were there. However, there is no necessary contradiction here, since the term 'the eleven' can mean 'the disciples as a group', rather than implying that all of them were there without exception on every occasion. For instance, there are eleven players in an English cricket team. If a sports reporter said that he had gone to Lord's Cricket Ground in London to interview the English Eleven, his statement would not necessarily be taken to imply that he had seen all eleven players as a group, but only a representative group of them.[16]

Well-known historian Michael Grant of Edinburgh University writes:

> True, the discovery of the empty tomb is differently described by the various Gospels, but if we apply the same sort of criteria that we would apply to any other ancient literary sources, then the evidence is firm and plausible enough to necessitate the conclusion that the tomb was, indeed, found empty.[17]

Criterion 3 — The possible bias of witnesses

It is often said that, because the evidence for the resurrection of Jesus Christ comes predominantly from Christian sources, there is a danger of it being partisan, and therefore not carrying the weight of independent testimony. This objection sounds plausible at first, but it looks very different in the light of the following considerations. Those who were convinced by the evidence for the resurrection of Jesus became Christians, *but they were not necessarily Christians when they first heard of the resurrection.* The prime example of this is Saul of Tarsus. Far from being a Christian, he was a leading academic Pharisee who was fanatically opposed to the Christians. So much so, in fact, that he was persecuting the Christians, and having them imprisoned and tortured.

---

[16] For further discussion of the detailed historical questions involved in the events surrounding the burial and resurrection of Christ, the reader is referred to Wenham's *Easter Enigma.*
[17] *Jesus: An Historian's Review of the Gospels,* 176.

He wanted to destroy the resurrection story, and stamp out Christianity at its roots. When he heard that Christianity was beginning to spread beyond Jerusalem, he got permission from the high priest's office to go to Damascus in Syria and arrest all Christians. But by the time he got to Damascus something utterly unexpected had happened—he had become a Christian (Acts 9:1–19)! He would of course come to be better known as Paul (13:9).

Paul's conversion and subsequent writing have marked the history of Europe and of the world. In his lifetime he founded many churches, and even to the present day his writings (more than half of the New Testament books) have influenced millions of people from every nation under the sun. The conversion of Paul has proved a turning point in history, and demands once more an explanation big enough to explain that effect. His own explanation was: 'Last of all . . . he appeared also to me' (1 Cor 15:8). Paul's witness is significant, then, for the reason that he was not a believer when he met the risen Christ. It was that meeting which was the cause of his conversion.

But there is another question that should be asked in this connection. Where is the evidence, on the part of those who did not believe the resurrection of Jesus, to prove that he did not rise? The religious authorities who had condemned and executed Jesus could not afford to ignore, or dismiss, the Christian claim. They desperately wanted to stop a mass movement based on the resurrection. They had at their disposal all their own official resources, and the help of the Roman military machine if they wanted it. Yet strangely they seem to have produced no evidence, except for the patently silly story (for which they had to pay a great deal!) about the disciples stealing the body while the guards slept. So they resorted to crude scare tactics. They put the apostles in prison and tried to intimidate them by threatening them with serious consequences if they continued preaching the resurrection (Acts 4:17–22). The complete absence of contemporary evidence from the authorities or anyone else against the resurrection, tells its own eloquent story. There does not seem to have been any to publish!

Criterion 4 — The attitude of the witnesses

Hume would have us consider here the manner in which the Christians put forward their views. Were they overly hesitant? Or, just the opposite, too violent? Certainly they were not hesitant. In Acts, Luke gives us many examples of the courageous way in which the disciples gave their witness to the resurrection, often to very hostile audiences. But they were never violent. Indeed, one of the striking things about the early Christians is their non-violence, which they had learned from Christ himself. He had taught them not to use the sword to protect either him or his message (Matt 26:52). His kingdom was not the kind of kingdom where people fight (John 18:36). Think of the effect of conversion upon Paul. Before he was converted, he was a religious bigot and fanatic who persecuted his own fellow Jews when they had become Christians. After his conversion he did not persecute anyone, of any religion, ever again. On the contrary, for his belief in the resurrection of Christ he himself suffered grievous persecution and eventually gave his life.

It would seem, therefore, that in the case of the early disciples, Hume's criteria for credible witnesses are well satisfied.

Women as witnesses

To anyone who knows anything about the ancient laws regarding legal testimony, it is very striking that the first reports mentioned in the Gospels of appearances of the risen Christ were made by women. For, in first-century Jewish culture, women were not considered to be competent witnesses. At that time, therefore, anyone who wanted to invent a resurrection story would never have thought of commencing it in this way. The only value of including such a story would be if it were both true and easy to verify, whatever people thought of the fact that it figured women as witnesses. Its very inclusion, therefore, is a clear mark of historical authenticity.

The psychological evidence

The lack of attachment to the tomb

There is no mention in John 20:1–10 that John and Peter attempted to discuss with Mary the logical implications of the grave-clothes. Psychologically, it is most unlikely that they did, for she was weeping, evidently distraught at the thought of having irreparably lost the body of the one who had brought forgiveness, peace of heart and honour back into her life. And if 'resurrection' meant that she had lost all contact with him permanently, it would have been no comfort to her. After all, she had come to the tomb with the other women in order to complete the embalming of the body, and it is easy to see what was ultimately in their minds. Had the resurrection not happened, they would very quickly have made the tomb into a shrine, to which they could come, and pray, and show devotion to their dead spiritual hero. Yet the extraordinary thing is that there is no record of their ever doing any such thing. Nowhere in the New Testament do we find the apostles encouraging the faithful to make pilgrimages to the tomb of Christ for special blessing, or for healing. On the contrary, there is no evidence of any real interest in the tomb of Christ in the earliest Christian era.

> Had the resurrection not happened, they would very quickly have made the tomb into a shrine, to which they could come, and pray, and show devotion to their dead spiritual hero. Yet the extraordinary thing is that there is no record of their ever doing any such thing.

So what was powerful enough to break the strong, natural desire, particularly on the part of those early Christian women, to venerate the tomb? Mary is perhaps the best person to tell us, for she felt very strongly that desire to remain close to the tomb on the day she found it empty. Since she had come to complete the task of embalming the body, she needed to find that body (see John 20:10–18). As she stood there weeping, through her tears she was conscious of someone else nearby, whom she thought was the gardener. Perhaps he had taken the body? So she spoke to him: 'Tell me where you have laid him and I will take him away.' Together with the other women, she would have taken him away and reburied him with honour, in a place to be venerated forever.

But she didn't. Something so powerful happened in the garden that day that Mary and the others never showed any interest in the tomb again. John tells us that the one whom she had taken to be the gardener was actually the risen Christ. 'Mary', he said, and as she instantly recognised his voice, she knew that her quest was over. If Jesus was risen, what interest could there possibly be in holding on to his tomb? None whatsoever! No one makes a shrine to a person who is alive.

A new relationship

But there is another issue. Granted that the tomb was abandoned because the disciples were convinced that Jesus was risen from the dead, there then arises the important question of what was to be the relationship between the disciples and the risen Christ. Mary, having found that he was alive, wanted, very naturally, to cling on to him. But Christ had something to say to her—indeed a message for all his followers: 'Do not hold on to me [that is, in Greek, 'do not keep holding on to me', or 'stop holding on to me'], for I have not yet ascended to the Father. Go instead to my brothers and tell them, 'I am ascending to my Father and your Father, to my God and your God' (John 20:17 NIV).

Mary knew he was real and really there: she had heard his voice and touched him; but he was telling her that he was not going to remain with her in that way. She would keep him, but not in the same sense as before. Now, from the other side of death, he was assuring her and, through her, all of his followers, that he had created a new and permanent relationship between them and him and his Father that death itself could not destroy. It was this living relationship with the living Christ that satisfied her heart and the hearts of millions since. The bare fact of knowing that he had risen from the dead would not have been enough to do that.

The nature of the resurrection body

That evening, Christ appeared to the main group of disciples (John 20:19–23; Luke 24:36–49). They were meeting somewhere in Jerusalem in a room with the doors locked, because they were frightened of the Jewish authorities. He showed them his hands and side with the marks of the nails and spear. Now at last John knew what resurrection meant! The body that had come through the grave-clothes, had come through closed doors—but it was real, tangible and, above all, alive.

Now some readers will at once wish to raise the question: in this advanced scientific age, how can one possibly believe that a physical body came through grave-clothes, and through locked doors in a room? But perhaps this advanced scientific age has made such a thing more conceivable, rather than less. We know what the disciples did not know: matter consists of largely empty space; elementary particles can penetrate matter; some—like neutrinos—to immense depth.

In addition to that, there is the question of dimensionality. We are familiar with the four dimensions of space-time. But God is not limited to those four dimensions. Maybe nature itself involves more dimensions than we thought—string theory would suggest there may be more.

An analogy can help us here. In 1880 a delightful book was written by a mathematician, Edwin Abbott, as a satire on class structure.[18] Abbott asks us to imagine a two-dimensional world called Flatland, whose inhabitants are two dimensional figures, straight lines, triangles, squares, pentagons, etc., all the way up to circles. We are introduced to a Sphere from Spaceland (three-dimensions), who tries to explain to one of the creatures in Flatland what it means to be a sphere. The sphere passes through the plane of Flatland, appearing first as a point, then a circle that gets larger, then smaller until it disappears. This, of course, seems impossible to the Flatlanders, simply because they cannot conceive any dimension higher than two. The sphere mystifies them even further by saying that, by moving around above the plane of Flatland, it can see into their houses and can appear at will in them, without the doors having to be open. The sphere even takes one incredulous Flatlander out into space to give him a view of his world from outside. However, on his return, he cannot get his new knowledge accepted by the Flatlanders who know nothing other than their two-dimensional world.

Is it possible that our world is something like Flatland—but with four dimensions rather than two? If so, a reality of higher dimensionality could interact with our world, as the sphere does in the Flatland world.

The physics of matter, and such analogies as that of Flatland, can help us at least to see that it might be very short-sighted and premature to dismiss out of hand the New Testament account of the properties of Christ's resurrection body. If there is a God who transcends space and time, it is not surprising if the resurrection of his Son reveals aspects of reality that also transcend space and time.

Some will, however, take issue with the idea that the resurrection

---

[18] *Flatland.*

body of Christ is physical, by pointing out that the New Testament itself speaks of the resurrection body as a 'spiritual body' (1 Cor 15:44). The objection, then, asserts that 'spiritual' means 'non-physical'. But a moment's reflection shows that there are other possibilities. When we speak of a 'petrol engine', we do not mean an 'engine made of petrol'. No, we mean an engine powered by petrol. Thus the term 'spiritual body' could well be referring to the power behind that body's life, rather than a description of what it is made of.

> The eating of that fish proved beyond all doubt that his resurrection body was a physical reality. They must have spent a long time staring at the empty plate on the table after he had gone. Whatever the nature of the world to which he now belonged, he had taken a fish into it.

To decide between these possibilities we need only to refer to the text of the New Testament. For there we find that Christ says to his disciples: 'Look at my hands and my feet. It is I myself! Touch me and see; a ghost does not have flesh and bones, as you see I have' (Luke 24:39 NIV). That is, he was explicitly pointing out that his resurrection body was not 'made of spirit'. It had flesh and bone: it was tangible. And to prove the point even further, Christ asked them if they had anything to eat. He was offered a fish, and he ate it in front of them (Luke 24:41–43). The eating of that fish proved beyond all doubt that his resurrection body was a physical reality. They must have spent a long time staring at the empty plate on the table after he had gone. Whatever the nature of the world to which he now belonged, he had taken a fish into it. It certainly therefore had a physical dimension.

Doubt and the resurrection

The New Testament writers honestly tell us there were several occasions on which the first reaction of some of the disciples was to entertain doubts about the resurrection. For example, when the apostles first heard the report of the women, they simply did not believe them, and regarded what they said as nonsense (Luke 24:11). They were not in the end convinced, until they had seen Jesus for themselves.

Thomas was not with the other disciples on the evening in Jerusalem when the risen Christ appeared in the locked room; and he simply refused to believe their claim that they had seen him. He issued a challenge: 'Unless I see the nail marks in his hands and put my finger where the nails were, and put my hand into his side, I will not believe' (John 20:25 NIV). Thomas was not prepared to give in to group pressure—he wanted the evidence for himself. A week later, they all found themselves once more in the locked room in Jerusalem. Jesus appeared, spoke to Thomas, and invited him to put his finger in the nail marks, and his hand in the spear wound. Christ offered him the evidence that he demanded (which proves, incidentally, that the risen Christ had heard him ask for it), gently reproaching him for not believing what the others had said. We are not told whether Thomas did, in fact, touch Christ on this occasion. But we are told what his response was. He said: 'My Lord and my God' (John 20:28). He recognised the risen Jesus as God.

What about those who have not seen Christ?

In this lengthy section on the appearances of Christ we have been thinking of those early Christians who saw him. We also have made the point that after about forty days the appearances stopped—apart from Paul's experience on the Damascus road. It is, therefore, a simple, historical fact that the vast majority of Christians throughout history have become Christians without literally seeing Jesus. Christ said something very important about this to Thomas and the others: 'Have you believed because you have seen me? Blessed are those who have not seen and yet have believed' (John 20:29).

They saw and believed—but most have not seen. This does not, of course, mean that Christ is asking all the rest to believe without any evidence. That is not so; in the first place, the evidence that is offered to us is the eyewitness evidence of those who did see. But Christ is alerting us to the fact that there are different kinds of evidence. One of them is the way in which the communication of God's message penetrates the heart and conscience of the listener.

Christ's death and resurrection predicted by the Old Testament

There was among the disciples a deeper sort of incredulity than that of Thomas, which was not overcome simply by seeing. Luke tells us of two of Jesus' followers taking a journey from Jerusalem to the nearby village of Emmaus on that event-packed first day of the week (Luke 24:3–35). They were utterly dispirited at the events that had just taken place in Jerusalem. A stranger joined them. It was Jesus, but they did not recognise him. Luke explains that their eyes were 'kept from recognizing him' (v. 16), presumably supernaturally, and for the following reason. They had thought that Jesus was going to be their political liberator; but, to their dismay, he had allowed himself to be crucified. To their way of thinking, a liberator who allowed himself to be crucified by his opponents was useless as a liberator. Rumours spread by women about his resurrection were therefore irrelevant.

To solve their problem, Jesus did not immediately open their eyes to see who he was. What he did was to take them through a concise summary of the Old Testament, arguing that it was the consistent testimony of the Old Testament prophets that the Messiah, whoever he was, would be rejected by his nation, put to death, and then eventually be raised and glorified. This was news to the two travellers. Up until now they had read from the Old Testament what they had wanted to see. They had studied the prophecies about the triumphant coming of Messiah, but had overlooked the fact that Messiah also had to fulfil the role of the Suffering Servant; and, in order to do that, he must suffer and only then enter into his glory.

Perhaps the most remarkable of those predictions is contained in Isaiah 53:2–12. Over five hundred years before it occurred, the rejection, suffering and death of the Messiah for human sins is graphically portrayed:

> He was wounded for our transgressions; he was crushed for our iniquities; upon him was the chastisement that brought us peace, and with his stripes we are healed. (Isa 53:5)

Isaiah then speaks of his being 'cut off out of the land of the living' (Isa 53:8), and being put in a grave; after which we read the remarkable words: 'Out of the anguish of his soul he shall see and be satisfied' (Isa 53:11). According to Isaiah, then, the Messiah was going to die. Therefore, far from the death of Jesus proving that he was not the Messiah, it proved that he was. When the two travellers had grasped that, it made the story of Jesus' resurrection that they had heard from the women credible. It removed the grounds of their despair, and filled them with new hope.

But still they didn't recognise that the stranger was Jesus. It was enough, so far, that they had been brought to see the objective fact that the Old Testament proclaimed the death of Messiah. How, then, did they come to recognise him? The answer is that they recognised him by something he did when they invited him into their home. He performed an act that would be intensely revealing to those who belonged to the inner core of the early disciples. As they were partaking of a simple meal, Jesus broke the bread for them—and suddenly they recognised him! This detail has a powerful ring of genuineness and truth. They had seen Jesus break bread before—when he fed the multitudes, for instance—and there was something indefinable, but characteristic, about the way he did it, that was instantly recognisable.

We all know this kind of thing from our experience of family and friends: characteristic ways of doing things that are special to them, and which we would recognise anywhere. It was evidence, conclusive evidence, to the disciples that this really was Jesus. No impostor would ever have thought of imitating such a tiny detail.

THE OBJECTIVE AND THE PERSONAL

This has been a lengthy and detailed account—necessarily so, because of the importance of the topic. We give the last word on the evidence for the resurrection to Professor Sir Norman Anderson:

> The empty tomb, then, forms a veritable rock on which all rationalistic theories of the resurrection dash themselves in vain.[19]

This cannot, however, be the last word about the subject of our investigation, for the evidence that we have considered forces upon each one of us a decision, not about the truth of an event only, but about the truthfulness of a person. If the resurrection of Jesus Christ really did occur, as the weight of the evidence indicates that it did, then he really is alive today. That being so, the next word about the matter belongs to you, the reader. What will you do about this person who himself claims to be the response to our deepest questions?

---

[19] *Evidence for the Resurrection*, 11.

And it is not fear-mongering but the force of logic to point out further that, if he did rise again as he said he would, then he will have something to say eventually about how we have responded to him and to his claims. In that sense, the final word on this matter will be that of Christ. As Paul declared in the first century AD to the philosophers and citizens of Athens gathered in the Areopagus:

> The times of ignorance God overlooked, but now he commands all people everywhere to repent, because he has fixed a day on which he will judge the world in righteousness by a man whom he has appointed; and of this he has given assurance to all by raising him from the dead. (Acts 17:30–31)

APPENDIX:
THE SCIENTIFIC ENDEAVOUR

The doing of successful science follows
no set of cosy rules. It is as complex as
the human personalities that are involved
in doing it.

THE CLEAR VOICE OF SCIENCE

Science rightly has the power to fire the imagination. Who could read the story of how Francis Crick and James D. Watson unravelled the double helix structure of DNA without entering at least a little into the almost unbearable joy that they experienced at this discovery? Who could watch an operation to repair someone's eye with a delicately controlled laser beam without a sense of wonder at human creativity and invention? Who could see pictures from space showing astronauts floating weightless in the cabin of the International Space Station or watch them repair the Hubble telescope against the background of the almost tangible blackness of space without a feeling akin to awe? Science has a right to our respect and to our active encouragement. Getting young people into science and giving them the training and facilities to develop their intellectual potential is a clear priority for any nation. It would be an incalculable loss if the scientific instinct were in any way stifled by philosophical, economic or political considerations.

But since one of the most powerful and influential voices to which we want to listen is the voice of science, it will be very important for us, whether we are scientists or not, to have some idea of what science is and what the scientific method is before we try to evaluate what science says to us on any particular issue. Our aim, therefore, first of all is to remind ourselves of some of the basic principles of scientific thinking, some of which we may already know. Following this, we shall think about the nature of scientific explanation and we shall examine some of the assumptions that underlie scientific activity—basic beliefs without which science cannot be done.

Then what is science? It tends to be one of those things that we all know what it means until we come to try to define it. And then we find that precise definition eludes us. The difficulty arises because we use the word in different ways. First of all, *science* is used as shorthand for:

1. sciences—areas of knowledge like physics, chemistry, biology, etc.;
2. scientists—the people who work in these areas;
3. scientific method—the way in which scientists do their work.

Often, however, the word *science* is used in expressions like 'Science says...', or 'Science has demonstrated...', as if science were a conscious being of great authority and knowledge. This usage, though understandable, can be misleading. The fact is that, strictly speaking, there is no such thing as 'science' in this sense. Science does not say, demonstrate, know or discover anything—scientists do. Of course, scientists often agree, but it is increasingly recognised that science, being a very human endeavour, is very much more complex than is often thought and there is considerable debate about what constitutes scientific method.

SCIENTIFIC METHOD

It is now generally agreed among philosophers of science that there is no one 'scientific method', so it is easier to speak of the kind of thing that doing science involves than to give a precise definition of science. Certainly observation and experimentation have primary

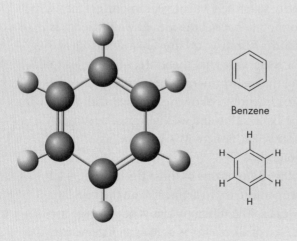

Benzene

H
H   H

H   H
H

FIGURE Ap.1. Benzene Molecule.

In 1929 crystallographer Kathleen Lonsdale confirmed Kekulé's earlier theory about the flat, cyclic nature of benzene, an important milestone in organic chemistry.

Reproduced with permission of ©iStock/hromatos.

roles to play, as well as do the reasoning processes that lead scientists to their conclusions. However, a glance at the history of science will show that there is much more to it than this. We find, for example, that inexplicable hunches have played a considerable role. Even dreams have had their place! The chemist Friedrich August Kekulé was studying the structure of benzene and dreamed about a snake that grabbed its own tail, thus forming itself into a ring. As a result he was led to the idea that benzene might be like the snake. He had a look and found that benzene indeed contained a closed ring of six carbon atoms! The doing of successful science follows no set of cosy rules. It is as complex as the human personalities that are involved in doing it.

Observation and experimentation

It is generally agreed that a revolution in scientific thinking took place in the sixteenth and seventeenth centuries. Up to then one main method of thinking about the nature of the universe was to appeal to authority. For example, in the fourth century BC Aristotle had argued from philosophical principles that the only perfect motion was circular. Thus, if you wanted to know how the planets moved, then, since according to Aristotle they inhabited the realm of perfection beyond the orbit of the moon, they must move in circles. In a radical departure from this approach, scientists like Galileo insisted that the best way to find out how the planets moved was to take his telescope and go and have a look! And through that telescope he saw things like the moons of Jupiter which, according to the Aristotelian system, did not exist. Galileo comes to embody for many people the true spirit of scientific enquiry: the freedom to do full justice to observation and experimentation, even if it meant seriously modifying or even abandoning the theories that he had previously held. That freedom should be retained and jealously guarded by us all.

Data, patterns, relationships and hypotheses

In summary form, the most widespread view, often attributed to Francis Bacon and John Stuart Mill, is that the scientific method consists of:

1. the collection of data (facts, about which there can be no dispute) by means of observation and experiment, neither of them influenced by presuppositions or prejudices;
2. the derivation of hypotheses from the data by looking for patterns or relationships between the data and then making an inductive generalisation;
3. the testing of the hypotheses by deducing predictions from them and then constructing and doing experiments designed to check if those predictions are true;
4. the discarding of hypotheses that are not supported by the experimental data and the building up of the theory by adding confirmed hypotheses.

Scientists collect data, experimental observations and measurements that they record. As examples of data, think of a set of blood pressure measurements of your class just before and just after a school examination, or of the rock samples collected by astronauts from the surface of the moon.

There are, however, many other things that are equally real to us, but which scarcely can count as data in the scientific sense: our subjective experience of a sunset, or of friendship and love, or of dreams. With dreams, of course, heart rate, brain activity and eye movement can be observed by scientists as they monitor people who are asleep and dreaming, but their subjective experience of the dream itself cannot be measured. Thus we see that the scientific method has certain built-in limits. It cannot capture the whole of reality.

Scientists are in the business of looking for relationships and patterns in their data and they try to infer some kind of hypothesis or theory to account for those patterns. Initially the hypothesis may be an intelligent or inspired guess that strikes the scientists from their experience as being a possible way of accounting for what they have observed. For example, a scientist might suggest the (very reasonable) hypothesis that the blood pressure measurements in your class can be accounted for by the fact that examinations cause stress in most people! To test the hypothesis a scientist will then work out what he or she would expect to find if the hypothesis were true and then will proceed to devise an experiment or a series of experiments to check if such is indeed the case. If the experiments fail to confirm expectation, the hypothesis may be modified or discarded in favour of another and the process repeated. Once a hypothesis has been successfully tested by repeated experimentation then it is dignified by being called a theory.[1]

It is now generally agreed by scientists themselves and philosophers of science that our account so far of what the scientific method is, is not only highly idealised but also flawed. In particular, contrary to what is asserted about observation and experimentation above, it is now widely accepted that no scientist, however honest and careful, can come to his or her work in a completely impartial way, without presuppositions and assumptions. This fact will be of importance for our understanding of science's contribution to our worldview. It is easier, however, to consider that topic after we have first had a look at some of the logical concepts and procedures that underlie scientific argumentation and proof.

Induction

Induction is probably the most important logical process that scientists use in the formulation of laws and theories.[2] It is also a process that is familiar to all of us from a very early age whether we are scientists or not, though we may well not have been aware of it. When we as young children first see a crow we notice it is black. For all we know, the next crow we see may well be white or yellow. But after observing crows day after day, there comes a point at which our feeling that any other crow we see is going to be black is so strong that we would be prepared to say that all crows are black. We have taken what is called an inductive step based on our own data—we have seen, say, 435 crows—to make a universal statement about all crows. Induction, then, is the process of generalising from a finite set of data to a universal or general statement.

---

[1] The terms *hypothesis* and *theory* are in fact almost indistinguishable, the only difference in normal usage being that a hypothesis is sometimes regarded as more tentative than a theory.

[2] Note for mathematicians: the process of induction described above is not the same as the principle of mathematical induction by which (typically) the truth of a statement $P(n)$ is established for all positive integers n from two propositions:

(1) $P(1)$ is true;

(2) for any positive integer k, we can prove that the truth of $P(k+1)$ follows from the truth of $P(k)$.

The key difference is that (2) describes an infinite set of hypotheses, one for each positive integer, whereas in philosophical induction we are generalising from a finite set of hypotheses.

A famous example of the use of induction in science is the derivation of Mendel's laws of heredity. Gregor Mendel and his assistants made a number of observations of the frequency of occurrence of particular characteristics in each of several generations of peas, like whether seeds were wrinkled or smooth, or plants were tall or short, and then made an inductive generalisation from those observations to formulate the laws that now bear his name.

> Induction, then, is the process of generalising from a finite set of data to a universal or general statement.

But, as may well have occurred to you, there is a problem with induction. To illustrate this, let's turn our minds to swans rather than the crows we thought about just now. Suppose that from childhood every swan you have seen was white. You might well conclude (by induction) that all swans are white. But then one day you are shown a picture of an Australian black swan and discover that your conclusion was false. This illustrates what the problem with induction is. How can you ever really know that you have made enough observations to draw a universal conclusion from a limited set of observations?

But please notice what the discovery of the black swan has done. It has proved wrong the statement that all swans are white, but it has not proved wrong the modified statement that if you see a swan in Europe, the high probability is that the swan will be white.

Let's look at another example of induction, this time from chemistry.

Particular observations:

Time	Date	Substance	Litmus test result
0905	2015-08-14	sulphuric acid	turned red
1435	2015-09-17	citric acid	turned red
1045	2015-09-18	hydrochloric acid	turned red
1900	2015-10-20	sulphuric acid	turned red

Universal or general statement (law): litmus paper turns red when dipped in acid.

This law, based on induction from the finite set of particular observations that are made of particular acids at particular times in particular places, is claimed to hold for all acids at all times in all places. The problem with induction is, how can we be sure that such a general statement is valid, when, in the very nature of things, we can only make a finite number of observations of litmus paper turning red on the application of acid? The story of the black swan makes us aware of the difficulty.

Well, we cannot be absolutely sure, it is true. But every time we do the experiment and find it works, our confidence in the litmus test is increased to the extent that if we dipped some paper in a liquid and found it did not go red we would be likely to conclude, not that the litmus test did not work, but that either the paper we had was not litmus paper or the liquid was not acid! Of course it is true that underlying our confidence is the assumption that nature behaves in a uniform way, that if I repeat an experiment tomorrow under the same conditions as I did it today, I will get the same results.

Let's take another example that Bertrand Russell used to illustrate the problem of induction in a more complex situation: Bertrand Russell's inductivist turkey. A turkey observes that on its first day at the turkey farm it was fed at 9 a.m. For two months it collects observations and notes that even if it chooses days at random, it is fed at 9 a.m. It finally concludes by induction that it always will be fed at 9 a.m. It therefore gets an awful shock on Christmas Eve when, instead of being fed, it is taken out and killed for Christmas dinner!

So how can we know for certain that we have made enough observations in an experiment? How many times do we have to check that particular metals expand on heating to conclude that all metals expand on heating? How do we avoid the inductivist turkey shock? Of course we can see that the problem with the turkey is that it did not have (indeed could not have) the wider experience of the turkey farmer who could replace the turkey's incorrect inductivist conclusion with a more complicated correct one: namely the law that each turkey will experience a sequence of days of feeding followed by execution!

The point of what we are saying here is not to undermine science by suggesting that induction is useless, nor that science in itself cannot lead us to any firm conclusions. It simply teaches us to recognise the limits of any one method and to found our conclusions, wherever possible, on a combination of them.

The role of deduction

Once a law has been formulated by induction, we can test the validity of the law by using it to make predictions. For example, assuming Mendel's laws to be true, we can deduce from them a prediction as to what the relative frequency of occurrence, say, of blue eyes in different generations of a family, should be. When we find by direct observation that the occurrence of blue eyes is what we predicted it to be, our observations are said to confirm the theory, although this sort of confirmation can never amount to total certainty. Thus deduction plays an important role in the confirmation of induction.

Deduction plays an important role in the confirmation of induction.

It may be that what we have said about induction has given the impression that scientific work always starts by looking at data and reasoning to some inductive hypothesis that accounts for those data. However, in reality, scientific method tends to be somewhat more complicated than this. Frequently, scientists start by deciding what kind of data they are looking for. That is, they already have in their mind some hypothesis or theory they want to test, and they look for data that will confirm that theory. In this situation deduction will play a dominant role.

For example, as we mentioned above regarding observation and experimentation, in the ancient world, Greek philosophers supposed as a hypothesis that the planets must move in circular orbits around the earth, since, for them, the circle was the perfect shape. They then deduced what their hypothesis should lead them to observe in the heavens. When their observations did not appear to confirm their original hypothesis completely, they modified it. They did this by replacing the original hypothesis by one in which other circular motions are imposed on top of the original one (epicycles, they were called). They then used this more complicated hypothesis from which to deduce their predictions. This theory of epicycles dominated astronomy for a long time, and was overturned and replaced by the revolutionary suggestions of Copernicus and Kepler.

Kepler's work in turn again illustrates the deductive method. Using the observations the astronomer Tycho Brahe had made available, Kepler tried to work out the shape that the orbit of Mars traced against the background of 'fixed' stars. He did not get anywhere until he hit on an idea that was prompted by geometrical work he had done on the ellipse. That idea was to suppose as a hypothesis that the orbit of Mars was an ellipse, then to use mathematical calculations to deduce what should be observed on the basis of that hypothesis, and finally to compare those predictions with the actual observations. The validity of the elliptical orbit hypothesis would then be judged by how closely the predictions fit the observations.

This method of inference is called the deductive or hypothetico-deductive method of reasoning: deducing predictions from a hypothesis, and then comparing them with actual observations.

Since deduction is such an important procedure it is worth considering it briefly. Deduction is a logical process by which an assertion we want to prove (the conclusion) is logically deduced from things we already accept (the premises). Here is an example of logical deduction, usually called a syllogism:

P1: All dogs have four legs.
P2: Fido is a dog.
_____
C: Fido has four legs.

Here statements P1 and P2 are the premises and C is the conclusion. If P1 and P2 are true then C is true. Or to put it another way, to have P1 and P2 true and C false, would involve a logical contradiction. This is the essence of a logically valid deduction.

Let's now look at an example of a logically invalid deduction:

P1: Many dogs have a long tail.
P2: Albert is a dog.
_____
C: Albert has a long tail.

Here statement C does not necessarily follow from P1 and P2. It is clearly possible for P1 and P2 to be true and yet for C to be false.

It all appears to be so simple that there is danger of your switching off. But don't do that quite yet or you might miss something very important. And that is that deductive logic cannot establish the truth of any of the statements involved in the procedure. All that the logic can tell us (but this much is very important!) is that if the premises are true and the argument is logically valid, then the conclusion is true. In order to get this clear let us look at a final example:

P1: All planets have a buried ocean.

P2: Mercury is a planet.

C: Mercury has a buried ocean.

This is a logically valid argument even though statement P1 and statement C are (so far as we know) false. The argument says only that if P1 and P2 were true, then C should be true, which is perfectly valid. This sort of thing may seem strange to us at first, but it can help us grasp that logic can only criticise the argument and check whether it is valid or not. It cannot tell us whether any or all of the premises or conclusion are true. Logic has to do with the way in which some statements are derived from others, not with the truth of those statements.

Logic has to do with the way in which some statements are derived from others, not with the truth of those statements.

We should also note that deductive inference plays a central role in pure mathematics where theories are constructed by means of making deductions from explicitly given axioms, as in Euclidean geometry. The results (or theorems, as they are usually called) are said to be true if there is a logically valid chain of deductions deriving them from the axioms. Such deductive proofs give a certainty (granted the consistency of the axioms) that is not attainable in the inductive sciences.

In practice induction and deduction are usually both involved in establishing scientific theories. We referred above to Kepler's use of deduction in deriving his theory that Mars moved in an ellipse round the sun. However, he first thought of the ellipse (rather than, say, the parabola or the hyperbola) because the observations of Brahe led Kepler to believe the orbit of Mars was roughly egg-shaped. The egg shape was initially conjectured as a result of induction from astronomical observations.

Competing hypotheses can cover the same data

But here we should notice that when it comes to interpreting the data we have collected, different hypotheses can be constructed to cover that data. We have two illustrations of this.

Illustration from astronomy. Under the role of deduction above we discussed two hypotheses from ancient astronomy that were put forward to explain the motion of the planets. Successive refinements of the epicyclic model appeared to cover the data at the expense of greater and greater complication in that more and more circles were necessary. Kepler's proposal, by contrast, covered the data by the simple device of replacing the complex array of circles by one single ellipse, which simplified the whole business enormously. Now, if we knew nothing of gravity and the deduction of elliptical orbits that can be made from it by means of Newton's laws, how would we choose between the two explanations?

At this point, scientists might well invoke the principle sometimes called 'Occam's razor', after William of Occam. This is the belief that simpler explanations of natural phenomena are more likely to be correct than more complex ones. More precisely, the idea is that if we have two or more competing hypotheses covering the same data, we should choose the one that involves the least number of assumptions or complications. The metaphorical use of the word 'razor' comes from this cutting or shaving down to the smallest possible number of assumptions. Occam's razor has proved very useful but we should observe that it is a philosophical preference, and it is not something that you can prove to be true in every case, so it needs to be used with care.

Illustration from physics. Another illustration of the way in which different hypotheses can account for the same data is given by a common exercise in school physics. We are given a spring, a series of weights and a ruler and asked to plot a graph of the length of the spring against the weight hanging on the end of it. We end up with a series, say, of 10 points on the paper that look as if they might (with a bit of imagination!) lie on a straight line. We take an inductive step and draw a straight line that goes through most of the points

The principle sometimes called 'Occam's razor', after William of Occam . . . is the belief that simpler explanations of natural phenomena are more likely to be correct than more complex ones.

and we claim that there is a linear relationship between the length of spring and the tension it is put under by the weights (Hooke's law). But then we reflect that there is an infinite number of curves that can be drawn through our ten points. Changing the curve would change the relation between spring length and tension. Why not choose one of those other curves in preference to the straight line? That is, in the situation just described, there are many different hypotheses that cover the same set of data. How do you choose between them?

Application of Occam's razor would lead to choosing the most elegant or economical solution—a straight line is simpler than a complicated curve. We could also repeat the experiment with 100 points, 200 points, etc. The results would build up our confidence that the straight line was the correct answer. When we build up evidence in this way, we say that we have cumulative evidence for the validity of our hypothesis.

So far we have been looking at various methods employed by scientists and have seen that none of them yields 100% certainty, except in deductive proofs in mathematics where the certainty is that particular conclusions follow from particular axioms. However, we would emphasise once more that this does not mean that the scientific enterprise is about to collapse! Far from it. What we mean by 'not giving 100% certainty' can be interpreted as saying that there is a small probability that a particular result or theory is false. But that does not mean that we cannot have confidence in the theory.

Indeed there are some situations, as in the litmus-paper test for acid where there has been 100% success in the past. Now whereas this does not formally guarantee 100% success in the future, scientists will say that it is a fact that litmus paper turns red on being dipped in acid. By a 'fact', they mean, as palaeontologist Stephen Jay Gould has delightfully put it, 'confirmed to such a degree that it would be perverse to withhold provisional assent to it'.[3]

On other occasions we are prepared to trust our lives to the findings of science and technology even though we know we do not have 100% certainty. For example, before we travel by train, we know that it is theoretically possible for something to go wrong, maybe for the brakes or signalling to fail and cause the train to crash. But we also know from the statistics of rail travel that the probability of such an event is very small indeed (though it is not zero—trains have from time to time crashed). Since the probability of a crash is so small, most of us who travel by train do so without even thinking about the risk.

On the other hand we must not assume that we can accept all proposed hypotheses arrived at by scientific method as absolute fact without testing them.

---

[3] Gould, 'Evolution as Fact and Theory', 119.

One of the criteria of testing is called falsifiability.

Falsifiability

Karl Popper put the emphasis not on the verifiability of a hypothesis but on its falsifiability. It is unfortunate that Popper's terminology can be a real source of confusion, since the adjective 'falsifiable' does not mean 'will turn out to be false'! The confusion is even worse when one realises, on the other hand, that the verb 'to falsify' means 'to demonstrate that something is false'! The term 'falsifiable' has in fact a technical meaning. A hypothesis is said to be falsifiable if you can think of a logically possible set of observations that would be inconsistent with it.

It is, of course, much easier to falsify a universal statement than to verify it. As an illustration, take one of our earlier examples. The statement 'All swans are white' is, from the very start, falsifiable. One would only have to discover one swan that was black and that would falsify it. And since we know that black swans do exist, the statement has long since been falsified.

However, there can be problems. Most scientific activity is much more complex than dealing with claims like 'All swans are white'!

For example, in the nineteenth century observations of the planet Uranus appeared to indicate that its motion was inconsistent with predictions made on the basis of Newton's laws. Therefore, it appeared to threaten to demonstrate Newton's laws to be false. However, instead of immediately saying that Newton's laws had been falsified, it was suggested by French mathematician Urbain Le Verrier and English astronomer John Couch Adams (unknown to each other) that there might be a hitherto undetected planet in the neighbourhood of Uranus that would account for its apparently anomalous behaviour. As a result another scientist, German astronomer Johann Galle, was prompted to look for a new planet and discovered the planet Neptune.

It would, therefore, have been incorrect to regard the behaviour of Uranus as falsifying Newton's laws. The problem was ignorance

> The term 'falsifiable' has in fact a technical meaning: a hypothesis is said to be falsifiable if you can think of a logically possible set of observations that would be inconsistent with it.

of the initial conditions—there was a planet missing in the configuration being studied. In other words, some of the crucial data was missing. This story demonstrates one of the problems inherent in Popper's approach. When observation does not fit theory, it could be that the theory is false, but it could equally well be that the theory is correct but the data is incomplete or even false, or that some of the auxiliary assumptions are incorrect. How can you judge what is the correct picture?

Most scientists in fact feel that Popper's ideas are far too pessimistic and his methodology too counter-intuitive. Their experience and intuition tell them that their scientific methods in fact enable them to get a better and better understanding of the universe, that they are in this sense getting a tighter grip on reality. One benefit of Popper's approach, however, is its insistence that scientific theories be testable.

Repeatability and abduction

The scientific activity we have been thinking of so far is characterised by *repeatability*. That is, we have considered situations where scientists are looking for universally valid laws that cover repeatable phenomena, laws which, like Newton's laws of motion, may be experimentally tested again and again. Sciences of this sort are often called inductive or nomological sciences (Gk. *nomos* = law) and between them they cover most of science.

However there are major areas of scientific enquiry where repeatability is not possible, notably study of the origin of the universe and the origin and development of life.

Now of course we do not mean to imply that science has nothing to say about phenomena that are non-repeatable. On the contrary, if one is to judge by the amount of literature published, particularly, but not only, at the popular level, the origin of the universe and of life, for example, are among the most interesting subjects by far that science addresses.

But precisely because of the importance of such non-repeatable phenomena, it is vital to see that the way in which they are accessible to science is not the same in general as the way in which repeatable phenomena are. For theories about both kinds of phenomena tend to be presented to the public in the powerful name of science as though they had an equal claim to be accepted. Thus there is a real danger that the public ascribes the same authority and validity to conjectures about non-repeatable events that are not capable of experimental verification as it does to those theories that have been confirmed by repeated experiment.

Physical chemist and philosopher Michael Polanyi points out that the study of how something originates is usually very different from the study of how it operates, although, of course, clues to how something originated may well be found in how it operates. It is one thing to investigate something repeatable in the laboratory, such as dissecting a frog to see how its nervous system functions, but it is an altogether different thing to study something non-repeatable, such as how frogs came to exist in the first place. And, on the large scale, how the universe works is one thing, yet how it came to be may be quite another.

How the universe works is one thing, yet how it came to be may be quite another.

The most striking difference between the study of non-repeatable and repeatable phenomena is that the method of induction is no longer applicable, since we no longer have a sequence of observations or experiments to induce from, nor any repetition in the future to predict about! The principal method that applies to non-repeatable phenomena is *abduction*.

Although this term, introduced by logician Charles Peirce in the nineteenth century, may be unfamiliar, the underlying idea is very familiar. For abduction is what every good detective does in order to clear up a murder mystery! With the murder mystery a certain event has happened. No one doubts that it has happened. The question is: who or what was the cause of it happening? And often in the search for causes of an event that has already happened, abduction is the only method available.

As an example of abductive inference, think of the following:

Data: Ivan's car went over the cliff edge and he was killed.

Inference: If the car brakes had failed, then the car would have gone over the cliff.

Abductive conclusion: There is reason to suppose that the brakes failed.

However, an alternative suggests itself (especially to avid readers of detective stories): if someone had pushed Ivan's car over the cliff, the result would have been the same! It would be fallacious and very foolish to assume that just because we had thought of one explanation of the circumstances, that it was the only one.

The basic idea of abduction is given by the following scheme:

Data: A is observed.

Inference: If B were true then A would follow.

Abductive conclusion: There is reason to suppose B may be true.

Of course, there may well be another hypothesis, C, of which we could say: if C were true A would follow. Indeed, there may be many candidates for C.

The detective in our story has a procedure for considering them one by one. He may first consider the chance hypothesis, B, that the brakes failed. He may then consider the hypothesis C that it was no chance event, but deliberately designed by a murderer who pushed the car over the cliff. Or the detective may consider an even more sophisticated hypothesis, D, combining both chance and design, that someone who wanted to kill Ivan had tampered with the brakes of the car so that they would fail somewhere, and they happened to fail on the clifftop!

Inference to the best explanation. Our detective story illustrates how the process of abduction throws up plausible hypotheses and forces upon us the question as to which of the hypotheses best fits the data. In order to decide that question, the hypotheses are compared for their explanatory power: how much of the data do they cover, does the theory make coherent sense, is it consistent with other areas of our knowledge, etc.?

In order to answer these further questions, deduction will often be used. For example, if B in the detective story is true, then we would expect an investigation of the brakes of the wrecked car to reveal worn or broken parts. If C is true we would deduce that the brakes might well be found in perfect order, whereas if D were the case, we might expect to find marks of deliberate damage to the hydraulic braking system. If we found such marks then D would immediately be regarded as the best of the competing explanations given so far, since it has a greater explanatory power than the others.

Thus, abduction together with the subsequent comparison of competing hypotheses may be regarded as an 'inference to the best explanation'. This is the essence not only of detective and legal work but also of the work of the historian. Both detective and historian have to infer the best possible explanation from the available data after the events in which they are interested have occurred.

For more on the application of abduction in the natural sciences, particularly in cosmology and biology, see the books by John Lennox noted at the end of this Appendix. Here we need to consider a few more of the general issues related to the scientific endeavour.

EXPLAINING EXPLANATIONS

Levels of explanation

Science explains. This, for many people encapsulates the power and the fascination of science. Science enables us to understand what we did not understand before and, by giving us understanding, it gives us power over nature. But what do we mean by saying that 'science explains'?

In informal language we take an explanation of something to be adequate when the person to whom the explanation is given understands plainly what he or she did not understand before. However, we must try to be more precise about what we mean by the process of 'explanation', since it has different aspects that are often confused. An illustration can help us. We have considered a similar idea in relation to roses. Let's now take further examples.

Suppose Aunt Olga has baked a beautiful cake. She displays it to a gathering of the world's top scientists and we ask them for an explanation of the cake. The nutrition scientists will tell us about the number of calories in the cake and its nutritional effect; the biochemists will inform us about the structure of the proteins, fats, etc. in the cake and what it is that causes them to hold together; the chemists will enumerate the elements involved and describe their bonding; the physicists will be able to analyse the cake in terms of fundamental particles; and the mathematicians will offer us a set of beautiful equations to describe the behaviour of those particles. Suppose, then, that these experts have given us an exhaustive description of the cake, each in terms of his or her scientific discipline. Can we say that the cake is now completely explained? We have certainly been given a description of how the cake was made and how its various constituent elements relate to each other. But suppose we now ask the assembled group of experts why the cake was made. We notice the grin on Aunt Olga's face. She knows the answer since, after all, she made the cake! But if she does not reveal the answer by telling us, it is clear that no amount of scientific analysis will give us the answer.

Thus, although science can answer 'how' questions in terms of causes and mechanisms, it cannot answer 'why' questions, questions of purpose and intention—teleological questions, as they are sometimes called (Gk. *telos* = end or goal).

However, it would be nonsensical to suggest that Aunt Olga's answer to the teleological question, that she made the cake for Sam's birthday, say, contradicted the scientific analysis of the cake! No. The two kinds of answer are clearly logically compatible.

And yet exactly the same confusion of categories is evidenced when atheists argue that there is no longer need to bring in God and the supernatural to explain the workings of nature, since we now have a scientific explanation for them. As a result, the general public has come to think that belief in a creator belongs to a primitive and unsophisticated stage of human thinking and has been rendered both unnecessary and impossible by science.

> Although science can answer 'how' questions in terms of causes and mechanisms, it cannot answer 'why' questions, questions of purpose and intention.

But there is an obvious fallacy here. Think of a Ford motor car. It is conceivable that a primitive person who was seeing one for the first time and who did not understand the principles of an internal combustion engine, might imagine that there was a god (Mr Ford) inside the engine, making it go. He might further imagine that when the engine ran sweetly that was because Mr Ford inside the engine liked him, and when it refused to go that was because Mr Ford did not like him. Of course, if eventually this primitive person became civilised, learned engineering, and took the engine to pieces, he would discover that there was no Mr Ford inside the engine, and that he did not need to introduce Mr Ford as an explanation for the working of the engine.

His grasp of the impersonal principles of internal combustion would be altogether enough to explain how the engine worked. So far, so good. But if he then decided that his understanding of the principles of the internal combustion engine made it impossible to believe in the existence of a Mr Ford who designed the engine, this would be patently false!

FIGURE Ap.2. Model T Ford Motor Car.
Introducing the world's first moving assembly line in 1913, Ford Motor Company built more than 15 million Model Ts from 1908 until 1927.

Reproduced with permission of ©iStock/Peter Mah.

It is likewise a confusion of categories to suppose that our understanding of the impersonal principles according to which the universe works makes it either unnecessary or impossible to believe in the existence of a personal creator who designed, made and upholds the great engine that is the universe. In other words, we should not confuse the mechanisms by which the universe works with its Cause. Every one of us knows how to distinguish between the consciously willed movement of an arm for a purpose and an involuntary spasmodic movement of an arm induced by accidental contact with an electric current.

Michael Poole, Visiting Research Fellow, Science and Religion, at King's College London, in his published debate on science and religion with Richard Dawkins, puts it this way:

> There is no logical conflict between reason-giving explanations which concern mechanisms, and reason-giving explanations which concern the plans and purposes of an agent, human or divine. This is a logical point, not a matter of whether one does or does not happen to believe in God oneself.[4]

---

[4]   Poole, 'Critique of Aspects of the Philosophy and Theology of Richard Dawkins', 49.

One of the authors, in a debate with Richard Dawkins, noted how his opponent was confusing the categories of mechanism and agency:

When Isaac Newton, for example, discovered his law of gravity and wrote down the equations of motion, he didn't say, 'Marvellous, I now understand it. I've got a mechanism therefore I don't need God.' In fact it was the exact opposite. It was because he understood the complexity of sophistication of the mathematical description of the universe that his praise for God was increased. And I would like to suggest, Richard, that somewhere down in this you're making a category mistake, because you're confusing mechanism with agency. We have a mechanism that does XYZ, therefore there's no need for an agent. I would suggest that the sophistication of the mechanism, and science rejoices in finding such mechanisms, is evidence for the sheer wonder of the creative genius of God.[5]

In spite of the clarity of the logic expressed in these counterpoints, a famous statement made by the French mathematician Laplace is constantly misappropriated to support atheism. On being asked by Napoleon where God fitted in to his mathematical work, Laplace replied: 'Sir, I have no need of that hypothesis.' Of course, God did not appear in Laplace's mathematical description of how things work, just as Mr Ford would not appear in a scientific description of the laws of internal combustion. But what does that prove? Such an argument can no more be used to prove that God does not exist than it can be used to prove that Mr Ford does not exist.

To sum up, then, it is important to be aware of the danger of confusing different levels of explanation and of thinking that one level of explanation tells the whole story.

This leads us at once to consider the related question of reductionism.

---

[5] Lennox's response to Dawkins's first thesis 'Faith is blind; science is evidence-based', 'The God Delusion Debate', hosted by Fixed Point Foundation, University of Alabama at Birmingham, filmed and broadcast live 3 October 2007, http://fixed-point.org/index.php/video/35-full-length/164-the-dawkins-lennox-debate. Transcript provided courtesy of ProTorah, http://www.protorah.com/god-delusion-debate-dawkins-lennox-transcript/.

Reductionism

In order to study something, especially if it is complex, scientists often split it up into separate parts or aspects and thus 'reduce' it to simpler components that are individually easier to investigate. This kind of reductionism, often called methodological or structural reductionism, is part of the normal process of science and has proved very useful. It is, however, very important to bear in mind that there may well be, and usually is, more to a given whole than simply what we obtain by adding up all that we have learned from the parts. Studying all the parts of a watch separately will never enable you to grasp how the complete watch works as an integrated whole.

Besides methodological reductionism there are two further types of reductionism, epistemological and ontological. *Epistemological reductionism* is the view that higher level sciences can be explained without remainder by the sciences at a lower level. That is, chemistry is explained by physics; biochemistry by chemistry; biology by biochemistry; psychology by biology; sociology by brain science; and theology by sociology. As Francis Crick puts it: 'The ultimate aim of the modern development in biology is in fact to explain all biology in terms of physics and chemistry.'[6] The former Charles Simonyi Professor of the Public Understanding of Science at Oxford, Richard Dawkins, holds the same view: 'My task is to explain elephants, and the world of complex things, in terms of the simple things that physicists either understand, or are working on.'[7] The ultimate goal of reductionism is to reduce all human behaviour, our likes and dislikes, the entire mental landscape of our lives, to physics.

> The ultimate goal of reductionism is to reduce all human behaviour, our likes and dislikes, the entire mental landscape of our lives, to physics.

However, both the viability and the plausibility of this programme are open to serious question. The outstanding Russian psychologist Leo Vygotsky (1896–1934) was critical of certain aspects of this reductionist philosophy as applied to psychology. He pointed out that such

---

6   Crick, *Of Molecules and Men*, 10.
7   Dawkins, *Blind Watchmaker*, 15.

reductionism often conflicts with the goal of preserving all the basic features of a phenomenon or event that one wishes to explain. For example, one can reduce water (H_2O) into H and O. However, hydrogen burns and oxygen is necessary for burning, whereas water has neither of these properties, but has many others that are not possessed by either hydrogen or oxygen. Thus, Vygotsky's view was that reductionism can only be done up to certain limits. Karl Popper says: 'There is almost always an unresolved residue left by even the most successful attempts at reduction.'[8]

Furthermore, Michael Polanyi argues the intrinsic implausibility of expecting epistemological reductionism to work in every circumstance.[9] Think of the various levels of process involved in building an office building with bricks. First of all there is the process of extracting the raw materials out of which the bricks have to be made. Then there are the successively higher levels of making the bricks, they do not make themselves; bricklaying, the bricks do not self-assemble; designing the building, it does not design itself; and planning the town in which the building is to be built, it does not organise itself. Each level has its own rules. The laws of physics and chemistry govern the raw material of the bricks; technology prescribes the art of brick making; architecture teaches the builders, and the architects are controlled by the town planners. Each level is controlled by the level above, but the reverse is not true. The laws of a higher level cannot be derived from the laws of a lower level (although, of course what can be done at a higher level will depend on the lower levels: for example, if the bricks are not strong there will be a limit on the height of a building that can be safely built with them).

Consider the page you are reading just now. It consists of paper imprinted with ink or, in the case of an electronic version, text rendered digitally. It is obvious that the physics and chemistry of ink and paper can never, even in principle, tell you anything about the significance of the shapes of the letters on the page. And this is nothing to do with the fact that physics and chemistry are not yet sufficiently advanced to deal with this question. Even if we allow these sciences another 1,000 years of development, we can see that it will make no difference, because

---

[8] Popper, 'Scientific Reduction.'
[9] Polanyi, *Tacit Dimension*.

the shapes of those letters demand a totally new and higher level of explanation than that of which physics and chemistry are capable. In fact, explanation can only be given in terms of the concepts of language and authorship—the communication of a message by a person. The ink and paper are carriers of the message, but the message certainly does not emerge automatically from them. Furthermore, when it comes to language itself, there is again a sequence of levels—you cannot derive a vocabulary from phonetics, or the grammar of a language from its vocabulary, etc.

As is well known, the genetic material DNA carries information. We shall describe this later on in some detail, but the basic idea is simply this. DNA, a substance found in every living cell, can be looked at as a long tape on which there is a string of letters written in a four-letter chemical language. The sequence of letters contains coded instructions (information) that the cell uses to make proteins. Physical biochemist and theologian Arthur Peacocke writes: 'In no way can the concept of "information", the concept of conveying a message, be articulated in terms of the concepts of physics and chemistry, even though the latter can be shown to explain how the molecular machinery (DNA, RNA and protein) operates to carry information.'[10]

In each of the situations we have described above, we have a series of levels, each one higher than the previous one. What happens on a higher level is not completely derivable from what happens on the level beneath it, but requires another level of explanation.

In this kind of situation it is sometimes said that the higher level phenomena 'emerge' from the lower level. Unfortunately, however, the word 'emerge' is easily misunderstood to mean that the higher level properties emerge automatically from the lower level properties. This is clearly false in general, as we showed by considering brick making and writing on paper. Yet notwithstanding the fact that both writing on paper and DNA have in common the fact that they encode a 'message', those scientists committed to materialistic philosophy insist that the information carrying properties of DNA must have emerged automatically out of mindless matter. For if, as materialism insists, matter and energy are all that there is, then it logically follows that they must

---

[10] Peacocke, *Experiment of Life*, 54.

possess the inherent potential to organise themselves in such a way that eventually all the complex molecules necessary for life, including DNA, will emerge.[11]

There is a third type of reductionism, called *ontological reductionism*, which is frequently encountered in statements like the following: The universe is nothing but a collection of atoms in motion, human beings are 'machines for propagating DNA, and the propagation of DNA is a self-sustaining process. It is every living object's sole reason for living'.[12]

Words such as 'nothing but', 'sole' or 'simply' are the telltale sign of (ontological) reductionist thinking. If we remove these words we are usually left with something unobjectionable. The universe certainly is a collection of atoms and human beings do propagate DNA. The question is, is there nothing more to it than that? Are we going to say with Francis Crick, who won the Nobel Prize jointly with James D. Watson for his discovery of the double helix structure of DNA: ' "You", your joys and your sorrows, your memories and your ambitions, your sense of personal identity and free will, are in fact no more than the behaviour of a vast assembly of nerve cells and their associated molecules'?[13]

What shall we say of human love and fear, of concepts like beauty and truth? Are they meaningless?

Ontological reductionism, carried to its logical conclusion, would ask us to believe that a Rembrandt painting is nothing but molecules of paint scattered on canvas. Physicist and theologian John Polkinghorne's reaction is clear:

There is more to the world than physics can ever express.

One of the fundamental experiences of the scientific life is that of wonder at the beautiful structure of the world. It is the pay-off for all the weary hours of labour involved in the pursuit of research. Yet in the world described by science where would that wonder find its lodging? Or our experiences of beauty? Of moral obligation? Of the presence of God? These seem to me to be quite

---

[11] Whether matter and energy do have this capacity is another matter that is discussed in the books noted at the end of this appendix.

[12] Dawkins, *Growing Up in the Universe* (study guide), 21.

[13] Crick, *Astonishing Hypothesis*, 3.

as fundamental as anything we could measure in the laboratory. A worldview that does not take them adequately into account is woefully incomplete.[14]

The most devastating criticism of ontological reductionism is that it is self-destructive. Polkinghorne describes its programme as ultimately suicidal:

> For, not only does it relegate our experiences of beauty, moral obligation, and religious encounter to the epiphenomenal scrapheap. It also destroys rationality. Thought is replaced by electrochemical neural events. Two such events cannot confront each other in rational discourse. They are neither right nor wrong. They simply happen. . . . The very assertions of the reductionist himself are nothing but blips in the neural network of his brain. The world of rational discourse dissolves into the absurd chatter of firing synapses. Quite frankly, that cannot be right and none of us beliaeves it to be so.[15]

BASIC OPERATIONAL PRESUPPOSITIONS

So far we have been concentrating on the scientific method and have seen that this is a much more complex (and, for that reason, a much more interesting) topic than may first appear. As promised earlier, we must now consider the implications of the fact that scientists, being human like the rest of us, do not come to any situation with their mind completely clear of preconceived ideas. The widespread idea that any scientist, if only he or she tries to be impartial, can be a completely dispassionate observer in any but the most trivial of situations, is a fallacy, as has been pointed out repeatedly by philosophers of science and by scientists themselves. At the very least scientists must already

The widespread idea that any scientist, if only he or she tries to be impartial, can be a completely dispassionate observer in any but the most trivial of situations, is a fallacy.

---

[14] Polkinghorne, *One World*, 72–3.
[15] Polkinghorne, *One World*, 92–3.

have formed some idea or theory about the nature of what they are about to study.

Observation is dependent on theory

It is simply not possible to make observations and do experiments without any presuppositions. Consider, for example, the fact that science, by its very nature, has to be selective. It would clearly be impossible to take every aspect of any given object of study into account. Scientists must therefore choose what variables are likely to be important and what are not. For example, physicists do not think of taking into account the colour of billiard balls when they are conducting a laboratory investigation of the application of Newton's laws to motion: but the shape of the balls is very important—cubical balls would not be much use! In making such choices, scientists are inevitably guided by already formed ideas and theories about what the important factors are likely to be. The problem is that such ideas may sometimes be wrong and cause scientists to miss vital aspects of a problem to such an extent that they draw false conclusions. A famous story about the physicist Heinrich Hertz illustrates this.

Maxwell's electromagnetic theory predicted that radio and light waves would be propagated with the same velocity. Hertz designed an experiment to check this and found that the velocities were different. His mistake, only discovered after his death, was that he did not think that the shape of his laboratory could have any influence on the results of his experiment. Unfortunately for him, it did. Radio waves were reflected from the walls and distorted his results.

The validity of his observations depended on the (preconceived) theory that the shape of the laboratory was irrelevant to his experiment. The fact that this preconception was false invalidated his conclusions.

This story also points up another difficulty. How does one decide in this kind of situation whether it is the theory or the experiment that is at fault, whether one should trust the results of the experiment and abandon the theory and look for a better one, or whether one should keep on having faith in the theory and try to discover what was wrong with the experiment? There is no easy answer to this question. A great deal will depend on the experience and judgment of the scientists involved, and, inevitably, mistakes can and will be made.

Knowledge cannot be gained without making certain assumptions to start with

Scientists not only inevitably have preconceived ideas about particular situations, as illustrated by the story about Hertz, but their science is done within a framework of general assumptions about science as such. World-famous Harvard geneticist Richard Lewontin writes: 'Scientists, like other intellectuals, come to their work with a world view, a set of preconceptions that provides the framework for their analysis of the world.'[16]

And those preconceptions can significantly affect scientists' research methods as well as their results and interpretations of those results, as we shall see.

We would emphasise, however, that the fact that scientists have presuppositions is not to be deprecated. That would, in fact be a nonsensical attitude to adopt. For the voice of logic reminds us that we cannot get to know anything if we are not prepared to presuppose something. Let's unpack this idea by thinking about a common attitude. 'I am not prepared to take anything for granted', says someone, 'I will only accept something if you prove it to me.' Sounds reasonable—but it isn't. For if this is your view then you will never accept or know anything! For suppose I want you to accept some proposition A. You will only accept it if I prove it to you. But I shall have to prove it to you on the basis of some other proposition B. You will only accept B if I prove it to you. I shall have to prove B to you on the basis of C. And so it will go on forever in what is called an infinite regress—that is, if you insist on taking nothing for granted in the first place!

We must all start somewhere with things we take as self-evident, basic assumptions that are not proved on the basis of something else. They are often called *axioms*.[17] Whatever axioms we adopt, we then proceed to try to make sense of the world by building on those

---

[16] Lewontin, *Dialectical Biologist*, 267.

[17] It should be borne in mind, however, that the axioms which appear in various branches of pure mathematics, for example, the theory of numbers or the theory of groups, do not appear out of nowhere. They usually arise from the attempt to encapsulate and formalise years, sometimes centuries, of mathematical research, into a so-called 'axiomatic system'.

axioms. This is true, not only at the worldview level but also in all of our individual disciplines. We retain those axioms that prove useful in the sense that they lead to theories which show a better 'fit' with nature and experience, and we abandon or modify those which do not fit so well. One thing is absolutely clear: none of us can avoid starting with assumptions.

Gaining knowledge involves trusting our senses and other people

There are essentially two sources from which we accumulate knowledge:

1. directly by our own 'hands-on' experience, for example, by accidentally putting our finger in boiling water, we learn that boiling water scalds;
2. we learn all kinds of things from sources external to ourselves, for example, teachers, books, parents, the media, etc.

In doing so we all constantly exercise faith. We intuitively trust our senses, even though we know they deceive us on times. For example, in extremely cold weather, if we put our hand on a metal handrail outside, the rail may feel hot to our touch.

We have faith, too, in our minds to interpret our senses, though here again we know that our minds can be deceived.

We also normally believe what other people tell us—teachers, parents, friends, etc. Sometimes we check what we learn from them because, without insulting them, we realise that even friends can be mistaken, and other people may set out to deceive us. However, much more often than not, we accept things on authority—if only because no one has time to check everything! In technical matters we trust our textbooks. We have faith in what (other) scientists have done. And it is, of course, reasonable so to do, though those experts themselves would teach us to be critical and not just to accept everything on their say-so. They would remind us also that the fact that a statement appears in print in a book, does not make it automatically true!

Gaining scientific knowledge involves belief in the rational intelligibility of the universe

We all take so much for granted the fact that we can use human reason as a probe to investigate the universe that we can fail to see that this is really something to be wondered at. For once we begin to think about the intelligibility of the universe, our minds demand an explanation. But where can we find one? Science cannot give it to us, for the very simple reason that science has to assume the rational intelligibility of the universe in order to get started. Einstein himself, in the same article we quoted earlier, makes this very clear in saying that the scientist's belief in the rational intelligibility of the universe goes beyond science and is in its very nature essentially religious:

> Science can only be created by those who are thoroughly imbued with the aspiration toward truth and understanding. This source of feeling, however, springs from the sphere of religion. To this there also belongs the faith in the possibility that the regulations valid for the world of existence are rational, that is, comprehensible to reason. I cannot conceive of a genuine scientist without that profound faith.[18]

Einstein saw no reason to be embarrassed by the fact that science involves at its root belief in something that science itself cannot justify.

Allied to belief in the rational intelligibility of the universe is the belief that patterns and law-like behaviour are to be expected in nature. The Greeks expressed this by using the word *cosmos* which means 'ordered'. It is this underlying expectation of order that lies behind the confidence with which scientists use the inductive method. Scientists speak of their belief in the uniformity of nature—the idea that the order in nature and the laws that describe it are valid at all times and in all parts of the universe.

Many theists from the Jewish, Islamic or Christian tradition would want to modify this concept of the uniformity of nature by adding their conviction that God the Creator has built regularities

---

[18] Einstein, *Out of My Later Years*, 26.

FIGURE Ap.3. Milky Way Galaxy.

The Milky Way galaxy is visible from earth on clear nights away from urban areas. Appearing as a cloud in the night sky, our galaxy's spiral bands of dust and glowing nebulae consist of billions of stars as seen from the inside.

into the working of the universe so that in general we can speak of uniformity—the norms to which nature normally operates. But because God is the Creator, he is not a prisoner of those regularities but can vary them by causing things to happen that do not fit into the regular pattern.

Here, again, commitment to the uniformity of nature is a matter of belief. Science cannot prove to us that nature is uniform, since we must assume the uniformity of nature in order to do science. Otherwise we would have no confidence that, if we repeat an experiment under the same conditions as it was done before, we shall get the same result. Were it so, our school textbooks would be useless. But surely, we might say, the uniformity of nature is highly probable since assuming it has led to such stunning scientific advance. However, as C. S. Lewis has observed: 'Can we say that Uniformity is at any rate very probable? Unfortunately not. We have just seen that all probabilities depend on *it*. Unless Nature is uniform, nothing is either probable or improbable.'[19]

---

[19] Lewis, *Miracles*, 163.

Operating within the reigning paradigms

Thomas Kuhn in his famous book *The Structure of Scientific Revolutions* (1962) pictured science as preceding through the following stages: pre-science, normal science, crisis revolution, new normal science, new crisis, and so on. Pre-science is the diverse and disorganised activity characterised by much disagreement that precedes the emergence of a new science that gradually becomes structured when a scientific community adheres to a paradigm. The paradigm is a web of assumptions and theories that are more or less agreed upon and are like the steelwork around which the scientific edifice is erected. Well-known examples are the paradigms of Copernican astronomy, Newtonian mechanics and evolutionary biology.

Normal science is then practised within the paradigm. It sets the standards for legitimate research. The normal scientist uses the paradigm to probe nature. He or she does not (often) look critically at the paradigm itself, because it commands so much agreement, much as we look down the light of a torch to illuminate an object, rather than look critically at the light of the torch itself. For this reason the paradigm will be very resistant to attempts to demonstrate that it is false. When anomalies, difficulties and apparent falsifications turn up, the normal scientists will hope to be able to accommodate them preferably within the paradigm or by making fine adjustments to the paradigm. However, if the difficulties can no longer be resolved and keep on piling up, a crisis situation develops, which leads to a scientific revolution involving the emergence of a new paradigm that then gains the ground to such an extent that the older paradigm is eventually completely abandoned. The essence of such a paradigm shift is the replacing of an old paradigm by a new one, not the refining of the old one by the new. The best known example of a major paradigm shift is the transition from Aristotelian geocentric (earth-centred) astronomy to Copernican heliocentric (sun-centred) astronomy in the sixteenth century.

Although Kuhn's work is open to criticism at various points, he has certainly made scientists aware of a number of issues that are important for our understanding of how science works:

1. the central role that metaphysical ideas play in the development of scientific theories;
2. the high resistance that paradigms show to attempts to prove them false;
3. the fact that science is subject to human frailty.

The second of these points has both a positive and a negative outworking. It means that a good paradigm will not be overturned automatically by the first experimental result or observation that appears to speak against it. On the other hand, it means that a paradigm which eventually proves to be inadequate or false, may take a long time to die and impede scientific progress by constraining scientists within its mesh and not giving them the freedom they need to explore radically new ideas that would yield real scientific advance.

It is important to realise that paradigms themselves are often influenced at a very deep level by worldview considerations. We saw earlier that there are essentially two fundamental worldviews, the materialistic and the theistic. It seems to be the case in science that there is sometimes a tacit understanding that only paradigms which are based on materialism are admissible as scientific. Richard Dawkins, for example, says, 'the kind of explanation we come up with must not contradict the laws of physics. Indeed it will make use of the laws of physics, and nothing more than the laws of physics.'[20] It is the words 'nothing more than' that show that Dawkins is only prepared to accept reductionist, materialistic explanations.

Further reading

Books by John Lennox:

Can Science Explain Everything? (Good Book Company, 2019)

God and Stephen Hawking: Whose Design Is It Anyway? (Lion, 2011)

God's Undertaker: Has Science Buried God? (Lion, 2009)

Gunning for God: A Critique of the New Atheism (Lion, 2011)

Miracles: Is Belief in the Supernatural Irrational? VeriTalks Vol. 2. (The Veritas Forum, 2013)

Seven Days That Divide the World (Zondervan, 2011)

---

[20] Dawkins, *Blind Watchmaker*, 24.

SERIES BIBLIOGRAPHY

See also reading lists given on p. 203.

BOOKS

A

Abbott, Edwin. *Flatland: A Romance of Many Dimensions*. London, 1884. Repr. Oxford: Oxford University Press, 2006.

Ambrose, E. J. *The Nature and Origin of the Biological World*. New York: Halsted Press, 1982.

Ammon, Otto. *Die Gesellschaftsordnung und ihre natürlichen Grundlagen*. Jena: Gustav Fisher, 1895.

Anderson, J. N. D. (Norman). *Christianity: The Witness of History*. London: Tyndale Press, 1969.

Anderson, J. N. D. (Norman). *The Evidence for the Resurrection*. 1950. Leicester: InterVarsity Press, 1990.

Anderson, J. N. D. (Norman). *Islam in the Modern World*. Leicester: Apollos, 1990.

Andreyev, G. L. *What Kind of Morality Does Religion Teach?* Moscow: 'Znaniye', 1959.

Aristotle. *Metaphysics*. Tr. W. D. Ross, *Aristotle's Metaphysics: A Revised Text with Introduction and Commentary*. Vol. 2. Oxford: Clarendon Press, 1924.

Aristotle. *Nicomachean Ethics*. Tr. W. D. Ross. Oxford: Clarendon Press, 1925. Repr. Kitchener, Ont.: Batoche Books, 1999. Also tr. David Ross. Oxford: Oxford University Press, 1980.

Arnold, Thomas. *Christian Life, Its Hopes, Its Fears, and Its Close: Sermons preached mostly in the chapel of Rugby School, 1841–1842*. 1842. New edn, London: Longmans, 1878.

Ashman, Keith M. and Philip S. Baringer, eds. *After the Science Wars*. London: Routledge, 2001.

Atkins, Peter. *Creation Revisited*. Harmondsworth: Penguin, 1994.

Augustine of Hippo. *Confessions*. AD 397–400. Tr. Henry Chadwick, *The Confessions*. Oxford, 1991. Repr. Oxford World's Classics. Oxford: Oxford University Press, 2008.

Avise, John C. *The Genetic Gods, Evolution and Belief in Human Affairs*. Cambridge, Mass.: Harvard University Press, 1998.

Ayer, A. J., ed. *The Humanist Outlook*. London: Pemberton, 1968.

B

Bacon, Francis. *Advancement of Learning*. 1605. Ed. G. W. Kitchin, 1915. Repr. London: Dent, 1930. Online at http://archive.org/details/ advancementlearn00bacouoft (facsimile of 1915 edn).

Bādarāyana, Śankarācārya and George Thibaut. *The Vedānta Sūtras of Bādarāyana*. Vol. 34 of *Sacred books of the East*. Oxford: Clarendon Press, 1890.

Baier, Kurt. *The Moral Point of View: A Rational Basis of Ethics*. Ithaca, N.Y.: Cornell University Press, 1958.

Behe, Michael J. *Darwin's Black Box: The Biochemical Challenge to Evolution*. 1988. 10th ann. edn with new Afterword, New York: Simon & Schuster, 2006.

Bentham, Jeremy. *An Introduction to the Principles of Morals and Legislation*. 1780, 1789. Dover Philosophical Classics. Repr. of Bentham's 1823 rev. edn, Mineola, N.Y.: Dover Publications, 2007.

Berdyaev, N. A. *The Beginning and The End*. Tr. R. M. French. London: Geoffrey Bles, 1952.

Berlinski, David. *The Deniable Darwin and Other Essays*. Seattle, Wash.: Discovery Institute, 2009.

Bickerton, Derek. *Language and Species*. 1990. Repr. Chicago: University of Chicago Press, 1992.

Biddiss, M. D. *Father of Racist Ideology: The Social and Political Thought of Count Gobineau*. New York: Weybright & Talley, 1970.

Bouquet, A. C. *Comparative Religion*. Harmondsworth: Penguin (Pelican), 1962.

Breck, John. *The Sacred Gift of Life: Orthodox Christianity and Bioethics*. Crestwood, N.Y.: St. Vladimir's Seminary Press, 1998.

Bronowski, Jacob. *The Identity of Man*. Harmondsworth: Penguin, 1967.

Brow, Robert. *Religion, Origins and Ideas*. London: Tyndale Press, 1966.

Bruce, F. F. *1 and 2 Corinthians*. New Century Bible Commentary. London: Oliphants, 1971.

Bruce, F. F. *The New Testament Documents: Are They Reliable?* 1943. 6th edn, Nottingham: Inter-Varsity Press, 2000.

Butterfield, Herbert. *Christianity and History*. London: Bell, 1949. Repr. London: Fontana, 1958.

C

Cairns-Smith, A. G. *The Life Puzzle*. Edinburgh: Oliver & Boyd, 1971.

Caputo, John D., ed. *Deconstruction in a Nutshell: A Conversation with Jacques Derrida*. Perspectives in Continental Philosophy No. 1. 1997. Repr. New York: Fordham University Press, 2004.

Cary, M. and T. J. Haarhoff. *Life and Thought in the Greek and Roman World*. 5th edn, London: Methuen, 1951.

Chalmers, David J. *The Conscious Mind: In Search of a Fundamental Theory*. Oxford: Oxford University Press, 1996.

Chamberlain, Paul. *Can We Be Good Without God?: A Conversation about Truth, Morality, Culture and a Few Other Things That Matter.* Downers Grove, Ill.: InterVarsity Press, 1996.

Chomsky, Noam. *Knowledge of Language: Its Nature, Origin and Use.* New York: Praeger, 1986.

Chomsky, Noam. *Language and Mind.* 1972. 3rd edn, Cambridge: Cambridge University Press, 2006.

Chomsky, Noam. *Syntactic Structures.* The Hague: Mouton, 1957.

Cicero, Marcus Tullius. *Cicero, Selected Political Speeches.* Tr. Michael Grant. Harmondsworth: Penguin Books, 1969.

Cicero, Marcus Tullius. *De Natura Deorum.* Tr. H. Rackham, Loeb Classical Library, No. 268. Cambridge, Mass.: Harvard University Press, 1933.

Cicero, Marcus Tullius. *The Nature of the Gods.* Tr. H. C. P. McGregor. London: Penguin, 1972.

Cicero, Marcus Tullius. *Pro Rabirio.*

Clement of Alexandria. *Stromata* [or, Miscellanies]. In Kirk, G. S., J. E. Raven and M. Schofield. *The Presocratic Philosophers: A Critical History with a Selection of Texts.* 1957. Rev. edn, Cambridge: Cambridge University Press, 1983. Online at http://www.ccel.org/ccel/schaff/anf02.vi.iv.html, accessed 29 Sept. 2015.

Cornford, F. M. *Before and After Socrates.* 1932. Repr. Cambridge: Cambridge University Press, 1999. doi: 10.1017/CBO9780511570308, accessed 29 Sept. 2015.

Craig, Edward, gen. ed. *Concise Routledge Encyclopaedia of Philosophy.* London: Routledge, 2000.

Craig, William Lane. *Reasonable Faith: Christian Truth and Apologetics.* 1994. 3rd edn, Wheaton, Ill.: Crossway, 2008.

Crane, Stephen. *War Is Kind.* New York: Frederick A. Stokes, 1899. Online at http://www.gutenberg.org/ebooks/9870, accessed 11 Sept. 2015.

Cranfield, C. E. B. *A Critical and Exegetical Commentary on the Epistle to the Romans.* Vol. 1. The International Critical Commentary. Edinburgh: T&T Clark, 1975.

Crick, Francis. *The Astonishing Hypothesis: The Scientific Search for the Soul.* New York: Scribner, 1994.

Crick, Francis. *Life Itself: Its Origin and Nature.* New York: Simon & Schuster, 1981.

Crick, Francis. *Of Molecules and Men.* 1966 Jessie and John Danz Lectures. Seattle, Wash.: University of Washington Press, 1966.

Cudakov. A. *Komsomol'skaja Pravda* (11 Oct. 1988).

Culler, Jonathan. *On Deconstruction: Theory and Criticism after Structuralism.* 1982. 25th ann. edn, Ithaca, N.Y.: Cornell University Press, 2007.

D

Darwin, Charles. *The Descent of Man, and Selection in Relation to Sex.* 1871. 2nd edn, New York: A. L. Burt, 1874. Ed. James Moore and Adrian Desmond, Penguin Classics, London: Penguin Books, 2004.

Darwin, Charles. *On the Origin of Species*. 1859. Repr. World's Classics Edition, Oxford: Oxford University Press, 2008. Also cited is the 6th edn (1872) reprinted by New York University Press, 1988. Citations to one or the other edition are indicated as such.

Darwin, Francis. *The Life and Letters of Charles Darwin*. London: John Murray, 1887. doi: 10.5962/bhl.title.1416, accessed 29 June 2015.

Davies, Paul. *The Cosmic Blueprint: New Discoveries in Nature's Creative Ability to Order the Universe*. 1988. Repr. West Conshohocken, Pa.: Templeton Foundation Press, 2004.

Davies, Paul. *The Fifth Miracle: The Search for the Origin and Meaning of Life*. 1999. Repr. New York: Touchstone, 2000.

Davies, Paul. *God and the New Physics*. London: J. M. Dent, 1983. Repr. London: Penguin Books, 1990.

Davies, Paul. *The Mind of God: Science and the Search for Ultimate Meaning*. 1992. Repr. London: Simon & Schuster, 2005.

Davies, Paul and John Gribbin. *The Matter Myth: Dramatic Discoveries that Challenge Our Understanding of Physical Reality*. London, 1991. Repr. London: Simon & Schuster, 2007.

Davis, Percival and Dean H. Kenyon. *Of Pandas and People: The Central Question of Biological Origins*. 1989. 2nd edn, Dallas, Tex.: Haughton Publishing, 1993.

Dawkins, Richard. *The Blind Watchmaker*. 1986. Rev. edn, 2006. Repr. London: Penguin, 2013.

Dawkins, Richard. *Climbing Mount Improbable*. New York: Norton, 1996.

Dawkins, Richard. *Growing Up in the Universe*. The Royal Institution Christmas Lectures for Children, 1991. Five one-hour episodes directed by Stuart McDonald for the BBC. 2-Disc DVD set released 20 April 2007 by the Richard Dawkins Foundation. Available on the Ri Channel, http://www.rigb.org/christmas-lectures/watch/1991/growing-up-in-the-universe. Study Guide with the same title. London: BBC Education, 1991.

Dawkins, Richard. *River Out of Eden: A Darwinian View of Life*. 1995. Repr. London: Phoenix, 2004.

Dawkins, Richard. *The Selfish Gene*. 1976. Repr. 30th ann. edn, Oxford: Oxford University Press, 2006.

Dawkins, Richard. *Unweaving the Rainbow: Science, Delusion and the Appetite for Wonder*. 1998. Repr. London: Penguin Books, 2006.

Dawkins, Richard and John Lennox. 'The God Delusion Debate', hosted by Fixed Point Foundation, University of Alabama at Birmingham, filmed and broadcast live 3 October 2007, online at http://fixed-point.org/video/richard-dawkins-vs-john-lennox-the-god-delusion-debate/. Transcript provided courtesy of ProTorah.com, http://www.protorah.com/god-delusion-debate-dawkins-lennox-transcript/.

Deacon, Terrence. *The Symbolic Species: The Co-Evolution of Language and the Human Brain*. London: Allen Lane, 1997.

Dembski, William A. *Being as Communion: A Metaphysics of Information*. Ashgate Science and Religion. Farnham, Surrey: Ashgate, 2014.

Dembski, William A. *The Design Inference: Eliminating Chance through Small Probabilities*. Cambridge Studies in Probability, Induction and Decision Theory. Cambridge: Cambridge University Press, 1998.

Dembski, William A., ed. *Uncommon Dissent: Intellectuals Who Find Darwinism Unconvincing*. Wilmington, Del.: Intercollegiate Studies Institute, 2004.

Dennett, Daniel. *Darwin's Dangerous Idea: Evolution and the Meanings of Life*. 1995; London: Penguin, 1996.

Denton, Michael. *Evolution: A Theory in Crisis*. 1986. 3rd rev. edn, Bethesda, Md.: Adler & Adler, 1986.

Derrida, Jacques. *Of Grammatology*. 1967 (French). Tr. G. C. Spivak, 1974. Repr. Baltimore, Md.: Johns Hopkins University Press, 1997.

Derrida, Jacques. *Positions*. 1972 (French). Tr. and ed. Alan Bass, 1981. 2nd edn 2002. Repr. London: Continuum, 2010.

Derrida, Jacques. *Writing and Difference*. 1967 (French). Tr. Alan Bass, Chicago, 1978. Repr. London: Routledge Classics, 2001.

Descartes, René. *Discourse on the Method of Rightly Conducting Reason and Reaching the Truth in the Sciences*. 1637. Online at https://www.gutenberg.org/files/59/59-h/59-h.htm, accessed 11 Sept. 2015.

Descartes, René. *Meditations on First Philosophy*. Paris, 1641.

Deutsch, David. *The Fabric of Reality*. London: Penguin, 1997.

Dewey, John. *A Common Faith*. New Haven: Yale University Press, 1934.

Dostoevsky, F. *The Collected Works of Dostoevsky*. Tr. Rodion Raskolnikoff [German]. Munich: Piper, 1866.

Dostoevsky, Fyodor. *The Karamazov Brothers*. 1880 (Russian). Tr. and ed. David McDuff, Penguin Classics, 1993. Rev. edn, London: Penguin Books, 2003.

E

Eastwood, C. Cyril. *Life and Thought in the Ancient World*. Derby: Peter Smith, 1964.

Easwaran, Eknath. *The Bhagavad Gita*. 1985. Berkeley, Calif.: Nilgiri Press, 2007.

Easwaran, Eknath. *The Upanishads*. 1987. Berkeley, Calif.: Nilgiri Press, 2007.

Eccles, John C. *Evolution of the Brain, Creation of the Self*. 1989. Repr. London: Routledge, 2005.

Einstein, A. *Letters to Solovine: 1906–1955*. New York: Philosophical Library, 1987.

Einstein, A. *Out of My Later Years: The Scientist, Philosopher, and Man Portrayed Through His Own Words*. 1956. Secaucus, N.J.: Carol Publishing, 1995.

Eldredge, Niles. *Reinventing Darwin: The Great Debate at the High Table of Evolutionary Theory*. New York: Wiley, 1995.

Eldredge, Niles. *Time Frames: The Evolution of Punctuated Equilibria*. 1985. Corr. edn, Princeton, N.J.: Princeton University Press, 1989.

Ellis, John M. *Against Deconstruction*. Princeton, N.J.: Princeton University Press, 1989.

The Encyclopedia Britannica. 15th edn (*Britannica 3*), ed. Warren E. Preece and Philip W. Goetz. Chicago: Encyclopaedia Britannica, 1974–2012.

Engels, Friedrich. *Ludwig Feuerbach and the End of Classical German Philosophy.* German original first published in 1886, in *Die Neue Zeit.* Moscow: Progress Publishers, 1946.

Erbrich, Paul. *Zufall: Eine Naturwissenschaftlich-Philosophische Untersuchung.* Stuttgart: Kohlhammer, 1988.

Euripides. *The Bacchae.* Tr. James Morwood, *Bacchae and Other Plays.* Oxford World's Classics. 1999. Repr. Oxford: Oxford University Press, 2008.

Evans-Pritchard, E. E. *Nuer Religion.* 1956. 2nd edn, London: Oxford University Press, 1971.

F

Feuerbach, Ludwig. *The Essence of Christianity.* 1841. Ed. and tr. George Eliot (Mary Ann Evans). New York: Harper Torchbooks, 1957.

Feynman, Richard. *Six Easy Pieces.* 1963. Repr. London: Penguin Books, 1995.

Fischer, Ernst. *Marx in His Own Words.* Tr. Anna Bostock. London: Penguin Books, 1973.

Fish, Stanley. *Is There a Text in This Class? The Authority of Interpretive Communities.* Cambridge, Mass.: Harvard University Press, 1980.

Fish, Stanley. *There's No Such Thing as Free Speech, and It's a Good Thing Too.* New York: Oxford University Press, 1994.

Flew, Antony with Roy Abraham Varghese. *There Is a God: How the World's Most Notorious Atheist Changed His Mind.* London: HarperCollins, 2007.

Fox, S. W., ed. *The Origins of Prebiological Systems and of Their Molecular Matrices.* New York: Academic Press, 1965.

Frazer, J. G. *The Golden Bough.* 1890, 1900, 1906–15, 1937.

Fromm, Erich. *You Shall be as Gods: A Radical Interpretation of the Old Testament and its Tradition.* New York: Holt, Rinehart & Winston, 1966.

G

Gates, Bill. *The Road Ahead.* 1995. Rev. edn, Harmondsworth: Penguin, 1996.

Geisler, Norman L., and William E. Nix, *A General Introduction to the Bible* (Chicago: Moody Press, 1986), 475. Gerson, Lloyd P. *Plotinus.* London: Routledge, 1994.

Gilligan, Carol. *In a Different Voice: Psychological Theory and Women's Development.* Cambridge, Mass.: Harvard University Press, 1982.

Goldschmidt, Richard. *The Material Basis of Evolution.* The Silliman Memorial Lectures Series. 1940. Repr. Yale University Press, 1982.

Gooding, David W. and John C. Lennox. *The Human Quest for Significance: Forming a Worldview* [in Russian]. Minsk: Myrtlefield Trust, 1999.

Gould, Stephen Jay. *The Lying Stones of Marrakech: Penultimate Reflections in Natural History.* 2000. Repr. Cambridge, Mass.: Harvard University Press, 2011.

Gould, Stephen Jay. *Wonderful Life: The Burgess Shale and the Nature of History.* 1989. Repr. London: Vintage, 2000.

Grant, Michael. *Jesus: An Historian's Review of the Gospels.* New York: Scribner, 1977.

Grene, Marjorie. *A Portrait of Aristotle*. London: Faber & Faber, 1963.

Groothuis, Douglas. *Truth Decay: Defending Christianity against the Challenges of Postmodernism*. Leicester: Inter-Varsity Press, 2000.

Guthrie, W. K. C. *The Greek Philosophers from Thales to Aristotle*. 1950. Repr. London: Methuen, 2013.

Guthrie, W. K. C. *Plato: the man and his dialogues, earlier period*. Vol. 4 of *A History of Greek Philosophy*. 1875. Repr. Cambridge: Cambridge University Press, 2000.

H

Haldane, J. B. S. *Possible Worlds*. 1927. London: Chatto & Windus, 1945.

Harrison, E. *Masks of the Universe*. 1985. 2nd edn, New York: Macmillan, 2003. Citations are to the first Macmillan edition.

Harvey, William. *On the Motion of the Heart and the Blood of Animals*. 1628. Online at https://ebooks.adelaide.edu.au/h/harvey/william/motion/complete .html, accessed 4 Sept. 2018.

Hawking, Stephen. *A Brief History of Time*. 1988. Updated and expanded 10th ann. edn, London: Bantam Press, 1998.

Hawking, Stephen and Leonard Mlodinow. *The Grand Design*. New York: Bantam Books, 2010.

Hegel, G. W. F. *Hegel's Logic*. Being Part One of the Encyclopaedia of the Philosophical Sciences (1830). Tr. William Wallace, 1892. Repr. Oxford: Clarendon Press, 1984–87.

Hegel, G. W. F. *The Phenomenology of the Mind* (Spirit). 1807. 2nd edn 1841. Tr. J. B. Baillie, London, 1910. Repr. Dover Philosophical Classics, New York: Dover Publications, 2003.

Hegel, G. W. F. *The Philosophy of History*. 1861. Tr. J. Sibree, 1857. Repr. New York: Dover Publications, 1956. Repr. Kitchener, Ont.: Batoche Books, 2001. Online at Internet Archive: https://archive.org/details/lecturesonphilos00hegerich/, accessed 19 Oct. 2018.

Hegel, G. W. F. *Wissenschaft der Logik* [The Science of Logic]. Nurnberg, 1812–16.

Hemer, Colin. *The Book of Acts in the Setting of Hellenistic History*. Tübingen: J. C. B. Mohr, Paul Siebeck, 1989.

Hengel, Martin. *Judaism and Hellenism: Studies in their Encounter in Palestine during the Early Hellenistic Period*. Tr. John Bowden. London: SCM Press, 1974. Repr. Eugene, Oreg.: Wipf & Stock, 2003.

Hengel, Martin. *Studies in Early Christology*. Tr. Rollin Kearns. Edinburgh: T&T Clark, 1995.

Herodotus. *The Histories*. Tr. Robin Waterfield, 1998, Oxford World's Classics. Repr. New York: Oxford University Press, 2008.

Herzen, Alexander Ivanovich. *Byloe i dumy*. London, 1853. Tr. C. Garnett, *My Past and Thoughts, The Memoirs of Alexander Herzen*. Revised by H. Higgens, introduced by I. Berlin, 1968. Repr. London: Chatto and Windus, 2008.

Hesiod. *Theogony*. In Charles Abraham Elton, tr. *The remains of Hesiod*. London: Lackington, Allen, 1812. Also in Dorothea Wender, tr. *Hesiod and Theognis*. Harmondsworth: Penguin, 1973.

Hippolytus, *Refutation of all Heresies*. In Kirk, G. S., J. E. Raven and M. Schofield. *The Presocratic Philosophers: A Critical History with a Selection of Texts*. 1957. Rev. edn, Cambridge: Cambridge University Press, 1983.

Holmes, Arthur F. *Ethics*. Downers Grove, Ill.: InterVarsity Press, 1984; 2nd edn, 2007.

Honderich, Ted, ed. *The Oxford Companion to Philosophy*. Oxford, 1995. 2nd edn, Oxford: Oxford University Press, 2005.

Hooper, Judith. *Of Moths and Men*. New York: Norton, 2002.

Hooykaas, R. *Religion and the Rise of Modern Science*. 1972. Repr. Edinbugh: Scottish Academic Press, 2000.

Hospers, John. *An Introduction to Philosophical Analysis*. 1953. 4th edn, Abingdon: Routledge, 1997.

Houghton, John. *The Search for God—Can Science Help?* Oxford: Lion Publishing, 1995.

Hoyle, Fred. *The Intelligent Universe*. London: Joseph, 1983.

Hoyle, Fred and Chandra Wickramasinghe. *Cosmic Life-Force, the Power of Life Across the Universe*. London: Dent, 1988.

Hoyle, Fred and Chandra Wickramasinghe. *Evolution from Space: A Theory of Cosmic Creationism*. New York: Simon & Schuster, 1984.

Hume, David. *David Hume: A Treatise of Human Nature*. 1739–40. Ed. Lewis Amherst Selby-Bigge and P. H. Nidditch. Oxford: Clarendon Press, 1888. Repr. 1978. Repr. Oxford: Oxford University Press, 2014. doi: 10.1093/actrade/9780198245872. book.1, accessed 11 Sept. 2015; also online at https://davidhume.org/texts/t/, accessed 4 Sept.2018.

Hume, David. *Dialogues Concerning Natural Religion*. 1779. Repr. ed. J. C. A. Gaskin, *Dialogues Concerning Natural Religion, and The Natural History of Religion*. Oxford World's Classics. Oxford: Oxford University Press, 2008. Online at https://davidhume.org/texts/d/, accessed 2 Aug. 2017. (Abbreviated as DNR.)

Hume, David. *An Enquiry Concerning Human Understanding*. London: A. Millar, 1748. Repr. Dover Philosophical Classics, Mineola, N.Y.: Dover Publications, 2012. Online at http://www.davidhume.org/texts/e/, accessed 2 Aug. 2017. (Abbreviated as EHU.)

Hume, David. *Treatise of Human Nature*. 1739–40. Eds. David Norton and Mary J. Norton, *David Hume: A Treatise of Human Nature: A critical edition*. Vol. 1 of The Clarendon Edition of The Works Of David Hume. Oxford: Oxford University Press, 2007. Online at http://www.davidhume.org/texts/thn.html, accessed 2 Aug. 2017. (Abbreviated as THN.)

Hunt, R. N. Carew. *The Theory and Practice of Communism*. Baltimore: Penguin Books, 1966.

Hurley, Thomas. *Method and Results: Collected Essays*. Vol. I. London: Macmillan, 1898.

Husserl, Edmund. *Ideas: General Introduction to Pure Phenomenology*. Ger. orig. *Ideen zu einer reinen Phänomenologie und phänomenologischen Philosophie. Erstes Buch:*

Allgemeine Einführung in die reine Phänomenologie (1913). Tr. W. R. Boyce Gibson. London: Macmillan, 1931.

Huxley, Julian. *Essays of a Humanist.* 1964. Repr. Harmondsworth: Penguin Books, 1969.

Huxley, Julian. *Religion Without Revelation.* New York: Mentor, 1957.

I

Isherwood, Christopher, ed. *Vedanta for Modern Man.* 1951. Repr. New York: New American Library, 1972.

J

Jacob, François. *Chance and Necessity: An Essay on the Natural Philosophy of Modern Biology.* Tr. Austryn Wainhouse. New York: Alfred A. Knopf, 1971.

Jacob, François. *The Logic of Life: A History of Heredity.* Tr. Betty E. Spillman. New York: Pantheon Books, 1973.

Jaeger, Werner. *The Theology of the Early Greek Philosophers.* The Gifford Lectures, 1936. Oxford: Oxford University Press, 1967.

James, E. O. *Christianity and Other Religions.* London: Hodder & Stoughton, 1968.

Jaroszwski, T. M. and P. A. Ignatovsky, eds. *Socialism as a Social System.* Moscow: Progress Publishers, 1981.

Jeremias, J. *New Testament Theology: The Proclamation of Jesus.* Tr. John Bowden. New York: Scribner, 1971.

Joad, C. E. M. *The Book of Joad: A Belligerent Autobiography* [= *Under the Fifth Rib*]. London: Faber & Faber, 1944.

Johnson, Phillip E. *Objections Sustained: Subversive Essays on Evolution, Law and Culture.* Downers Grove, Ill.: InterVarsity Press, 1998.

Jones, Steve. *In the Blood: God, Genes and Destiny.* London: Harper Collins, 1996.

Josephus, Flavius. *Antiquities of the Jews.* Tr. William Whiston, *The Works of Flavius Josephus.* 1737. Repr. Grand Rapids: Kregel, 1974. Repr. Peabody, Mass.: Hendrickson, 1995.

K

Kant, Immanuel. *Critique of Practical Reason.* 1788. Tr. and ed. Mary Gregor. Cambridge Texts in the History of Philosophy. 1997. Repr. Cambridge: Cambridge University Press, 2003.

Kant, Immanuel. *Critique of Pure Reason.* 1781. 2nd edn, 1787. Tr. Norman Kemp Smith. London: Macmillan, 1929. Repr. Blunt Press, 2007. Also Paul Guyer and Allen Wood, eds., Cambridge: Cambridge University Press, 1999.

Kant, Immanuel. *Groundwork of the Metaphysics of Morals.* 1785. In H. J. Paton, tr. *The Moral Law.* London: Hutchinson, 1972.

Kant, Immanuel. *The Metaphysics of Morals*. 1797. Tr. and ed. Mary J. Gregor. Cambridge Texts in the History of Philosophy. Cambridge: Cambridge University Press, 1996.

Kant, Immanuel. *Prolegomena to Any Future Metaphysics*. 1783. Tr. and ed. Gary Hatfield, *Prolegomena to Any Future Metaphysics with Selections from the Critique of Pure Reason*. Cambridge Texts in the History of Philosophy. 1997. Rev. edn, Cambridge: Cambridge University Press, 2004.

Kantikar, V. P. (Hemant) and W. Owen. *Hinduism—An Introduction: Teach Yourself*. 1995. Repr. London: Hodder Headline, 2010.

Kaye, Howard L. *The Social Meaning of Modern Biology, From Social Darwinism to Sociobiology*. 1986. Repr. with a new epilogue, New Brunswick, N.J.: Transaction Publishers, 1997.

Kenny, Anthony. *An Illustrated Brief History of Western Philosophy*. Oxford: Blackwell, 2006. First published as *A Brief History of Western Philosophy*, 1998.

Kenyon, D. H. and G. Steinman. *Biochemical Predestination*. New York: McGraw-Hill, 1969.

Kenyon, Frederic. *Our Bible and the Ancient Manuscripts*. 1895. 4th edn, 1938. Repr. Eugene, Oreg.: Wipf & Stock, 2011.

Kilner, J. F., C. C. Hook and D. B. Uustal, eds. *Cutting-Edge Bioethics: A Christian Exploration of Technologies and Trends*. Grand Rapids: Eerdmans, 2002.

Kirk, G. S., J. E. Raven and M. Schofield. *The Presocratic Philosophers: A Critical History with a Selection of Texts*. 1957. Rev. edn, Cambridge: Cambridge University Press, 1983.

Kirk, M. and H. Madsen. *After the Ball*. New York: Plume Books, 1989.

Knott, Kim. *Hinduism: A Very Short Introduction*. Oxford: Oxford University Press, 1998.

Koertge, Noretta, ed. *A House Built on Sand: Exposing Postmodernist Myths About Science*. Oxford: Oxford University Press, 1998.

Kolbanovskiy, V. N. *Communist Morality*. Moscow, 1951.

Krikorian, Yervant H., ed. *Naturalism and the Human Spirit*. 1944. Repr. New York: Columbia University Press, 1969.

Kuhn, Thomas. *The Structure of Scientific Revolutions*. 1962. 3rd edn, Chicago: University of Chicago Press, 1996.

Kurtz, Paul. *The Fullness of Life*. New York: Horizon Press, 1974.

Kurtz, Paul. *The Humanist Alternative*. Buffalo, N.Y.: Prometheus, 1973.

Kurtz, Paul, ed. *Humanist Manifestos I & II*. Buffalo, N.Y.: Prometheus, 1980.

Kurtz, Paul, ed. *Humanist Manifesto II*. Buffalo, N.Y.: Prometheus Books, 1980. Online at https://americanhumanist.org/what-is-humanism/manifesto2/, accessed 11 Sept. 2105.

L

Lamont, Corliss. *A Lifetime of Dissent*. Buffalo, N.Y.: Prometheus Books, 1988.

Lamont, Corliss. *The Philosophy of Humanism*. 1947. 8th edn, Emherst, N.Y.: Humanist Press, 1997.

Lapouge, G. Vacher de. *Les Sélections Sociales*. Paris: Fontemoing, 1899.

Leakey, Richard. *The Origin of Humankind*. London: Weidenfeld & Nicolson, 1994.

Leitch, Vincent B. *Deconstructive Criticism: An Advanced Introduction*. New York: Columbia University Press, 1982.

Lenin, V. I. *Complete Collected Works*. Tr. Andrew Rothstein. 4th Eng. edn, Moscow: Progress Publishers, 1960–78. Online at http://www.marx2mao.com/ Lenin/Index.html (facsimile), accessed 11 Sept. 2015. Repr. Moscow: Progress Publishers, 1982.

Lenin, V. I. *Materialism and Empirico-Criticism*. New York: International Publishers, 1927.

Lennox, John C. *Can Science Explain Everything?* Epsom, UK: Good Book Company, 2019.

Lennox, John C. *Determined to Believe: The Sovereignty of God, Freedom, Faith and Human*. Oxford: Monarch Books, 2017.

Lennox, John C. *God and Stephen Hawking: Whose Design is it Anyway?* Oxford: Lion, 2010.

Lennox, John C. *God's Undertaker: Has Science Buried God?* Oxford, Lion Books, 2007, 2009.

Leslie, John. *Universes*. London: Routledge, 1989.

Levinskaya, Irina. *The Book of Acts in its First Century Setting*. Vol. 5. Diaspora Setting. Grand Rapids: Eerdmans, 1996.

Lewis, C. S. *The Abolition of Man*. London, 1945. Repr. London: Collins, Fount, 1978.

Lewis, C. S. *Christian Reflections*. London, 1967. Repr. New York: HarperCollins, 1998.

Lewis, C. S. *God in the Dock*. London, 1979. Repr. Grand Rapids: Eerdmans, 2014.

Lewis, C. S. *Mere Christianity*. London, 1952. Rev. edn with new introduction and foreword by Kathleen Norris, New York: HarperCollins, 2001.

Lewis, C. S. *Miracles*. 1947. Repr. London: Collins, 2012.

Lewis, C. S. *The Problem of Pain*. 1940. Repr. London: Collins, 2009.

Lewis, C. S. *Transposition and other Addresses*. London: Geoffrey Bles, 1949.

Lewontin, Richard. *The Dialectical Biologist*. Cambridge, Mass.: Harvard University Press, 1987.

Locke, John. *An Essay Concerning Human Understanding*. London, 1689. Ed. Peter H. Nidditch, Oxford: Oxford University Press, 1975.

Long, A. A. *Hellenistic Philosophy*. 1974. 2nd edn, Berkeley, Calif.: University of California Press, 1986.

Lossky, N. O. *History of Russian Philosophy*. London: Allen & Unwin, 1952.

Lucretius (Titus Lucretius Carus). *De Rerum Natura*. 50 BC. Tr. A. E. Stallings as *The Nature of Things*. London: Penguin, 2007. Also tr. and ed. William Ellery Leonard. 1916. Online at: http://www.perseus.tufts.edu/hopper/text?doc=Lucr or http:// classics.mit.edu/Carus/nature_things.html.

Lumsden, Charles J. and Edward O. Wilson. *Promethean Fire: Reflections on the Origin of Mind*. Cambridge, Mass.: Harvard University Press, 1983.

M

Mabbott, J. D. *An Introduction to Ethics*. Hutchinson University Library. London: Hutchinson, 1966.

McKay, Donald. *The Clockwork Image: A Christian Perspective on Science*. London: Inter-Varsity Press, 1974.

Majerus, Michael. *Melanism: Evolution in Action*. Oxford: Oxford University Press, 1998.

Margenau, Henry and Roy Abraham Varghese, eds. *Cosmos, Bios, and Theos: Scientists Reflect on Science, God, and the Origins of the Universe, Life, and Homo Sapiens*. La Salle, Ill.: Open Court, 1992.

Marx, Karl. *Marx's Theses on Feuerbach*. 1845.

Mascall, E. L. *Words and Images, a study in the Possibility of Religious Discourse*. London: Longmans, 1957.

Mascaró, Juan, tr. *The Upanishads*. Harmondsworth: Penguin, 1965.

Maslow, Abraham. *Towards a Psychology of Being*. New York: Van Nostrand Reinhold, 1968.

Masterson, Patrick. *Atheism and Alienation*. Harmondsworth: Pelican Books, 1972.

May, Rollo. *Psychology and the Human Dilemma*. Princeton, N.J., 1967. Repr. New York: Norton, 1996.

Medawar, Peter. *Advice to a Young Scientist*. New York: Harper & Row, 1979.

Medawar, Peter. *The Limits of Science*. Oxford: Oxford University Press, 1985.

Medawar, Peter and Jean Medawar. *The Life Science*. London: Wildwood House, 1977.

Metzger, Bruce. *The Text of the New Testament, its Transmission, Corruption and Restoration*. 1964. 3rd edn, Oxford: Oxford University Press, 1992.

Mill, John Stuart. *Utilitarianism*. 1861, 1863. Repr. Mineola, N.Y.: Dover Publications, 2007.

Millard, Alan. *Reading and Writing in the Time of Jesus*. Sheffield: Sheffield Academic Press, 2000.

Miller, David, Janet Coleman, William Connolly, and Alan Ryan, eds. *The Blackwell Encyclopaedia of Political Thought*. 1987. Repr. Oxford: Blackwell, 1991.

Monod, Jacques. *Chance and Necessity: An Essay on the Natural Philosophy of Modern Biology*. 1970 (French). Tr. Austryn Wainhouse, 1971. Repr. London: Penguin Books, 1997. Citations are from Vintage Books 1972 edn.

Monod, Jacques. *From Biology to Ethics*. San Diego: Salk Institute for Biological Studies, 1969.

Morris, Simon Conway. *The Crucible of Creation: The Burgess Shale and the Rise of Animals*. 1998. New edn, Oxford: Oxford University Press, 1999.

Mossner, Ernest C., ed. *David Hume, A Treatise of Human Nature*. London: Penguin Classics, 1985.

Moule, C. F. D. *The Phenomenon of the New Testament: An Inquiry into the Implications of Certain Features of the New Testament*. London: SCM, 1967.

Murphy, John P. *Pragmatism: From Peirce to Davidson*. Boulder, Colo.: Westview Press, 1990.

N

Nagel, Thomas. *The Last Word*. Oxford: Oxford University Press, 1997.

Nagel, Thomas. *Mortal Questions*. Cambridge: Cambridge University Press. 1979.

Nahem, Joseph. *Psychology and Psychiatry Today: A Marxist View*. New York: International Publishers, 1981.

Nasr, Seyyed Hossein, and Oliver Leaman, eds. *History of Islamic Philosophy*. Part 1, Vol. 1 of *Routledge History of World Philosophies*. 1996. Repr. London: Routledge, 2001.

Nettleship, R. L. *Lectures on the Republic of Plato*. London: Macmillan, 1922.

Newton, Isaac. *Principia Mathematica*. London, 1687.

Nietzsche, Friedrich. *Beyond Good and Evil: Prelude to a Philosophy of the Future*. Leipzig, 1886. 1973. Repr. tr. R. J. Hollingdale, Harmondsworth: Penguin, 1975.

Noddings, Nel. *Caring: A Feminine Approach to Ethics and Moral Education*. 1984. Repr. Berkeley, Calif.: University of California Press, 2013.

Norris, Christopher. *Deconstruction: Theory and Practice*. 1982. 3rd edn, London: Methuen, 2002.

O

Olivelle, Patrick. *The Early Upanishads: Annotated Text and Translation*. 1996. Repr. Oxford: Oxford University Press, 1998.

O'Meara, Dominic J. *Plotinus: An Introduction to the Enneads*. Oxford: Clarendon Press, 1993.

P

Paley, William. *Natural Theology on Evidence and Attributes of Deity*. 1802. Repr. Oxford: Oxford University Press, 2006.

Patterson, Colin. *Evolution*. 1978. 2nd edn, Ithaca, N.Y.: Cornstock Publishing Associates, 1999.

Peacocke, Arthur. *The Experiment of Life*. Toronto: University of Toronto Press, 1983.

Pearsall, Judy and Bill Trumble, eds. *The Oxford English Reference Dictionary*. 2nd edn, Oxford: Oxford University Press, 1996.

Pearse, E. K. Victor. *Evidence for Truth: Science*. Guildford: Eagle, 1998.

Penfield, Wilder. *The Mystery of the Mind*. Princeton, N.J.: Princeton University Press, 1975.

Penrose, Roger. *The Emperor's New Mind*. 1986. Repr. with new preface, Oxford: Oxford University Press, 1999.

Penrose, Roger. *The Road to Reality: A Complete Guide to the Laws of the Universe*. London: Jonathan Cape, 2004.

Peterson, Houston, ed. *Essays in Philosophy*. New York: Pocket Library, 1959.

Pinker, Steven. *The Language Instinct: How the Mind Creates Language*. New York: Morrow, 1994.

Plantinga, Alvin. *Warranted Christian Belief*. Oxford: Oxford University Press, 2000.

Plato. *Apology*. Tr. Hugh Tredennick, 1954. Repr. Harmondsworth: Penguin Books, 1976. Also in *The Collected Dialogues of Plato including the letters*. 1961. Repr. with corrections, Princeton, N.J.: Princeton University Press, 1973.

Plato. *The Euthyphro*.

Plato. *The Last Days of Socrates*. Tr. Hugh Tredennick. Harmondsworth: Penguin Books, 1969.

Plato. *Phaedo*.

Plato. *Republic*. Tr. Desmond Lee. 2nd edn, Harmondsworth: Penguin, 1974. Also tr. Paul Shorey, Loeb Classical Library. Cambridge, Mass.: Harvard University Press, 1930. Also in *The Collected Dialogues of Plato including the letters*, 1961. Repr. with corrections, Princeton, N.J.: Princeton University Press, 1973.

Plato. *Timaeus*.

Pliny the Younger. *Letters*. Tr. Betty Radice as *The Letters of the Younger Pliny*. Harmondsworth: Penguin Books, 1963.

Plotinus. *Enneads*. Tr. Stephen MacKenna, 1917–30. Repr. London: Penguin, 2005.

Polanyi, Michael. *The Tacit Dimension*. New York: Doubleday, 1966.

Polkinghorne, John. *One World: The Interaction of Science and Theology*. London: SPCK, 1986.

Polkinghorne, John. *Reason and Reality: The Relationship between Science and Theology*. 1991. Repr. London: SPCK, 2011.

Polkinghorne, John. *Science and Creation: The Search for Understanding*. 1988. Rev. edn, West Conshohocken, Pa.: Templeton Foundation Press, 2009.

Polkinghorne, John. *Science and Providence: God's Interaction with the World*. 1989. Repr. West Conshohocken, Pa.: Templeton Foundation Press, 2011.

Popper, Karl R. *The World of Parmenides*. London: Routledge, 1998.

Popper, Karl R. and John C. Eccles. *The Self and Its Brain: An Argument for Interactionism*. 1977. Repr. Springer Berlin Heidelberg, 2012.

Pospisil, Leopold J. *Kapauku Papuans and their Law*. Yale University Publications in Anthropology 54. New Haven, 1958.

Pospisil, Leopold J. *The Kapauku Papuans of West New Guinea*. Case Studies in Cultural Anthropology. 1963. 2nd edn, New York: Holt, Rinehart and Winston, 1978.

Powers, B. Ward. *The Progressive Publication of Matthew*. Nashville: B&H Academic, 2010.

Poythress, Vern S. *Inerrancy and the Gospels: A God-Centered Approach to the Challenges of Harmonization*. Wheaton, Ill.: Crossway, 2012.

Pritchard, J. B., ed. *Ancient Near Eastern Texts Relating to the Old Testament*. Princeton, 1950. 3rd edn, Princeton, N.J.: Princeton University Press, 1969.

Putnam, Hilary. *Reason, Truth and History*. Cambridge: Cambridge University Press, 1981.

R

Rachels, James. *Elements of Moral Philosophy*. New York: McGraw-Hill, 1986.

Ragg, Lonsdale and Laura Ragg, eds. *The Gospel of Barnabas*. Oxford: Clarendon Press, 1907.

Ramsay, William. *St. Paul the Traveller and the Roman Citizen*. London: Hodder & Stoughton, 1895.

Randall, John H. *Cosmos*. New York: Random House, 1980.

Raphael, D. D. *Moral Philosophy*. 1981. 2nd edn, Oxford: Oxford University Press, 1994.

Rawls, John. *A Theory of Justice*. Cambridge, Mass.: Harvard University Press, 1971.

Redford, Donald B., ed. *The Oxford Encyclopaedia of Ancient Egypt*. Oxford: Oxford University Press, 2001. doi: 10.1093/acref/9780195102345.001.0001.

Reid, Thomas. *An Enquiry Concerning Human Understanding*. Oxford: Clarendon Press, 1777.

Reid, Thomas. *An Inquiry into the Human Mind on the Principles of Common Sense*. 1764. Repr. Cambridge: Cambridge University Press, 2011.

Renfrew, Colin. *Archaeology and Language: The Puzzle of Indo-European Origins*. 1987. Repr. Cambridge: Cambridge University Press, 1999.

Ricoeur, Paul. *Hermeneutics and the Human Sciences*. 1981. Ed. and tr. J. B. Thompson. Repr. Cambridge: Cambridge University Press, 1998.

Ricoeur, Paul. *Interpretation Theory: Discourse and the Surplus of Meaning*. Fort Worth, Tex.: Texas Christian University Press, 1976.

Ridley, Mark. *The Problems of Evolution*. Oxford: Oxford University Press, 1985.

Rodwell, J. M., tr. *The Koran*. Ed. Alan Jones. London: Phoenix, 2011.

Rorty, Richard. *Consequences of Pragmatism: Essays, 1972–1980*. Minneapolis, Minn.: University of Minnesota Press, 1982.

Rose, Steven. *Lifelines: Biology, Freedom, Determinism*. 1998. Repr. New York: Oxford University Press, 2003.

Ross, Hugh. *The Creator and the Cosmos*. Colorado Springs: NavPress, 1995.

Ross, W. D. *The Right and the Good*. Oxford: Clarendon Press, 1930. Repr. 2002.

Rousseau, Jean Jacques. *The Social Contract*. 1762.

Russell, Bertrand. *The Autobiography of Bertrand Russell*. 1967–69. Repr. London: Routledge, 1998.

Russell, Bertrand. *History of Western Philosophy*. 1946. New edn, London: Routledge, 2004.

Russell, Bertrand. *Human Society in Ethics and Politics*. New York: Mentor, 1962.

Russell, Bertrand. *The Problems of Philosophy*. 1912. Repr. New York: Cosimo Classics, 2010.

Russell, Bertrand. *Religion and Science*. Oxford: Oxford University Press, 1970.

Russell, Bertrand. *Understanding History*. 1943. New York: Philosophical Library, 1957.

Russell, Bertrand. *Why I Am Not a Christian and Other Essays on Religion and Related Subjects*. New York: Simon & Schuster, 1957.

Russell, L. O. and G. A. Adebiyi. *Classical Thermodynamics*. Oxford: Oxford University Press, 1993.

Ryle, Gilbert. *The Concept of Mind*. London, 1949. Repr. London: Routledge, 2009.

S

Sagan, Carl. *The Cosmic Connection: An Extraterrestrial Perspective*. New York: Anchor Press, 1973.

Sagan, Carl. *Cosmos: The Story of Cosmic Evolution, Science and Civilisation*. 1980. Repr. London: Abacus, 2003.

Sagan, Carl. *The Demon-Haunted World: Science as a Candle in the Dark*. London: Headline, 1996.

Sandbach, F. H. *The Stoics*. 1975. Rev. edn, London: Bloomsbury, 2013.

Sartre, Jean-Paul. *Being and Nothingness: An Essay on Phenomenological Ontology*. 1943. Tr. Hazel E. Barnes. 1956. Repr. New York: Pocket Books, 1984.

Sartre, Jean-Paul. *Existentialism and Human Emotions*. Tr. Bernard Frechtman. New York: Philosophical Library, 1957.

Sartre, Jean-Paul. *Existentialism and Humanism*. Tr. and ed. P. Mairet. London: Methuen, 1948.

Sartre, Jean-Paul. *The Flies*. 1943 (French). Tr. Stuart Gilbert. New York: Knopf, 1947.

Schaff, Adam. *A Philosophy of Man*. London: Lawrence and Wishart, 1963.

Scherer, Siegfried. *Evolution. Ein kritisches Lehrbuch*. Weyel Biologie, Giessen: Weyel Lehrmittelverlag, 1998.

Schmidt, W. *The Origin and Growth of Religion*. Tr. J. Rose. London: Methuen, 1931.

Scruton, Roger. *Modern Philosophy*. 1994; London: Arrow Books, 1996.

Searle, John R. *The Construction of Social Reality*. London: Penguin, 1995.

Searle, John R. *Minds, Brains and Science*. 1984 Reith Lectures. London: British Broadcasting Corporation, 1984.

Selsam, Howard. *Socialism and Ethics*. New York: International Publishers, 1943.

Sen, Amartya and Bernard Williams, eds. *Utilitarianism and Beyond*. Cambridge: Cambridge University Press, 1982. 8th repr. in association with La Maison Des Sciences De L'Homme, Paris, 1999.

Shakespeare, William. *As You Like It*.

Sherrington, Charles S. *The Integrative Action of the Nervous System*. 1906. Repr. with new preface, Cambridge: Cambridge University Press, 1947.

Sherwin-White, A. N. *Roman Society and Roman Law in the New Testament*. The Sarum Lectures 1960–61. Oxford: Clarendon Press, 1963. Repr. Eugene, Oreg.: Wipf & Stock, 2004.

Simplicius. *Commentary on Aristotle's Physics* [or, Miscellanies]. In Kirk, G. S., J. E. Raven, and M. Schofield. *The Presocratic Philosophers: A Critical History with a Selection of Texts*. 1957. Rev. edn, Cambridge: Cambridge University Press, 1983.

Simpson, George Gaylord. *The Meaning of Evolution: A Study of the History of Life and of Its Significance for Man*. The Terry Lectures Series. 1949. Rev. edn, New Haven, Conn.: Yale University Press, 1967.

Singer, Peter. *Practical Ethics.* 1979. 2nd edn, Cambridge: Cambridge University Press, 1993.

Singer, Peter. *Rethinking Life and Death: The Collapse of Our Traditional Ethics.* Oxford: Oxford University Press, 1994.

Singer, Peter and Helga Kuhse. *Should the Baby Live?: The Problem of Handicapped Infants* (Studies in Bioethics). Oxford: Oxford University Press, 1985.

Sire, James. *The Universe Next Door.* Downers Grove, Ill.: InterVarsity Press, 1988.

Skinner, B. F. *Beyond Freedom and Dignity.* 1971; Harmondsworth: Penguin, 1974.

Skinner, B. F. *Lectures on Conditioned Reflexes.* New York: International Publishers, 1963.

Skinner, B. F. *Science and Human Behaviour.* New York: Macmillan, 1953.

Sleeper, Raymond S. *A Lexicon of Marxist-Leninist Semantics.* Alexandria, Va.: Western Goals, 1983.

Smart, J. J. C. and Bernard Williams. *Utilitarianism For and Against.* 1973. Repr. Cambridge: Cambridge University Press, 1998.

Smith, Adam. *An Enquiry into the Nature and Causes of the Wealth of Nations.* 1776. With introduction by Mark G. Spencer, Ware, UK: Wordsworth Editions, 2012.

Smith, John Maynard and Eörs Szathmary. *The Major Transitions in Evolution.* 1995. Repr. Oxford: Oxford University Press, 2010.

Smith, Wilbur. *Therefore Stand.* Grand Rapids: Baker, 1965.

Sober, E. *Philosophy of Biology.* 1993. Rev. 2nd edn, Boulder, Colo.: Westview Press, 2000.

Social Exclusion Unit. *Teenage Pregnancy.* Cmnd 4342. London: The Stationery Office, 1999.

Sophocles. *Antigone.* Tr. F. H. Storr, *Sophocles* Vol. 1. London: Heinemann, 1912.

Spencer, Herbert. *Social Statics.* New York: D. Appleton, 1851.

Stalin, Joseph. *J. Stalin Works.* Moscow: Foreign Languages Publishing House, 1953.

Stam, James H. *Inquiries into the Origin of Language: The Fate of a Question.* New York: Harper & Row, 1976.

Starkey, Mike. *God, Sex, and the Search for Lost Wonder: For Those Looking for Something to Believe In.* 1997. 2nd edn, Downers Grove, Ill.: InterVarsity Press, 1998.

Stauber, Ethelbert. *Jesus—Gestalt und Geschichte.* Bern: Francke Verlag, 1957.

Storer, Morris B., ed. *Humanist Ethics: Dialogue on Basics.* Buffalo, N.Y.: Prometheus Books, 1980.

Stott, John R. W. *The Message of Romans.* Leicester: Inter-Varsity Press, 1994.

Strabo. *Geography.* Tr. with introduction Duane W. Roller as *The Geography of Strabo*, Cambridge: Cambridge University Press, 2014. Tr. H. C. Hamilton and W. Falconer, London, 1903. Online at Perseus, Tufts University, http://www.perseus.tufts.edu/hopper/text?doc=Perseus%3Atext%3A1999.01.0239, accessed 11 Sept. 2015.

Strickberger, Monroe. *Evolution.* 1990. 3rd edn, London: Jones and Bartlett, 2000.

Strobel, Lee. *The Case for Christ: A Journalist's Personal Investigation of the Evidence for Jesus*. Grand Rapids: Zondervan, 1998.

Suetonius. *Lives of the Caesars*. Tr. Catharine Edwards. 2000. Repr. Oxford World's Classics. Oxford: Oxford University Press, 2008.

Sunderland, Luther D. *Darwin's Enigma*. Green Forest, Ark.: Master Books, 1998.

Swinburne, Richard. *The Existence of God*. 1979. Repr. Oxford: Oxford University Press, 2004.

Swinburne, Richard. *Faith and Reason*. 1981. Repr. Oxford: Clarendon Press, 2002.

Swinburne, Richard. *Is There a God?* Oxford: Oxford University Press, 1996.

Swinburne, Richard. *Providence and the Problem of Evil*. Oxford: Oxford University Press, 1998.

T

Tacitus, Cornelius. *Annals*. Tr. Alfred John Church and William Jackson Brodribb as *Complete Works of Tacitus*. New York: Random House, 1872. Repr. 1942. Online at Sara Byrant, ed., Perseus Digital Library, Tufts University, Medford, MA: http://www.perseus.tufts.edu/hopper/text?doc=Perseus:text:1999.02.0078, accessed 2 Aug. 2017.

Tada, Joni Eareckson and Steven Estes. *When God Weeps: Why Our Sufferings Matter to the Almighty*. Grand Rapids: Zondervan, 1997.

Tax, Sol and Charles Callender, eds. *Issues in Evolution*. Chicago: University of Chicago Press, 1960.

Thaxton, Charles B., Walter L. Bradley and Roger L. Olsen. *The Mystery of Life's Origin*. Dallas: Lewis & Stanley, 1992.

Thibaut, George, tr. *The Vedānta Sūtras of Bādarāyana* with the Commentary by Śankara, 2 Parts. New York: Dover, 1962.

Torrance, T. F. *The Ground and Grammar of Theology*. Belfast: Christian Journals Limited, 1980; and Charlottesville: The University Press of Virginia, 1980. Repr. with new preface, Edinburgh: T&T Clark, 2001.

Torrance, T. F. *Theological Science*. Oxford: Oxford University Press, 1978.

U

Unamuno, Don Miguel de. *The Tragic Sense of Life*. Tr. J. E. Crawford. 1921. Repr. Charleston, S.C.: BiblioBazaar, 2007.

V

Von Neumann, John. *Theory of Self-Reproducing Automata*. Ed. and completed by Arthur W. Burks, Urbana: University of Illinois Press, 1966.

W

Waddington, C. H., ed. *Science and Ethics: An Essay*. London: Allen & Unwin, 1942.

Wallis, R. T. *Neoplatonism*. 1972. Repr. London: Duckworth, 1985.

Ward, Keith. *God, Chance and Necessity*. 1996. Repr. Oxford: Oneworld Publications, 2001.

Warner, Richard, and Tadeusz Szubka. *The Mind-Body Problem*. Oxford: Blackwell, 1994.

Weiner, Jonathan. *The Beak of the Finch*. London: Cape, 1994.

Welch, I. David, George A. Tate and Fred Richards, eds. *Humanistic Psychology*. Buffalo, N.Y.: Prometheus Books, 1978.

Wenham, John. *Easter Enigma—Do the Resurrection Stories Contradict One Another?* Exeter: Paternoster Press, 1984. Repr. as *Easter Enigma: Are the Resurrection Accounts in Conflict?*, Eugene, Oreg.: Wipf & Stock, 2005.

Wesson, Paul. *Beyond Natural Selection*. 1991. Repr. Cambridge, Mass.: Massachusetts Institute of Technology Press, 1997.

Westminster Shorter Catechism. 1647. [Widely available in print and online.]

Wetter, Gustav A. *Dialectical Materialism*. Westport, Conn.: Greenwood Press, 1977.

Whitehead, Alfred North. *Process and Reality*. Gifford Lectures 1927–28. London: Macmillan, 1929. Repr. New York: The Free Press, 1978.

Wilson, Edward O. *Consilience*. London: Little, Brown, 1998.

Wilson, Edward O. *Genes, Mind and Culture*. Cambridge, Mass.: Harvard University Press, 1981.

Wilson, Edward O. *On Human Nature*. Cambridge, Mass.: Harvard University Press, 1978.

Wilson, Edward O. *Sociobiology: The New Synthesis*. Cambridge, Mass.: Harvard University Press, 1975.

Wimsatt, William K. and Monroe Beardsley. *The Verbal Icon: Studies in the Meaning of Poetry*. 1954. Repr. Lexington, Ky.: University of Kentucky Press, 1982.

Wippel, John F., ed. *Studies in Medieval Philosophy*. Vol. 17 of *Studies in Philosophy and the History of Philosophy*. Washington D.C.: Catholic University of America Press, 1987.

Wittgenstein, L. *On Certainty*. Ed. G. E. M. Anscombe and G. H. von Wright; tr. Denis Paul and G. E. M. Anscombe. Oxford, 1969. Repr. New York: Harper & Row, 1972.

Wolpert, Lewis. *The Unnatural Nature of Science*. London: Faber & Faber, 1992.

Wolstenholme, Gordon, ed. *Man and His Future*. A Ciba Foundation Volume. London: J. & A. Churchill, 1963.

Wolters, Clifton, tr. *The Cloud of Unknowing*. 1961. Repr. London: Penguin, 1978.

Wolterstorff, Nicholas. *Divine Discourse: Philosophical Reflections on the Claim that God Speaks*. 1995. Repr. Cambridge: Cambridge University Press, 2000.

X

Xenophon. *Memorabilia*. Tr. E. C. Marchant. *Memorabilia. Oeconomicus. Symposium. Apology*. Vol. 4. Loeb Classical Library, Vol. 168. 1923. Repr. Cambridge, Mass.: Harvard University Press, 1997.

Y

Yancey, Philip. *Soul Survivor: How my Faith Survived the Church*. London: Hodder & Stoughton, 2001.

Yockey, Hubert. *Information Theory and Biology*. Cambridge: Cambridge University Press, 1992.

Z

Zacharias, Ravi. *Jesus Among Other Gods: The Absolute Claims of the Christian Message*. Nashville, Tenn.: Thomas Nelson, 2000.

Zacharias, Ravi. *The Real Face of Atheism*. Grand Rapids: Baker, 2004.

Zaehner, Z. C., ed. *The Concise Encyclopedia of Living Faiths*. 1959. 2nd edn, 1971. Repr. London: Hutchinson, 1982.

ARTICLES, PAPERS, CHAPTERS AND LECTURES

A

Adams, R. M. 'Religious Ethics in a Pluralistic Society.' In G. Outka and J. P. Reeder, Jr., eds. *Prospects for a Common Morality*. Princeton, N.J.: Princeton University Press, 1993.

Alberts, Bruce. 'The Cell as a Collection of Protein Machines: Preparing the Next Generation of Molecular Biologists.' *Cell* 92/3 (6 Feb. 1998), 291–4. doi: 10.1016/S0092-8674(00)80922-8.

Almond, Brenda. 'Liberty or Community? Defining the Post-Marxist Agenda.' In Brenda Almond, ed. *Introducing Applied Ethics*. Oxford: Wiley Blackwell, 1995.

Alpher, R. A., H. Bethe and G. Gamow. 'The Origin of Chemical Elements.' *Physical Review* 73/7 (Apr. 1948), 803–4. doi: 10.1103/PhysRev.73.803.

Anscombe, G. E. M. 'Modern Moral Philosophy.' *Philosophy* 33 (1958), 1–19.

Asimov, Isaac (interview by Paul Kurtz). 'An Interview with Isaac Asimov on Science and the Bible.' *Free Enquiry* 2/2 (Spring 1982), 6–10.

Auer, J. A. C. F. 'Religion as the Integration of Human Life.' *The Humanist* (Spring 1947).

Austin, J. L., P. F. Strawson and D. R. Cousin. 'Truth.' *Proceedings of the Aristotelian Society, Supplementary Volumes, Vol. 24, Physical Research, Ethics and Logic* (1950), 111–72. Online at http://www.jstor.org/stable/4106745. Repr. in Paul Horwich, ed. *Theories of Truth*. Aldershot: Dartmouth Publishing, 1994.

B

Bada, Jeffrey L. 'Stanley Miller's 70th Birthday.' *Origins of Life and Evolution of Biospheres* 30/2 (2000), 107–12. doi: 10.1023/A:1006746205180.

Baier, Kurt E. M. 'Egoism.' In P. Singer, ed. *A Companion to Ethics*. Oxford: Blackwell, 1991. Repr. 2000, 197–204.

Baier, Kurt E. M. 'Freedom, Obligation, and Responsibility.' In Morris B. Storer, ed. *Humanist Ethics: Dialogue on Basics*. Buffalo, N.Y.: Prometheus Books, 1980, 75–92.

Baier, Kurt E. M. 'The Meaning of Life.' 1947. In Peter Angeles, ed. *Critiques of God*, Buffalo, N.Y.: Prometheus Books, 1976. Repr. in E. D. Klemke, ed. *The Meaning of Life*. New York: Oxford University Press, 1981, 81–117.

Baker, S. W. 'Albert Nyanza, Account of the Discovery of the Second Great Lake of the Nile.' *Journal of the Royal Geographical Society* 36 (1866). Also in *Proceedings of the Royal Geographical Society of London* 10 (13 Nov. 1856), 6–27.

Bates, Elizabeth, Donna Thal and Virginia Marchman. 'Symbols and Syntax: A Darwinian Approach to Language Development.' In Norman A. Krasnegor, Duane M. Rumbaugh, Richard L. Schiefelbusch and Michael Studdert-Kennedy, eds. *Biological and Behavioural Determinants of Language Development*. 1991. Repr. New York: Psychology Press, 2014, 29–65.

Behe, Michael J. 'Reply to My Critics: A Response to Reviews of *Darwin's Black Box: The Biochemical Challenge to Evolution*.' *Biology and Philosophy* 16 (2001), 685–709.

Berenbaum, Michael. 'T4 Program.' In *Encyclopaedia Britannica*. Online at https://www.britannica.com/event/T4-Program, accessed 2 Nov. 2017.

Berlinski, David. 'The Deniable Darwin.' *Commentary* (June 1996), 19–29.

Bernal, J. D. 'The Unity of Ethics.' In C. H. Waddington, ed. *Science and Ethics: An Essay*. London: Allen & Unwin, 1942.

Black, Deborah L. 'Al-Kindi.' In Seyyed Hossein Nasr and Oliver Leaman, eds. *History of Islamic Philosophy*. Part 1, Vol. 1 of *Routledge History of World Philosophies*. 1996. Repr. London: Routledge, 2001, 178–97.

Boghossian, Paul A. 'What the Sokal hoax ought to teach us: The pernicious consequences and internal contradictions of "postmodernist" relativism.' *Times Literary Supplement*, Commentary (13 Dec. 1996), 14–15. Reprinted in Noretta Koertge, ed. *A House Built on Sand: Exposing Postmodernist Myths about Science*. Oxford: Oxford University Press, 1998, 23–31.

Briggs, Arthur E. 'The Third Annual Humanist Convention.' *The Humanist* (Spring 1945).

Bristol, Evelyn. 'Turn of a Century: Modernism, 1895–1925.' Ch. 8 in C. A. Moser, ed. *The Cambridge History of Russian Literature*. 1989. Rev. edn, 1992. Repr. 1996, Cambridge: Cambridge University Press, 387–457.

C

Caputo, John D. 'The End of Ethics.' In Hugh LaFollette, ed. *The Blackwell Guide to Ethical Theory*. Oxford: Blackwell, 1999, 111–28.

Cartmill, Matt. 'Oppressed by Evolution.' *Discover* Magazine 19/3 (Mar. 1998), 78–83. Reprinted in L. Polnac, ed. *Purpose, Pattern, and Process*. 6th edn, Dubuque: Kendall-Hunt, 2002, 389–97.

Cavalier-Smith, T. 'The Blind Biochemist.' *Trends in Ecology and Evolution* 12 (1997), 162–3.

Chaitin, Gregory J. 'Randomness in Arithmetic and the Decline and Fall of Reductionism in Pure Mathematics.' Ch. 3 in John Cornwell, ed. *Nature's Imagination: The Frontiers of Scientific Vision*. Oxford: Oxford University Press, 1995, 27–44.

Chomsky, Noam. 'Review of B. F. Skinner.' *Verbal Behavior*. *Language* 35/1 (1959), 26–58.

Chomsky, Noam. 'Science, Mind, and Limits of Understanding.' Transcript of talk given at the Science and Faith Foundation (STOQ), The Vatican (Jan. 2014). No pages. Online at https://chomsky.info/201401__/, accessed 3 Aug. 2017.

Coghlan, Andy. 'Selling the family secrets.' *New Scientist* 160/2163 (5 Dec. 1998), 20–1.

Collins, Harry. 'Introduction: Stages in the Empirical Programme of Relativism.' *Social Studies of Science* 11/1 (Feb. 1981), 3–10. Online at http://www.jstor.org/stable/284733, accessed 11 Sept. 2015.

Collins, R. 'A Physician's View of College Sex.' *Journal of the American Medical Association* 232 (1975), 392.

Cook, Sidney. 'Solzhenitsyn and Secular Humanism: A Response.' *The Humanist* (Nov./Dec. 1978), 6.

Cookson, Clive. 'Scientist Who Glimpsed God.' *Financial Times* (29 Apr. 1995), 20.

Cottingham, John. 'Descartes, René.' In Ted Honderich, ed. *The Oxford Companion to Philosophy*. Oxford, 1995. 2nd edn, Oxford: Oxford University Press, 2005.

Crick, Francis. 'Lessons from Biology.' *Natural History* 97 (Nov. 1988), 32–9.

Crosman, Robert. 'Do Readers Make Meaning?' In Susan R. Suleiman and Inge Crosman, eds. *The Reader in the Text: Essays on Audience and Interpretation*. Princeton, N.J.: Princeton University Press, 1980.

D

Davies, Paul. 'Bit before It?' *New Scientist* 2171 (30 Jan. 1999), 3.

Dawkins, Richard. 'Put Your Money on Evolution.' Review of Maitland A. Edey and Donald C. Johanson. *Blueprint: Solving the Mystery of Evolution*. Penguin, 1989. *The New York Times Review of Books* (9 Apr. 1989), sec. 7, 34–5.

Dembski, William. 'Intelligent Design as a Theory of Information.' *Perspectives on Science and Christian Faith* 49/3 (Sept. 1997), 180–90.

Derrida, Jacques. 'Force of Law: The "Mystical Foundation of Authority".' In Drucilla Cornell, Michel Rosenfeld and David Gray Carlson, eds. *Deconstruction and the Possibility of Justice*. 1992. Repr. Abingdon: Routledge, 2008.

Dirac, P. A. M. 'The Evolution of the Physicist's Picture of Nature.' *Scientific American* 208/5 (1963), 45–53. doi: 10.1038/scientificamerican0563-45.

Dobzhansky, Theodosius. 'Chance and Creativity in Evolution.' Ch. 18 in Francisco J. Ayala and Theodosius Dobzhansky, eds. *Studies in the Philosophy of Biology: Reduction and Related Problems*. Berkeley, Calif.: University of California Press, 1974, 307–36.

Dobzhansky, Theodosius. Discussion of paper by Gerhard Schramm, 'Synthesis of Nucleosides and Polynucleotide with Metaphosphate Esters.' In Sidney W. Fox, ed. *The Origins of Prebiological Systems and of Their Molecular Matrices*, 299–315. Proceedings of a Conference Conducted at Wakulla Springs, Florida, on 20–30 October 1963 under the auspices of the Institute for Space Biosciences, the Florida State University and the National Aeronautics and Space Administration. New York: Academic Press, 1965.

Dobzhansky, Theodosius. 'Evolutionary Roots of Family Ethics and Group Ethics.' In *The Centrality of Science and Absolute Values*, Vol. I of *Proceedings of the Fourth International Conference on the Unity of the Sciences*. New York: International Cultural Foundation, 1975.

Documents of the 22nd Congress of the Communist Party of the Soviet Union. 2 vols. Documents of Current History, nos. 18–19. New York: Crosscurrents Press, 1961.

Dose, Klaus. 'The Origin of Life: More Questions Than Answers.' *Interdisciplinary Science Reviews* 13 (Dec. 1988), 348–56.

Druart, Th.-A. 'Al-Fārābī and Emanationism.' In J. F. Wippel, ed. *Studies in Medieval Philosophy*. Vol. 17 of Studies in Philosophy and the History of Philosophy. Washington D.C.: Catholic University of America Press, 1987, 23–43.

Dyson, Freeman. 'Energy in the Universe.' *Scientific American* 225/3 (1971), 50–9.

E

Eddington, Arthur. 'The End of the World: From the Standpoint of Mathematical Physics.' *Nature* 127 (21 Mar. 1931), 447–53. doi: 10.1038/127447a0.

Edwards, William. 'On the Physical Death of Jesus Christ.' *Journal of the American Medical Association* 255/11 (21 Mar. 1986), 1455–63.

Eigen, Manfred, Christof K. Biebricher, Michael Gebinoga and William C. Gardiner. 'The Hypercycle: Coupling of RNA and Protein Biosynthesis in the Infection Cycle of an RNA Bacteriophage.' *Biochemistry* 30/46 (1991), 11005–18. doi: 10.1021/bi00110a001.

Einstein, Albert. 'Physics and Reality.' 1936. In Sonja Bargmann, tr. *Ideas and Opinions.* New York: Bonanza, 1954.

Einstein, Albert. 'Science and Religion.' 1941. Published in *Science, Philosophy and Religion, A Symposium.* New York: The Conference on Science, Philosophy and Religion in Their Relation to the Democratic Way of Life, 1941. Repr. in *Out of My Later Years,* 1950, 1956. Repr. New York: Open Road Media, 2011.

Eysenck, H. J. 'A Reason with Compassion.' In Paul Kurtz, ed. *The Humanist Alternative.* Buffalo, N.Y.: Prometheus Books, 1973.

F

Feynman, Richard P. 'Cargo Cult Science.' Repr. in *Engineering and Science* 37/7 (1974), 10–13. Online at http://calteches.library.caltech.edu/51/2/CargoCult.pdf (facsimile), accessed 11 Sept. 2015. (Originally delivered as Caltech's 1974 commencement address in Pasadena, Calif.)

Fletcher, J. 'Comment by Joseph Fletcher on Nielsen Article.' In Morris B. Storer, ed. *Humanist Ethics: Dialogue on Basics.* Buffalo, N.Y.: Prometheus Books, 1980, 70.

Flew, Anthony. 'Miracles.' In Paul Edwards, ed. *The Encyclopedia of Philosophy.* New York: Macmillan, 1967, 5:346–53.

Flew, Anthony. 'Neo-Humean Arguments about the Miraculous.' In R. D. Geivett and G. R. Habermas, eds. *In Defence of Miracles.* Leicester: Apollos, 1997, 45–57.

Flieger, Jerry Aline. 'The Art of Being Taken by Surprise.' *Destructive Criticism: Directions. SCE Reports* 8 (Fall 1980), 54–67.

Fodor, J. A. 'Fixation of Belief and Concept Acquisition.' In M. Piattelli-Palmarini, ed., *Language and Learning: The Debate Between Jean Piaget and Noam Chomsky.* Cambridge, Mass.: Harvard University Press, 1980, 143–9.

Fotion, Nicholas G. 'Logical Positivism.' In Ted Honderich, ed. *The Oxford Companion to Philosophy.* 2nd edn, Oxford: Oxford University Press, 2005.

Frank, Lawrence K. 'Potentialities of Human Nature.' *The Humanist* (Apr. 1951).

Frankena, William K. 'Is morality logically dependent on religion?' In G. Outka and J. P. Reeder, Jr., eds. *Religion and Morality.* Garden City, N.Y.: Anchor, 1973.

G

Genequand, Charles. 'Metaphysics.' Ch. 47 in Seyyed Nossein Nasr and Oliver Leaman, eds. *History of Islamic Philosophy.* Vol. 1 of *Routledge History of World Philosophies.* London: Routledge, 1996, 783–801.

Genné, William H. 'Our Moral Responsibility.' *Journal of the American College Health Association* 15/Suppl (May 1967), 55–60.

Gilbert, Scott F., John Opitz and Rudolf A Raff. 'Resynthesizing Evolutionary and Developmental Biology.' *Developmental Biology* 173/2 (1996), 357–72.

Ginsburg, V. L. *Poisk* 29–30 (1998).

Gould, Stephen Jay. 'Evolution as Fact and Theory.' In Ashley Montagu, ed. *Science and Creationism*. Oxford: Oxford University Press, 1984.

Gould, Stephen Jay. 'Evolution's Erratic Pace.' *Natural History* 86/5 (May 1977), 12–16.

Gould, Stephen Jay. 'Evolutionary Considerations.' Paper presented at the McDonnell Foundation Conference, 'Selection vs. Instruction'. Venice, May 1989.

Gould, Stephen Jay. 'In Praise of Charles Darwin.' Paper presented at the Nobel Conference XVIII, Gustavus Adolphus College, St. Peter, Minn. Repr. in Charles L. Hamrum, ed. *Darwin's Legacy*. San Francisco: Harper & Row, 1983.

Gould, Stephen Jay. 'The Paradox of the Visibly Irrelevant.' *Annals of the New York Academy of Sciences* 879 (June 1999), 87–97. doi: 10.1111/j.1749-6632.1999 .tb10407.x. Repr. in *The Lying Stones of Marrakech: Penultimate Reflections in Natural History*. 2000. Repr. Cambridge, Mass.: Harvard University Press, 2011.

Gribbin, John. 'Oscillating Universe Bounces Back.' *Nature* 259 (1 Jan. 1976), 15–16. doi: 10.1038/259015c0.

Grigg, Russell. 'Could Monkeys Type the 23rd Psalm?' *Interchange* 50 (1993), 25–31.

Guth, A. H. 'Inflationary Universe: A Possible Solution to the Horizon and Flatness Problems.' *Physical Review D* 23/2 (1981), 347–56.

Guttmacher Institute. 'Induced Abortion in the United States', Fact Sheet. New York: Guttmacher Institute, Jan. 2018. Online at https://www.guttmacher.org/fact-sheet/ induced-abortion-united-states, accessed 1 Feb. 2018.

H

Haldane, J. B. S. 'When I am Dead.' In *Possible Worlds*. [1927] London: Chatto & Windus, 1945, 204–11.

Hansen, Michèle; Jennifer J. Kurinczuk, Carol Bower and Sandra Webb. 'The Risk of Major Birth Defects after Intracytoplasmic Sperm Injection and in Vitro Fertilization.' *New England Journal of Medicine* 346 (2002), 725–30. doi: 10.1056/ NEJMoa010035.

Hardwig, John. 'Dying at the Right Time: Reflections on (Un)Assisted Suicide.' In Hugh LaFollette, ed. *Ethics In Practice*. Blackwell Philosophy Anthologies. 2nd edn, Oxford: Blackwell, 1997, 101–11.

Hawking, S. W. 'The Edge of Spacetime: Does the universe have an edge and time a beginning, as Einstein's general relativity predicts, or is spacetime finite without boundary, as quantum mechanics suggests?' *American Scientist* 72/4 (1984), 355–9. Online at http://www.jstor.org/stable/27852759, accessed 15 Sept. 2015.

Hawking, S. W. Letters to the Editors. Reply to letter by J. J. Tanner relating to article 'The Edge of Spacetime'. *American Scientist* 73/1 (1985), 12. Online at http:// www.jstor.org/stable/27853056, accessed 15 Sept. 2015.

Hawking, S. W. and R. Penrose. 'The Singularities of Gravitational Collapse and Cosmology.' *Proceedings of the Royal Society London A* 314/1519 (1970), 529–48. doi: 10.1098/rspa.1970.0021.

Hocutt, Max. 'Does Humanism Have an Ethic of Responsibility?' In Morris B. Storer, ed. *Humanist Ethic: Dialogue on Basics*. Buffalo, N.Y.: Prometheus Books, 1980, 11–24.

Hocutt, Max. 'Toward an Ethic of Mutual Accommodation.' In Morris B. Storer, ed. *Humanist Ethics: Dialogue on Basics*. Buffalo, N.Y.: Prometheus Books, 1980, 137–46.

Hookway, C. J. 'Scepticism.' In Ted Honderich, ed. *The Oxford Companion to Philosophy*. Oxford, 1995. 2nd edn, Oxford: Oxford University Press, 2005.

Hoyle, Fred. 'The Universe: Past and Present Reflections.' *Annual Reviews of Astronomy and Astrophysics* 20 (1982), 1–35. doi: 10.1146/annurev.aa.20.090182 .000245.

Hursthouse, Rosalind. 'Virtue theory and abortion.' *Philosophy and Public Affairs* 20, 1991, 223–46.

Huxley, Julian. 'The Emergence of Darwinism.' In Sol Tax, ed. *The Evolution of Life: Its Origins, History, and Future*. Vol. 1 of *Evolution after Darwin*. Chicago: University of Chicago Press, 1960, 1–21.

Huxley, Julian. 'The Evolutionary Vision: The Convocation Address.' In Sol Tax and Charles Callender, eds. *Issues in Evolution*. Vol. 3 of *Evolution after Darwin*. Chicago: University of Chicago Press, 1960, 249–61.

I

Inwood, M. J. 'Feuerbach, Ludwig Andreas.' In Ted Honderich, ed. *The Oxford Companion to Philosophy*. Oxford, 1995. 2nd edn, Oxford: Oxford University Press, 2005.

J

Jeeves, Malcolm. 'Brain, Mind, and Behaviour.' In Warren S. Brown, Nancey Murphy and H. Newton Malony, eds. *Whatever Happened to the Soul: Scientific and Theological Portraits of Human Nature*. Minneapolis: Fortress Press, 1998.

Johnson, Barbara. 'Nothing Fails Like Success.' *Deconstructive Criticism: Directions. SCE Reports* 8 (Fall 1980), 7–16.

Josephson, Brian. Letters to the Editor. *The Independent* (12 Jan. 1997), London.

K

Kant, Immanuel. 'Beantwortung der Frage: Was ist Aufklärung?' *Berlinische Monatsschrift* 4 (Dec. 1784), 481–94. Repr. in *Kant's Gesammelte Schriften*. Berlin: Akademie Ausgabe, 1923, 8:33–42.

Khrushchev, Nikita. *Ukrainian Bulletin* (1–15 Aug. 1960), 12.

Klein-Franke, Felix. 'Al-Kindī.' In Seyyed Hossein Nasr and Oliver Leaman, eds. *History of Islamic Philosophy*. Vol. 1, Part 1 of *Routledge History of World Philosophies*. 1996. Repr. London: Routledge, 2001, 165–77.

Kurtz, Paul. 'A Declaration of Interdependence: A New Global Ethics.' *Free Inquiry* 8/4 (Fall 1988), 4–7. Also published in Vern L. Ballough and Timothy J. Madigan, ed. *Toward a New Enlightenment: The Philosophy of Paul Kurtz*. New Brunswick, N.J.: Transaction Publishers, 1994 (ch. 3, 'The Twenty-First Century and Beyond: The Need for a New Global Ethic and a Declaration of Interdependence').

Kurtz, Paul. 'Does Humanism Have an Ethic of Responsibility?' In Morris B. Storer, ed. *Humanist Ethics: Dialogue on Basics*. Buffalo, N.Y.: Prometheus Books, 1980, 11–24.

Kurtz, Paul. 'Is Everyone a Humanist?' In Paul Kurtz, ed. *The Humanist Alternative*. Buffalo, N.Y.: Prometheus Books, 1973.

L

Lamont, Corliss. 'The Ethics of Humanism.' In Frederick C. Dommeyer, ed. *In Quest of Value: Readings in Philosophy and Personal Values*. San Francisco: Chandler, 1963, 46–59. Repr. from ch. 6 of Corliss Lamont. *Humanism as a Philosophy*. Philosophical Library, 273–97.

Larson, Erik. 'Looking for the Mind.' (Review of David J. Chalmers. *The Conscious Mind: In Search of a Fundamental Theory*.) *Origins & Design* 18/1(34) (Winter 1997), Colorado Springs: Access Research Network, 28–9.

Leitch, Vincent B. 'The Book of Deconstructive Criticism.' *Studies in the Literary Imagination* 12/1 (Spring 1979), 19–39.

Lewis, C. S. 'The Funeral of a Great Myth.' In Walter Hooper, ed. *Christian Reflections*. Grand Rapids: Eerdmans, 1967, 102–116.

Lewis, C. S. 'The Weight of Glory.' In *Transposition and other Addresses*. London: Geoffrey Bles, 1949. Repr. in *The Weight of Glory and Other Addresses*. HarperOne, 2001.

Lewontin, Richard C. 'Billions and Billions of Demons.' *The New York Review of Books* 44/1 (9 Jan. 1997).

Lewontin, Richard C. 'Evolution/Creation Debate: A Time for Truth.' *BioScience* 31/8 (Sept. 1981), 559. Reprinted in J. Peter Zetterberg, ed. *Evolution versus Creationism*. Phoenix, Ariz.: Oryx Press, 1983. doi: 10.1093/bioscience/31.8.559, accessed 15 Sept. 2015.

Lieberman, Philip and E. S. Crelin. 'On the Speech of Neanderthal Man.' *Linguistic Inquiry* 2/2 (Mar. 1971), 203–22.

Louden, Robert. 'On Some Vices of Virtue Ethics.' Ch. 10 in R. Crisp and M. Slote, eds. *Virtue Ethics*. Oxford: Oxford University Press, 1997.

M

Mackie, J. L. 'Evil and Omnipotence.' *Mind* 64/254 (Apr. 1955), 200–12.

McNaughton, David and Piers Rawling. 'Intuitionism.' Ch. 13 in Hugh LaFollette, ed. *The Blackwell Guide to Ethical Theory*. Oxford: Blackwell, 2000, 268–87. Ch. 14 in 2nd edn, Wiley Blackwell, 2013, 287–310.

Maddox, John. 'Down with the Big Bang.' *Nature* 340 (1989), 425. doi: 10.1038/340425a0.

Marx, Karl. 'The Difference between the Natural Philosophy of Democritus and the Natural Philosophy of Epicurus.' In *K. Marx and F. Engels on Religion*. Moscow: Foreign Languages Publishing House, 1955.

Marx, Karl. 'Economic and Philosophical Manuscripts.' In T. B. Bottomore, tr. and ed. *Karl Marx: Early Writings*. London: Watts, 1963.

Marx, Karl. 'Theses on Feuerback.' In Frederick Engels, *Ludwig Feuerback*. New York: International Publishers, 1941.

May, Rollo. 'The Problem of Evil: An Open Letter to Carl Rogers.' *Journal of Humanistic Psychology* (Summer 1982).

Merezhkovsky, Dmitry. 'On the Reasons for the Decline and on the New Currents in Contemporary Russian Literature.' 1892 lecture. In Dmitry Merezhkovsky. *On the reasons for the decline and on the new currents in contemporary Russian literature*. Petersburg, 1893.

Meyer, Stephen C. 'The Explanatory Power of Design: DNA and the Origin of Information.' In William A. Dembski, ed. *Mere Creation: Science, Faith and Intelligent Design*. Downers Grove, Ill.: InterVarsity Press, 1998, 114–47.

Meyer, Stephen C. 'The Methodological Equivalence of Design and Descent.' In J. P. Moreland, ed. *The Creation Hypothesis*. Downers Grove, Ill.: InterVarsity Press, 1994, 67–112.

Meyer, Stephen C. 'Qualified Agreement: Modern Science and the Return of the "God Hypothesis".' In Richard F. Carlson, ed. *Science and Christianity: Four Views*. Downers Grove, Ill.: InterVarsity Press, 2000, 129–75.

Meyer, Stephen C. 'The Return of the God Hypothesis.' *Journal of Interdisciplinary Studies* 11/1&2 (Jan. 1999), 1–38. Online at http://www.discovery.org/a/642, accessed 3 Aug. 2017. Citations are to the archived version, which is repaginated, and online at http://www.discovery.org/scripts/viewDB/filesDB-download.php?command=download&id=12006, accessed 3 Aug. 2017.

Miller, J. Hillis. 'Deconstructing the Deconstructors.' Review of Joseph N. Riddel. *The Inverted Bell: Modernism and the Counterpoetics of William Carlos Williams*. *Diacritics* 5/2 (Summer 1975), 24–31. Online at http://www.jstor.org/stable/464639, accessed 3 Aug. 2017. doi: 10.2307/464639.

Monod, Jacques. 'On the Logical Relationship between Knowledge and Values.' In Watson Fuller, ed. *The Biological Revolution*. Garden City, N.Y.: Doubleday, 1972.

N

Nagel, Ernest. 'Naturalism Reconsidered.' 1954. In Houston Peterson, ed. *Essays in Philosophy*. New York: Pocket Books, 1959. Repr. New York: Pocket Books, 1974.

Nagel, Thomas. 'Rawls, John.' In Ted Honderich, ed. *The Oxford Companion to Philosophy*. 1995. 2nd edn, Oxford: Oxford University Press, 2005.

Nagler, Michael N. 'Reading the Upanishads.' In Eknath Easwaran. *The Upanishads*. 1987. Repr. Berkeley, Calif.: Nilgiri Press, 2007.

Neill, Stephen. 'The Wrath of God and the Peace of God.' In Max Warren, *Interpreting the Cross*. London: SCM Press, 1966.

Newing, Edward G. 'Religions of pre-literary societies.' In Sir Norman Anderson, ed. *The World's Religions*. 4th edn, London: Inter-Varsity Press, 1975.

Nielsen, Kai. 'Religiosity and Powerlessness: Part III of "The Resurgence of Fundamentalism". *The Humanist* 37/3 (May/June 1977), 46–8.

O

The Oxford Reference Encyclopaedia. Oxford: Oxford University Press, 1998.

P

Palmer, Alasdair. 'Must Knowledge Gained Mean Paradise Lost?' *Sunday Telegraph.* London (6 Apr. 1997).

Penzias, Arno. 'Creation is Supported by all the Data So Far.' In Henry Margenau and Roy Abraham Varghese, eds. *Cosmos, Bios, Theos: Scientists Reflect on Science, God, and the Origins of the Universe, Life, and Homo Sapiens.* La Salle, Ill.: Open Court, 1992.

Pinker, Steven, and Paul Bloom. 'Natural Language and Natural Selection.' *Behavioral and Brain Sciences* 13/4 (Dec. 1990), 707–27. doi: 10.1017/S0140525X00081061.

Polanyi, Michael. 'Life's Irreducible Structure. Live mechanisms and information in DNA are boundary conditions with a sequence of boundaries above them.' *Science* 160/3834 (1968), 1308–12. Online at http://www.jstor.org/stable/1724152, accessed 3 Aug. 2017.

Poole, Michael. 'A Critique of Aspects of the Philosophy and Theology of Richard Dawkins.' *Christians and Science* 6/1 (1994), 41–59. Online at http://www.scienceandchristianbelief.org/serve_pdf_free.php?filename=SCB+6-1+Poole.pdf, accessed 3 Aug. 2017.

Popper, Karl. 'Scientific Reduction and the Essential Incompleteness of All Science.' In F. J. Ayala and T. Dobzhansky, ed. *Studies in the Philosophy of Biology, Reduction and Related Problems.* London: MacMillan, 1974.

Premack, David. '"Gavagai!" or The Future History of the Animal Controversy.' *Cognition* 19/3 (1985), 207–96. doi: 10.1016/0010-0277(85)90036-8.

Provine, William B. 'Evolution and the Foundation of Ethics.' *Marine Biological Laboratory Science* 3 (1988), 27–8.

Provine, William B. 'Scientists, Face it! Science and Religion are Incompatible.' *The Scientist* (5 Sept. 1988), 10–11.

R

Rachels, James. 'Naturalism.' In Hugh LaFollette, ed. *The Blackwell Guide to Ethical Theory.* Oxford: Blackwell, 2000, 74–91.

Randall, John H. 'The Nature of Naturalism.' In Yervant H. Krikorian, ed. *Naturalism*, 354–82.

Raup, David. 'Conflicts between Darwin and Palaeontology.' *Field Museum of Natural History Bulletin* 50/1 (Jan. 1979), 22–9.

Reidhaar-Olson, John F. and Robert T. Sauer. 'Functionally Acceptable Substitutions in Two α-helical Regions of λ Repressor.' *Proteins: Structure, Function, and Genetics* 7/4 (1990), 306–16. doi: 10.1002/prot.340070403.

Rescher, Nicholas. 'Idealism.' In Jonathan Dancy and Ernest Sosa, eds. *A Companion to Epistemology*. 1992. Repr. Oxford: Blackwell, 2000.

Ridley, Mark. 'Who Doubts Evolution?' *New Scientist* 90 (25 June 1981), 830–2.

Rogers, Carl. 'Notes on Rollo May.' *Journal of Humanistic Psychology* 22/3 (Summer 1982), 8–9. doi: 10.1177/0022167882223002.

Rorty, Richard. 'Untruth and Consequences.' *The New Republic* (31 July 1995), 32–6.

Ruse, Michael. 'Is Rape Wrong on Andromeda?' In E. Regis Jr., ed. *Extraterrestrials*. Cambridge: Cambridge University Press, 1985.

Ruse, Michael. 'Transcript: Speech by Professor Michael Ruse,' Symposium, 'The New Antievolutionism', 1993 Annual Meeting of the American Association for the Advancement of Science, 13 Feb. 1993. Online at http://www.arn.org/docs/orpages/or151/mr93tran.htm, accessed 3 Aug. 2017.

Ruse, Michael and Edward O. Wilson. 'The Evolution of Ethics.' *New Scientist* 108/1478 (17 Oct. 1985), 50–2.

Russell, Bertrand. 'A Free Man's Worship.' 1903. In *Why I Am Not a Christian*. New York: Simon & Schuster, 1957. Also in *Mysticism and Logic Including A Free Man's Worship*. London: Unwin, 1986.

Russell, Colin. 'The Conflict Metaphor and its Social Origins.' *Science and Christian Belief* 1/1 (1989), 3–26.

S

Sanders, Blanche. *The Humanist* 5 (1945).

Sanders, Peter. 'Eutychus.' *Triple Helix* (Summer 2002), 17.

Sayre-McCord, Geoffrey. 'Contractarianism.' In Hugh LaFollette, ed. *The Blackwell Guide to Ethical Theory*. Oxford: Blackwell, 2000, 247–67. 2nd edn, Wiley Blackwell, 2013, 332–53.

Scruton, Roger. *The Times* (Dec. 1997), London.

Searle, John. 'Minds, Brains and Programs.' In John Haugeland, ed. *Mind Design*. Cambridge, Mass.: Cambridge University Press, 1981.

Sedgh, Gilda, et al., 'Abortion incidence between 1990 and 2014: global, regional, and subregional levels and trends.' *The Lancet* 388/10041 (16 July 2016), 258–67. doi: 10.1016/S0140-6736(16)30380-4.

Shapiro, James A. 'In the Details . . . What?' *National Review* (16 Sept. 1996), 62–5.

Simpson, George Gaylord. 'The Biological Nature of Man.' *Science* 152/3721 (22 Apr. 1966), 472–8.

Singer, Peter. 'Hegel, Georg Wilhelm Friedrich.' In Ted Honderich, ed. *The Oxford Companion to Philosophy*. Oxford, 1995. 2nd edn, Oxford: Oxford University Press, 2005.

Skorupski, John. 'Mill, John Stuart.' In Ted Honderich, ed. *The Oxford Companion to Philosophy*. Oxford, 1995. 2nd edn, Oxford: Oxford University Press, 2005.

Slote, Michael. 'Utilitarianism.' In Ted Honderich, ed. *The Oxford Companion to Philosophy*. Oxford, 1995. 2nd edn, Oxford: Oxford University Press, 2005.

Slote, Michael. 'Virtue Ethics.' In Hugh LaFollette, ed. *The Blackwell Guide to Ethical Theory*. Oxford: Blackwell, 2000, 325–47.

Sokal, Alan D. 'Transgressing the boundaries: towards a transformative hermeneutic of Quantum Gravity.' *Social Text* (Spring/Summer 1996), 217–52.

Sokal, Alan D. 'What the Social Text Affair Does and Does Not Prove.' In Noretta Koertge, ed. *A House Built on Sand: Exposing Postmodernist Myths About Science.* Oxford: Oxford University Press, 1998, 9–22.

Solzhenitsyn, Alexander. 'Alexandr Solzhenitsyn—Nobel Lecture.' *Nobelprize.org.* Nobel Media AB 2014. Online at https://www.nobelprize.org/nobel_prizes/literature/laureates/1970/solzhenitsyn-lecture.html, accessed 15 Aug. 2017.

Spetner, L. M. 'Natural selection: An information-transmission mechanism for evolution.' *Journal of Theoretical Biology* 7/3 (Nov. 1964), 412–29.

Stalin, Joseph. Speech delivered 24 April 1924. New York, International Publishers, 1934.

Stolzenberg, Gabriel. 'Reading and relativism: an introduction to the science wars.' In Keith M. Ashman and Philip S. Baringer, eds. *After the Science Wars.* London: Routledge, 2001, 33–63.

T

Tarkunde, V. M. 'Comment by V. M. Tarkunde on Hocutt Article.' In Morris B. Storer, ed. *Humanist Ethics: Dialogue on Basics.* Buffalo, N.Y.: Prometheus Books, 1980, 147–8.

Taylor, Robert. 'Evolution is Dead.' *New Scientist* 160/2154 (3 Oct. 1998), 25–9.

W

Walicki, Andrzej. 'Hegelianism, Russian.' In Edward Craig, gen. ed. *Concise Routledge Encyclopedia of Philosophy.* London: Routledge, 2000.

Wallace, Daniel, "The Majority Text and the Original Text: Are They Identical?," *Bibliotheca Sacra*, April-June, 1991, 157-8.

Walton, J. C. 'Organization and the Origin of Life.' *Origins* 4 (1977), 16–35.

Warren, Mary Ann. 'On the Moral and Legal Status of Abortion.' Ch. 11 in Hugh LaFollette, ed. *Ethics in Practice: An Anthology*, 1997, 72–82. 4th edn, Oxford: Blackwell, 2014, 132–40.

Watters, Wendell W. 'Christianity and Mental Health.' *The Humanist* 37 (Nov./Dec. 1987).

Weatherford, Roy C. 'Freedom and Determinism.' In Ted Honderich, ed. *The Oxford Companion to Philosophy.* Oxford, 1995. 2nd edn, Oxford: Oxford University Press, 2005.

Wheeler, John A. 'Information, Physics, Quantum: The Search for Links.' In Wojciech Hubert Zurek. *Complexity, Entropy, and the Physics of Information.* The Proceedings of the 1988 Workshop on Complexity, Entropy, and the Physics of Information, held May–June, 1989, in Santa Fe, N. Mex. Redwood City, Calif.: Addison-Wesley, 1990.

Wigner, Eugene. 'The Unreasonable Effectiveness of Mathematics in the Natural Sciences', Richard Courant Lecture in Mathematical Sciences, delivered at New York University, 11 May 1959. *Communications in Pure and Applied Mathematics*, 13/1 (Feb. 1960), 1–14. Repr. in E. Wiger. *Symmetries and Reflections*. Bloomingon, Ind., 1967. Repr. Woodbridge, Conn.: Ox Bow Press, 1979, 222–37.

Wilford, John Noble. 'Sizing Up the Cosmos: An Astronomer's Quest.' *New York Times* (12 Mar. 1991), B9.

Wilkinson, David. 'Found in space?' Interview with Paul Davies. *Third Way* 22:6 (July 1999), 17–21.

Wilson, Edward O. 'The Ethical Implications of Human Sociobiology.' *Hastings Center Report* 10:6 (Dec. 1980), 27–9. doi: 10.2307/3560296.

Y

Yockey, Hubert. 'A Calculation of the Probability of Spontaneous Biogenesis by Information Theory.' *Journal of Theoretical Biology* 67 (1977), 377–98.

Yockey, Hubert. 'Self-Organisation Origin of Life Scenarios and Information Theory.' *Journal of Theoretical Biology* 91 (1981), 13–31.

STUDY QUESTIONS FOR TEACHERS AND STUDENTS

CHAPTER 1: DO ALL RELIGIONS LEAD TO THE SAME GOAL?

Introduction

1.1   How and why has religion got itself such a bad name in the course of the centuries?

1.2   Is there any justification for religious wars?

1.3   What would you say is the main purpose of religion?

1.4   What is the difference between moral philosophy and religion?

1.5   What has truth got to do with religion?

What the major religions mean by 'god', what they teach about the material world and how they deal with guilt

1.6   The Buddha himself originally abandoned Hinduism. How does that fact show up in the teaching of original Buddhism?

1.7   What is the difference between Hindu philosophy and popular Hindu religion?

1.8   What moral difficulties does the doctrine of pantheism run into?

1.9   'Some people find the doctrine of reincarnation attractive, because it seems to offer a second chance to those who feel they have not behaved too well in this life.' Comment.

1.10   Assess the moral implications of the doctrine of reincarnation.

1.11   What change, if any, would Hinduism and Mahayana Buddhism make to your evaluation of the material world and of the human body?

The question of salvation in the three monotheistic faiths

1.12   What attitude do Christians take to the holy book of Judaism? What is meant by saying that the New Testament is a Jewish book?

1.13   What attitude does the Qur'an take to the Old and New Testaments?

1.14   What is the 'problem of guilt'?

1.15   What do Muslims believe will happen at the final judgment?

1.16   What do Jews do every year on Yom Kippur, the Day of Atonement? What does it mean to them? (See Lev 16)

1.17   What do Christians believe to be the significance of the death of Jesus?

CHAPTER 2: THE HISTORICITY OF THE NEW TESTAMENT

The historical nature of the Christian gospel

2.1   What two books did Luke contribute to the New Testament?

2.2 What evidence is there to show that Luke intended both his books to be regarded as history, and not as myth or legend?

2.3 Why is history such an important element in the Christian gospel? How does Christianity differ from Buddhism in this respect?

2.4 According to Luke, how soon after the death of Christ was the first Christian sermon preached? What were its contents? (See Acts 2)

2.5 What is the connection between Old Testament history and the Christian gospel? Why is that connection important?

2.6 Suggestion for class work: have a student read the text of Acts 13:15–42 aloud while the others follow, and then ask the class what the major elements in the text are, comparing their ideas with the list under the heading 'Two samples of early Christian preaching'.

The reliability of the historical sources

2.7 What is the difference between the way historians work and the way natural scientists work?

2.8 What indicates that the writer of the Gospel of Luke and the Acts of the Apostles was a reliable historian?

2.9 Get the class to talk to their parents (or, better still, their grandparents) about some of their earliest memories. See how far back they go. See how far back the teacher can go! Compare your findings with the time gaps discussed above in connection with the New Testament. Discuss what the class thinks about the authenticity of the accounts.

Evidences from non-Christian sources

2.10 What can we learn about Jesus from the evidence that comes from ancient literature other than the New Testament?

2.11 What can we learn about the worship of Jesus from Pliny's letter to the emperor?

The manuscripts of the New Testament

2.12 How does the manuscript evidence for the text of the New Testament compare with that for other ancient texts?

2.13 How does the fact that we have many manuscripts of the New Testament help us to determine the original text?

2.14 What weaknesses do you see in the argument that the New Testament is unreliable because it has been copied out many times?

The canon of the New Testament

2.15 What is meant by the 'canon' of the New Testament? On what grounds were the books recognised as being authoritative, and therefore received into the canon?

2.16 Why is the Gospel of Barnabas regarded as non-canonical?

2.17 What is the strength of the evidence that Jesus actually died on the cross?

2.18 Why did the death of Christ figure so centrally in the preaching of the early Christians?

CHAPTER 3: THE FIGURE OF CHRIST: FICTION, MYTH, OR REALITY?

Is the figure of Jesus in the gospels an invention?

3.1 Read the first chapter of *The Master and Margarita*. Why did Berlioz and Bezdomny think that the character of Jesus was a literary invention?

3.2 Why does Socrates, as described to us by Plato, strike us as a real character?

3.3 What were the Jewish, Greek and Roman ideas of a hero? Give your reasons why Jesus fitted none of them. What significance has this for the status of Jesus as a historical rather than an invented figure?

3.4 Why did the preaching of the cross of Jesus scandalise the Jews, and appear to be foolish to the Greeks?

3.5 What evidence is there that the message that Jesus came to die for human sin goes back to Jesus himself and is not an invention of the early Christians?

3.6 Read Isaiah chapter 53, and discuss in class the accuracy of its depiction of the death of Messiah.

What is the evidence that Jesus claimed to be the Son of God?

3.7 What evidence is there that Jesus' claim to be the Son of God is not primitive superstition?

3.8 What did Jesus mean when he claimed to be the Son of God? Give your reasons.

3.9 What evidence would you adduce from Jesus' teaching and behaviour to show that he was neither a megalomaniac nor a fraud?

3.10 In what way can Christ's claim to forgive sins be used as evidence for the fact that he claimed to be God?

Where does the evidence ultimately come from, that Jesus is the Son of God?

3.11 What does it mean to say that God is, and must be, his own evidence?

3.12 Read John chapter 5. What can you learn from it about Jesus' relationship with the Father?

3.13 What is the condition Christ laid down for getting to know whether or not his teaching is true? Why do you think that there is such a condition?

3.14 Read the story of the blind man in John 9. What was the experiment that Jesus suggested he should do in order to receive sight? Do you think the man was right to try the experiment? Why?

3.15 Relate in your own words the discussion between the blind man and the Pharisees and others who were not convinced that a miracle had happened. What do you think about their arguments, and his replies?

3.16 What experiment can we perform, to check if the claim of Christ to be the Son of God is true?

CHAPTER 4: THE RESURRECTION OF CHRIST AND THE QUESTION OF MIRACLES

The prime miracle

4.1 Why is the resurrection of Christ so important to the Christian gospel?

David Hume and miracles

4.2   What does it mean to say that a law of nature is not only descriptive but predictive?

4.3   What is meant by 'the uniformity of nature'? Can the uniformity of nature be proved?

4.4   How does Hume's theory of causality undermine science? What do you think of Whitehead's argument about the light bulb?

Miracles and the laws of nature

4.5   'Miracles violate nature's laws and are therefore impossible.' Discuss.

4.6   'The writers of the New Testament were ignorant of the laws of nature, and so easily believed in miracles.' Say whether you agree or disagree, and why.

4.7   Why are the laws of nature important to the Christian position?

Evidence for the historical fact of the resurrection

4.8   What does it mean to proportion belief to evidence? Do we always do so?

4.9   How reasonable is it to suppose that when the disciples of Christ preached the resurrection they were knowingly committing a fraud?

4.10   What was the purpose for which the Christian church came into existence?

4.11   'Miracles threaten the foundations of naturalism.' Discuss.

4.12   Why does belief in order in nature ultimately depend on belief in a Creator?

CHAPTER 5: THE EVIDENCE FOR THE RESURRECTION

The death of Jesus

5.1   Why do the early Christians emphasise the fact that Christ was dead?

5.2   Why is the swoon-revival theory untenable?

5.3   What evidence is there that Jesus was really dead?

The burial of Jesus

5.4   Why is it important how, where and by whom the body of Christ was buried?

5.5   What is meant by saying that the authorities officially 'sealed' the stone that covered the mouth of Christ's tomb? What would be the implications of breaking that seal?

The fact of the empty tomb

5.6   The early Christians insist that on the day of the resurrection they found Christ's tomb empty. What does this show us about the meaning of the term 'resurrection', as the early Christians used it?

5.7   What may we deduce from the fact that, before the Christians said anything, the Jewish authorities circulated the story about the disciples stealing the body?

5.8   Do you think it is probable that the soldiers on guard at the tomb went to sleep?

5.9   Why, do you think, did Pilate make no attempt to arrest the early Christians when they began to preach that Jesus had risen from the dead?

5.10   Do you think that the disciples would have mistaken the tomb?

5.11   What did Peter and John deduce from the position of the grave-clothes?

Eyewitnesses of the appearances of Christ

5.12   What, according to the early Christians, was the nature of Christ's appearances to them between his resurrection and ascension?

5.13   Is there adequate ground for supposing that those appearances were simply hallucinations?

5.14   In what circumstances and to what kind of people did these appearances occur?

5.15   These appearances were always accompanied by words spoken by Christ, and/ or by demonstrations performed by him. What kind of messages did those words convey? What did those demonstrations prove?

The psychological evidence

5.16   What are Hume's criteria for witnesses? Do you think they are fair? How do you assess the strength of the eyewitness evidence of the resurrection?

5.17   How do you account for the lack of contrary evidence from the Jewish leaders?

5.18   Read the accounts of the conversion of Saul of Tarsus (Acts 9:1–19; 21:37–22:21; 26:1–32). Why was Saul persecuting the Christians? What do you think of Paul's explanation of what led to his becoming a Christian? Can you think of a more convincing explanation?

5.19   What was it that really convinced (*a*) John; (*b*) Mary, that Jesus had risen from the dead?

5.20   Why did the early disciples not start pilgrimages to the tomb of Jesus or make a shrine of it?

5.21   What is the nature of the 'new relationship' which Mary Magdalene and all followers of the risen Christ have with him?

The nature of the resurrection body

5.22   What evidence is offered by the early Christians that Christ's resurrection body was a physical body?

5.23   What differences were there between Christ's pre-resurrection body and that same body after the resurrection?

5.24   How might the *Flatland* analogy help us understand the properties of Christ's risen body?

5.25   What does the story of Thomas reveal about Jesus' attitude to doubt? What do you think really convinced Thomas in the end?

5.25   Is it necessary to see in order to believe? Is it possible for the physically blind to believe?

5.26   Why were the disciples on the road to Emmaus dispirited? What new things did they learn from the Old Testament that changed their opinion? What really convinced them that they had been talking with Jesus?

5.27   Say what piece of evidence for the resurrection discussed in this chapter you find most interesting, and why.

APPENDIX: THE SCIENTIFIC ENDEAVOUR

Scientific method

A.1 In what different ways have you heard the word 'science' used? How would you define it?

A.2 How is induction understood as part of our everyday experience and also of the scientific endeavour?

A.3 In what ways does deduction differ from induction, and what role does each play in scientific experiments?

A.4 Do you find the idea of 'falsifiability' appealing, or unsatisfactory? Why?

A.5 How does abduction differ from both induction and deduction, and what is the relationship among the three?

Explaining explanations

A.6 How many levels of explanation can you think of to explain a cake, in terms of how was it made, what was it made from, and why was it made? What can scientists tell us? What can 'Aunt Olga' tell us?

A.7 In what ways is reductionism helpful in scientific research, and in what ways could it be limiting, or even detrimental, to scientific research?

A.8 How do you react to physicist and theologian John Polkinghorne's statement that reductionism relegates 'our experiences of beauty, moral obligation, and religious encounter to the epiphenomenal scrapheap. It also destroys rationality'?

The basic operational presuppositions of the scientific endeavour

A.9 What is meant by the statement 'Observation is dependent on theory'?

A.10 What are some of the axioms upon which your thinking about scientific knowledge rests?

A.11 What does trust have to do with gaining knowledge?

A.12 What does belief have to do with gaining knowledge?

A.13 According to physicist and philosopher of science Thomas Kuhn, how do new scientific paradigms emerge?

SCRIPTURE INDEX

GENERAL INDEX

ABOUT THE AUTHORS

David W. Gooding is Professor Emeritus of Old Testament Greek at Queen's University Belfast and a Member of the Royal Irish Academy. He has taught the Bible internationally and lectured on both its authenticity and its relevance to philosophy, world religions and daily life. He has published scholarly articles on the Septuagint and Old Testament narratives, as well as expositions of Luke, John, Acts, Hebrews, the New Testament's use of the Old Testament, and several books addressing arguments against the Bible and the Christian faith. His analysis of the Bible and our world continues to shape the thinking of scholars, teachers and students alike.

John C. Lennox is Professor Emeritus of Mathematics at the University of Oxford and Emeritus Fellow in Mathematics and the Philosophy of Science at Green Templeton College. He is also an Associate Fellow of the Saïd Business School. In addition, he is an Adjunct Lecturer at the Oxford Centre for Christian Apologetics, as well as being a Senior Fellow of the Trinity Forum. In addition to academic works, he has published on the relationship between science and Christianity, the books of Genesis and Daniel, and the doctrine of divine sovereignty and human free will. He has lectured internationally and participated in a number of televised debates with some of the world's leading atheist thinkers.

David W. Gooding (right)
and John C. Lennox (left)

Photo credit: Barbara Hamilton.

Myrtlefield Encounters

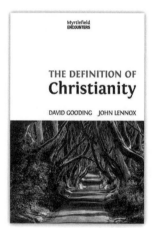

Key Bible Concepts

How can one book be so widely appreciated and so contested? Millions revere it and many ridicule it, but the Bible is often not allowed to speak for itself. Key Bible Concepts explores and clarifies the central terms of the Christian gospel. Gooding and Lennox provide succinct explanations of the basic vocabulary of Christian thought to unlock the Bible's meaning and its significance for today.

The Definition of Christianity

Who gets to determine what Christianity means? Is it possible to understand its original message after centuries of tradition and conflicting ideas? Gooding and Lennox throw fresh light on these questions by tracing the Book of Acts' historical account of the message that proved so effective in the time of Christ's apostles. Luke's record of its confrontations with competing philosophical and religious systems reveals Christianity's own original and lasting definition.

Myrtlefield Encounters

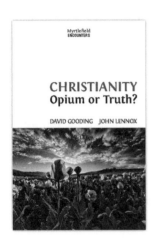

Christianity: Opium or Truth

Is Christianity just a belief that dulls the pain of our existence with dreams that are beautiful but false? Or is it an accurate account of reality, our own condition and God's attitude toward us? Gooding and Lennox address crucial issues that can make it difficult for thoughtful people to accept the Christian message. They answer those questions and show that clear thinking is not in conflict with personal faith in Jesus Christ.

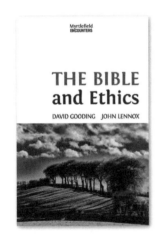

The Bible and Ethics

Why should we tell the truth or value a human life? Why should we not treat others in any way we like? Some say the Bible is the last place to find answers to such questions, but even its critics recognize the magnificence of Jesus' ethical teaching. To understand the ethics of Jesus we need to understand the values and beliefs on which they are based. Gooding and Lennox take us on a journey through the Bible and give us a concise survey of its leading events and people, ideas, poetry, moral values and ethics to bring into focus the ultimate significance of what Jesus taught about right and wrong.

Clear, simple, fresh and highly practical—this David Gooding/John Lennox series is a goldmine for anyone who desires to live Socrates' 'examined life'.

Above all, the books are comprehensive and foundational, so they form an invaluable handbook for negotiating the crazy chaos of today's modern world.

Os Guinness, author of *Last Call for Liberty*

These six volumes, totalling almost 2000 pages, were written by two outstanding scholars who combine careers of research and teaching at the highest levels. David Gooding and John Lennox cover well the fields of Scripture, science, and philosophy, integrating them with one voice. The result is a set of texts that work systematically through a potpourri of major topics, like being human, discovering ultimate reality, knowing truth, ethically evaluating life's choices, answering our deepest questions, plus the problems of pain and suffering. To get all this wisdom together in this set was an enormous undertaking! Highly recommended!

Gary R. Habermas, Distinguished Research Professor & Chair, Dept. of Philosophy, Liberty University & Theological Seminary

David Gooding and John Lennox are exemplary guides to the deepest questions of life in this comprehensive series. It will equip thinking Christians with an intellectual roadmap to the fundamental conflict between Christianity and secular humanism. For thinking seekers it will be a provocation to consider which worldview makes best sense of our deepest convictions about life.

Justin Brierley, host of the *Unbelievable?* radio show and podcast

I would recommend these books to anyone searching to answer the big questions of life. Both Gooding and Lennox are premier scholars and faithful biblicists—a rare combination.

Alexander Strauch, author of *Biblical Eldership*